A Portrait of Farnham

Classical excellence: the magnificent early 18th-century pine garden door-case on the east front of The Grange, Castle Hill. The mask on the apex of the interior arch is thought to be a representation of Flora, goddess of flowers, and is perhaps a portrait-mask of a lady associated with the property. On the reverse, facing west, is Fauna, possibly inspired by Sir Jonathan Trelawny Bt., Bishop of Winchester in 1707–1721, and whose secretary, Edward Forbes, is thought to have built the house.

A Portrait of Farnham

Jonathan Wood

Illustrated by Gareth Ball

Foreword by
Sir Ray Tindle

Farnham Herald

Acknowledgements

First and foremost my thanks go to Sir Ray Tindle, proprietor of the *Farnham Herald*, who not only conceived the idea of this book but also made its publication possible. I should also like to thank Sir Ray for contributing the Foreword.

Back in 1963, Ernest Langham, the *Herald's* proprietor in those days, published *Farnham Buildings and People*, written and illustrated by Nigel Temple. It would not have been possible to compile *A Portrait of Farnham* without this masterly book by my side. I acquired my copy soon after arriving in Farnham in 1970, and I would like to acknowledge my indebtedness to its author. I am also grateful to Dr Temple for his advice on some particular properties in the town and my thanks to him for the photographs on pages 15 (lower) and 17 which are courtesy of The Nigel Temple Collection.

I would like to record my thanks to the curator of the Museum of Farnham, Anne Jones, and her ever-helpful staff who offered every assistance with this project. It seemed at times that I had established squatter's rights in the Local History room! Apart from referring to the Museum's copious records of the town, I also drew on the files of one-time local historians, Bill Ewbank-Smith and F.W. Simmonds, which are held at Willmer House. Contemporary photographs, unless otherwise stated, are reproduced by courtesy of the Museum.

I must also record heartfelt thanks to historian Jean Parratt, the author of a fascinating series of books on the town, and the Museum's Chris Hellier. They both read the text and made many helpful suggestions, although I alone am responsible for any conclusions reached.

Illustrations are an integral part of any book on architecture and my collaborator, Gareth Ball, spent over a year researching and preparing the all-important drawings which follow. It will come as little surprise to learn that Gareth, who grew up in a West Street property located virtually opposite the home of the legendary Harold Falkner, knows Farnham intimately. Drawing every building in Castle Street was a feat in itself.

As might be expected, the past issues of the *Farnham Herald* have provided a mine of information and I would like to make particular acknowledgement to the regular *Environmental Viewpoint* column by Michael Blower and Susan Farrow that has recorded so many of the changes to the town in recent years.

I am also most grateful for the help provided by Joanne Aylwin, Michael Blower, Jane Brown, Pat Heather, Denise Todd and Max Lyons and my thanks to him for the photograph reproduced on page 98. I also undertook further research at the library of The Royal Institute of British Architects.

Staff at Farnham Library were of great assistance and my appreciation should also be extended to the proprietors and members of the staffs of many local businesses and the owners of houses in the town, all of whom readily shared with me the histories of their properties.

I should add that the opinions voiced throughout this work are entirely mine and should not be regarded as those of the *Farnham Herald*.

Jonathan Wood
Ludlow, Shropshire

Contents

Title page: The female cones of the hop plant which shaped Farnham's fortunes for some 200 years between the late 16th and 19th centuries.

Designed by: Aztec Design, 31, Artillery Road, Guildford, Surrey GU1 4NW

Editor: Philip de Ste. Croix

Printed by: Biddles Ltd., Woodbridge Park Estate, Woodbridge Road, Guildford, Surrey GU1 1DA

ISBN 0 95007 262 1

Foreword

Sir Ray Tindle
CBE DL FCIS FCIJ FCI Arb

Everyone who loves Farnham will love this book. This is because Jonathan Wood and Gareth Ball have not only done a splendid job in bringing our town to life in words and drawings but presented them in a truly unique way. After spending my whole life in print, that is quite a statement to make!

Jonathan and Gareth take you through Farnham as you might walk it. Everyone has heard the expression "I couldn't put this book down" and once you start reading this one you'll find yourself on an enthralling tour of the town that explores not only its principal streets, but also some of the yards and alleyways that make Farnham so special.

We get descriptions of its buildings, together with accounts of the people who lived and often traded in them. These can be read in conjunction with Gareth's superb drawings which illustrate, both in outline and fascinating detail, the infinite variety of Farnham's townscape.

Exactly 40 years ago, in 1963, Ernest Langham, my predecessor as proprietor of the *Farnham Herald*, published *Farnham Buildings and People*, written and illustrated by Nigel Temple. With The Woolmead development then in the offing, change was in the air and this scholarly and timely book became required reading for anyone with an interest in the town, its architecture and past inhabitants. It became my "bible".

Four decades on, the face of Farnham has, of course, changed. Whilst the heart of the town has remained essentially intact, once again there is further development pending in and around East Street.

I am very pleased to join with Jonathan and Gareth in publishing ***A Portrait of Farnham***. In addition to charting the evolution of the town's historic fabric, it also chronicles many of the changes that have taken place in our community over the past 40 years. I commend this book to anyone who, like me, loves Farnham.

Ray Tindle

The Fabric of Farnham

"The Town is alive! alive! It is changing under our very eyes! The old streets have to be widened to make room for its ever-expanding life, for the incessant rush of its traffic. See how the former wagon and corn-yards are making way for new business premises."

This was how George Sturt, a wheelwright by trade and an author by profession, described Farnham in 1925. Yet his optimism is tempered by an underlying caution and the "ever-expanding life" he identifies has been all too apparent since then. Sadly, in recent years it has resulted in the destruction of many of the houses and shops which constitute the very fabric of our town. And they have invariably been replaced by buildings of an inferior quality and style which survive today in uneasy juxtaposition with their older neighbours.

Since 1970 the centre of Farnham has been ringed within a Conservation Area but this does not mean that local vigilance should be relaxed. Such a provision is subject to constant commercial pressures and much of the town falls outside its protection. The loss of any building, like a stolen fragment of mosaic, should be seen in the context of the whole. This is because so much of the appeal of the town's architecture lies in the rich variety of its mellow brick frontages. These are usually enhanced by white-painted wooden door-cases and sash windows that are crowned by a lively roofscape of tile or slate.

Farnham has, rightly, been judged to be one of the finest Georgian towns in the country. But architecture is full of surprises. Many of its buildings are older than they might at first appear while, conversely, some – despite the apparent evidence – are of a more recent date. What is not in doubt is that they combine to produce streets, lanes and yards which delight the eye and uplift the spirit.

Castle Street, the jewel in Farnham's architectural crown, is an ideal starting point for our journey. In 1566,

Old Market House, built in 1566 and demolished in December 1865, when its building materials were auctioned, that occupied the lower part of Castle Street. The brick frontage and the wooden arcade below facing The Borough, together with the cupola, date from the 18th century.

when the first Queen Elizabeth had been on the throne for only eight years, and at about the spot where the fruit and vegetable stall now stands, John Clarke, senior bailiff of Farnham Corporation, built, at his own expense, a Market House for the town.

Raised on oak posts with space beneath where farmers used to congregate on wet market days, its external walls were constructed of a strong wooden frame which featured a type of construction that had served the community since Saxon times.

For Farnham in the 16th century was a town of timber buildings where the carpenter held sway; houses abounded with tiled gables, carved barge-boards, corner posts and decorated brackets. You do not have to look far to discover the evidence. It can still be found down alleyways and at the rear of buildings. Look to the west wall of the arch alongside Help the Aged's West Street shop – there you will see the beams of the ancient Swan Inn. More obviously, they are readily apparent on the sensitively restored Tanyard House in Bridge Square, built for a local man of importance in the 1480s. There are other examples, many of which are hidden behind the 18th- and 19th-century brick frontages of The Borough, Castle Street and West Street.

Most timber-framed dwellings were modest in scale although there were exceptions. In 1355 a house was deemed sufficiently important for it to be dismantled and removed to Sutton Sketeneye, today Sutton Scotney, Hampshire, an endeavour which cost the Bishop of Winchester £7.10s. (£7.50).

The bishopric had held the Manor of Farnham since at least the 9th century and in about 1138 Bishop Henry de Blois, a grandson of William the Conqueror, is generally credited with the building of Farnham Castle. It was one of seven such Episcopal establishments and included a residential palace which his successors would occupy almost continuously until 1927. Set on the commanding chalk ridge to the north of the town, the motte and bailey castle was protected by a wooden stockade. However, later in the 12th century this was replaced by walls of locally quarried clunch, which is a type of chalk and, in truth, not a particularly satisfactory building material.

Similarly, Waverley Abbey, set in an estate of 60 acres (24ha) of land to the south-east of the town, was stone-built, its walls being made of locally quarried ironstone with malmstone and clunch dressings. Established in 1128, this religious house had the distinction of being the first Cistercian monastery in Britain, although its end came with Henry VIII's Dissolution of the Monasteries in 1536.

All these materials would be similarly employed in Farnham with ironstone forming the basis of the town's distinctive pavements which, alas, were a little hard on the feet. As Gordon Home cautioned in his 1900 guide, they made the "Farnham man easily recognisable by his fondness for walking in the road in preference to the footway."

There were a few stone houses in the town and one perhaps socially conscious Farnham family took the name of "Stonehous" to underline its exceptional possession of such a property. The only other stone building (clunch again) of consequence in medieval Farnham was St Andrew's parish church, which mostly dates from the 15th century although it was extensively restored in 1855.

Built on higher ground on the north bank of the River Wey, this was the probable site of a Saxon place of worship

Many of Farnham's houses are timber-framed but were refronted in brick in the 18th century. This is readily apparent at 31 Lower Church Lane where the projecting jetty was also infilled.

A LEVY ON LIGHT

If you walk around the town, you will notice that some of its older buildings have "blind" windows, that is to say there is a recess which contains a painted representation of one, or there is just plain brick where the sash should be. One of many examples is 15/16 The Borough which has no less than three. While this effect can sometimes be what the builder intended to provide an element of symmetry to a facade, it usually indicates that at some stage the property's owner blocked up the aperture to avoid paying window tax.

This penalty was first levied in 1697, payment was due on the seventh window of a property, ☛

and in 2002 the chalk foundations of a two-cell church, which may date from the 10th or 11th centuries, were exposed beneath the floor of the nave. It seems likely that the original community grew up around this ancient site.

What today are named the Church Lanes and, probably, an east/west track, although whether it was along the line of the present West Street/Borough axis is not known, existed in Saxon times. A north/south highway may have crossed the Wey at Longbridge. The town had grown organically but radical changes would follow the Norman Conquest.

This was because by building the Castle, its position dictated by its defensive requirements, the Bishops of Winchester had effectively shifted Farnham's epicentre away from the old Saxon settlement around the church to a south-facing slope beneath its ramparts. With trade as its spur, by 1208 the construction of a wide new street flanked by regular half and whole burgage (rented) plots had been initiated. This is today's Castle Street with perhaps Bear Lane and a now absent track created on either side as back service lanes. The Borough was similarly developed.

Thus Farnham can now be seen as one of the Bishops of Winchester's seven planned towns, the others being Alresford, Clere, Overton, Downton, Knowle and Calburne.

The new street was also the ideal location for the town's market, its medieval mainspring, established by the bishop in 1216. Destined to be held there for nearly 700 years, George Sturt remembered it in the mid-19th century when the "sheep pens...stretched all up Castle Street," and it was

The late 15th-century Tanyard House in Bridge Square is the surviving fragment of a larger property that used to extend towards Red Lion Lane.

"thick with cattle of all sorts" to the hill and beyond.

In the 13th century the market was held within The Borough, the limits of which were underlined by the presence of a town ditch that is believed to have been dug in the late 12th century. In 1249 the bishop granted the burgesses their first chapter of liberties which gave them control of The Borough and town. Traders who wished to participate in the market had to pass through a bar, or gate, to pay their dues and eventually leave by another. Bear Lane takes its name from the latter barrier.

Much of the town's prosperity was based on the manufacture and sale of woollen cloth, although this activity had all but ceased by the 17th century. However, there was also a flourishing corn market which reached its peak in 1694 but was in decline 100 years later.

One legacy of those days are the yards where wagons could remain overnight. There were some 50 in all, and today, thankfully, some survive, mostly in West Street. This road had also expanded in the 13th century as the bishop laid out burgage plots when those in Castle Street were fully taken up. The buildings of the familiar timber-framed variety (Alice Holt Forest was a ready source) were infilled with lime-washed wattle and daub. This was made of hazel or cleft oak, woven, basket-style, and then daubed with a mixture of clay, dung and chopped straw that was usually applied as dry as possible to avoid shrinkage.

Although this construction material survived in some areas of the country until the 18th century, from about the 1500s in Farnham and other parts of the south-east wattle and daub began to be replaced by brick. Although visually more attractive – Tanyard House in Bridge Square is an example – it was actually less satisfactory, being heavy. It also retained damp and was a poor insulator. No matter. Its use marks the arrival of a building material in the town that was soon to be used in the structural form with which we are so familiar today.

Bricks had featured in Roman Britain, although they were used for specialist purposes, such as supporting heated floors, but not walls. Their use ceased when the legions departed. However, a limited revival began in the latter part of the 13th century, influenced by the increasing use of bricks in Holland and the Low Countries. It was not until the 16th century that, with supplies of timber dwindling, a truly national revival began.

the first six were exempt.
The idea was that those who lived in larger houses were in a position to pay more. These parameters were adjusted over the years and by 1747 the owner of a property with 20 or more windows was required to make an annual payment of 1s. (5p) for every window. It was not until 1851 that the by-then-discredited legislation, which was criticized as a tax on light and air, was repealed. By this time windows had, in any event, been getting larger. Tall and narrow three pane sash windows were an integral part of any Georgian facade, four panes followed in the late 18th century but by the 1800s the openings were enlarged, with margin panes being introduced on either side of the frame. A major advance came with the patenting, in 1838, of plate glass which meant that the number of glazing bars, which had been progressively slimmed down over the years, could be reduced. This allowed more light into houses, but, arguably, to the detriment of their outward appearances.

Blind windows at 15/16 Downing Street.

Bishop Wayneflete was an early user of brick and his gatehouse tower at Farnham Castle was built between 1470 and 1475. The turrets and crenellations are purely decorative. It bears no resemblance to any other surviving brick buildings of the period.

Opposite: The western wall of the Bailiffs' Hall in The Borough was briefly exposed during the construction of Town Hall Buildings in the early 1930s. The strapwork decoration below the roof line is readily apparent.

The evidence is readily apparent in Farnham. Stand at the bottom of Castle Street, outside Going Places premises, and look up the hill to the castle and the great brick gateway that overlooks the town. In 1470 Bishop William of Wayneflete began to improve his palace with the construction of this gatehouse tower which, paradoxically, is today known by the name of his successor, the blind Bishop Fox, who merely repaired it. But Wayneflete was an early user of brick: his tower predates the building of Hampton Court by some 50 years.

In 1927 a brick kiln was discovered at Hogshatch at the top of Folly Hill and it seems likely that this was the source of the material used. While the kiln was local, few people had experience of laying bricks in medieval Farnham. Bricklayers were therefore recruited from the Continent, probably the Low Countries. Cornelius Brekemason, a surname which clearly reflected his skill, and Jacob, his apprentice, worked on the project for 39 weeks, his relative, Adrian, for 28 and ffloraunce for 23. They were probably responsible for the elaborate decorative work on the exterior of the tower although Englishmen also assisted.

Now cast your eyes down Castle Street and look at the

plane trees on its eastern side. Behind them are Andrew Windsor's almshouses, which date from 1619, another modest but significant essay in local brick. In truth the construction of timber-framed buildings continued until the Restoration of Charles II in 1660. For instance, The Spinning Wheel on the south side of The Borough may date from the mid-17th century. But thereafter brick gained the ascendancy.

Fortunately there was an ample supply of local clay and this is why ours is essentially a brick-built town. Gault deposits at Wrecclesham were a source, along with outcrops of the Reading and London beds, while the presence of greensand provided an essential ingredient to the firing process.

Brick was used for the Bailiffs' Hall in The Borough, a few surviving parts of which may date from the 1650s. But an example of a Farnham house which reflects a more confident use of the material in the Classical idiom, although still embodying a rustic spirit, is Ivy House, better known as the Conservative Club, in Ivy Lane off Downing Street. It dates from the reign of Queen Anne and was completed in about 1700.

Ten Castle Street, now happily returned to its original appearance following the removal of Victorian "improvements" by the present owners, is only a few years younger and grander. Now compare it with 3 Downing Street, which bears the date of 1717. It is outwardly different, not only because of its rubbed brick decoration but, more significantly, for its parapeted frontage, which is

BEATING THE BRICK TAX

Like windows, bricks were subject to taxation and builders sometimes adopted ingenious methods to get around paying their dues. In 1769 Parliament legislated for bricks with dimensions of 8.25 x 4 x 2.5in (21 x 10 x 6.3cm). But 15 years later, in 1784, and faced with war in America, Parliament imposed a duty of 2s.6d. (12.5p) per 1000 bricks. Brickmakers responded by increasing the size of their stock while another ingenious solution was to produce tiles that resembled bricks. Look very carefully at the frontages of 1 and 2 Middle Church Lane. Although they appear to be brick, they are in fact faced with what were called mathematical tiles.

In 1803 the government retaliated by doubling the duty on bricks which had a capacity that exceeded 150 cubic inches (2460cu cm). In some areas this brought about changes in methods of house construction with a revival in weather-boarding and tile-hanging. Brick tax was eventually repealed in 1850.

The narrower the brick, the older it usually is.

Georgian Architecture
Strictly the term refers to the Classical architecture built in Britain during the reigns of the first four King Georges between 1714 and 1830. A movement which grew out of the Italian Renaissance in the 14th century and spread across Europe, it was based on rules of symmetry and proportion exemplified by the columns and pediments of the buildings of the Roman Empire, which were themselves Greek-inspired.

The style arrived in Britain in the 16th century but was invariably applied in an ☛

the forerunner of all such enhanced buildings in the town. This reflected the influence of London's Building Acts of 1707 and 1709 (see accompanying box).

The same builder may have been responsible for what, arguably, is the town's finest building, namely Willmer House in West Street. This was completed in 1718, and is today the home of the Museum of Farnham. While its splendid rubbed brick frontage would soon become unfashionable, its stature and three storeys would set the architectural pace in the town. The adjoining Sandford House, Bethune House at 88 West Street and 4 Downing Street all followed in its wake.

Most of these properties were built by individuals who had grown wealthy through the cultivation and sale of hops (see page 17), or sundry related businesses, which began around the town in the late 16th century. In 1800 William Cobbett described Farnham as occupying a "beautiful and fertile valley" and this was principally because of the presence of the River Wey and an outcrop of upper greensand, only a few hundred yards wide in places, which runs through the community. It provided the ideal conditions for growing hops and if there is one single

Ten Castle Street dates from the early 18th century and thus predates the parapet which features on many of Farnham's Georgian buildings. To the right is Long Garden Walk that was closed to road traffic in 1988.

reason why Farnham looks as it does today, look no further than the impact of this now vanished industry.

Hop grounds, "never gardens" insisted George Sturt, whose father was one of many growers, surrounded the town and many of the best of them lay only just behind the properties on the north sides of East and West Streets. By the 1850s about 1000 acres (405ha) were under cultivation.

For some 200 years, up until the 1880s, this highly lucrative crop, which was extremely vulnerable to both poor weather and disease, set the pace of Farnham's growth. Sturt recounts how in the summer anxieties began. "Were they coming into bloom properly? Were they at all 'lousy'? Was there any sign of 'blight' or 'mould' or 'mildew'?...Were the nights warm enough?"

With national beer consumption running at prodigious levels, partly because water supplies were inherently suspect, and Farnham's hops being some of the best and most expensive in the country, the profits were enormous. J. Alfred Eggar recorded that in 1850 bets were placed on the *duty*, levied at between 1.5 and 2d. (about 1p) a pound in weight that would be due on the annual crop. Forecasts for the latter ranged from £165,690 to £215,100, the equivilent of £7.7 to £10 million by today's values. And in a good year some £60,000 could be paid by an individual grower to the army of itinerant pickers who invaded Farnham in every September for the annual "hopping".

There were hops and kilns everywhere, many of the latter being built in the yards which had been such an integral part of medieval commercial life. Planter John Henry Knight remembered them "...in East Street, Bear Lane and West Street, and the smell of the sulphur used in drying was anything but pleasant." The entire crop was then dispatched by wagons – although from the 1850s it

undisciplined form – note the crudely interpreted Ionic volutes (miniature scrolls) on either side of the Bailiffs' Hall in The Borough. Renaissance architecture was not correctly interpreted in Britain until 1616 when Inigo Jones, inspired by the fine, understated work of the 16th-century Italian architect Andrea Palladio, built the Queen's House in Greenwich and followed it with the Banqueting House at Whitehall in 1619. To these were added, in the 1670s, the sash window, almost certainly an English invention.

A further significant influence was the Great Fire of London of 1666 which resulted in the capital's Building Act of 1707. This required potentially combustible timber eaves, ☛

Harold Falkner's 24 West Street, dated 1790.

Left: Just two of the many oasts that used to be found throughout the town. The cowl, with its attendant wind vane, was a hot air outlet. Its flat top is typical of South-East England, oasts in the West Midlands had pointed "witch's hat" cowls.

clearly visible, for example, at Ivy House, to be replaced by a fireproof stone cornice that was topped by a parapet, as at 3 Downing Street. A second Act of 1709 dictated for the same reasons that the sashes be recessed by four inches (10cm), see 9 Castle Street, which left a "reveal" of naked brickwork. Later, in 1774, came a further Building Act with the result that brickwork further encroached on the sash, only leaving a modicum of wood uncovered.

In the late 17th century architects of the standing of Sir Christopher Wren and Sir John Vanburgh had developed an indigenous version of the European baroque style noted for its freedom and vigour. Willmer House is in this spirit. The movement was abruptly curtailed from the 1720s onwards by the influential Lord Burlington and his circle who required that buildings should remain true to the works of Palladio and Inigo Jones. Later, from the 1780s, the Adam brothers provided lighter relief with decoration, often externally expressed with scalloped fanlights and decorated cornices, as at 90 West Street. Soon afterwards tiles began to be replaced by slates, and stucco, a plaster wall covering that resembled stone, also gained acceptance and its influence endured right up until the 1870s.

went by train – for sale at the Weyhill Fair in Hampshire. There Farnham's hops were mostly bought by West Country and Midlands brewers.

While the principal hop growers and maltsters built the largest properties, many of the occupants of smaller, but nonetheless delectable, town houses were similarly employed. But who designed them? Alas, we do not know. Until the mid-18th century Britain did not possess an established architectural profession, although there were many individuals who described themselves as such! And while the moving spirits behind the great country houses of those day are known, town properties, which Farnham possesses by the score, were generally the work of anonymous local craftsmen. So a builder, fortified by books of designs and working with a bricklayer and carpenter, would aim to place the emphasis on proportion, rather than decoration, making sure that one element of a house's frontage was harmoniously related to the other.

In later years architect Harold Falkner, who has made such an immeasurable contribution to Farnham's townscape, looked in vain for any names of such people. He reported: "I have searched the ratepayers' lists, directories, and parish registers, before 1800 and I can find neither the name of an architect nor of a surveyor."

But during the first half of the 19th century, the identities of builders and architects begin to emerge from the shadows. Pigot's Directory of Surrey of 1839 lists just one Farnham architect, James Harding, who was also a builder and surveyor. Resident at 59 West Street, he may have been responsible for 118 West Street and is credited with the nave of Froyle Church and the north aisle of St Mary's, Frensham.

Such was the hold that the Classical Orders had on the town that Farnham, with a few notable exceptions, escaped the worst excesses of the Victorian age. And when houses began to be fashionably faced with stucco, it invariably concealed well proportioned brickwork more associated with the previous century. 118 West Street, today occupied by Currys, and Zingari Terrace in East Street are examples. More significantly, the appearance of this cladding did not supplant brick that was out-of-favour nationally. Farnham Station, the nearby Exchange pub and Still House in East Street look "Georgian". In fact they all date from about the middle of the 19th century.

By contrast, there could be no doubting the date of Farnham's new Corn Exchange and Town Hall that was completed in 1866 on the prime south-eastern corner site of Castle Street and The Borough. It was a development that had seen the demolition of John Clarke's by then *Old* Market House, the idea being to bring the market under cover. Other benefits were the creation of an assembly room, together with offices and a range of shops facing The Borough.

It was built in a style which *The Builder* described as "an adaptation of that prevalent in Italy during the 11th and 12th centuries". No doubt at the request of the architect, local bricks were dispensed with, and it was instead built, inside and out, in white Huntingdon stock. The corner was dominated by an 88ft (27m) tower surmounted by a belfry and slated spire. As far as the

Hops Are Tops

Hops – specifically the plant's female flowers or cones – not only imbue beer with its bitter taste, they also act as a preservative. And while the oasts, where hops are dried, are seen to be as English as the pint of best bitter they help to produce, beer was a Continental import that arrived in this country from Holland at the beginning of the 15th century. At that time the national drink was ale, made from malt and flavoured with herbs and spices.

The hop bines took root in Britain in the 1520s, first in Kent, and then spread throughout the country as beer rapidly overtook ale in popularity. Hops came to Farnham later in that century and, as John Aubrey wrote in *The Natural History and Antiquities of Surrey* published in 1673, "about this Town are Hops in as great plenty as in any part of England, if not greater...And ever since they have planted larger quantities...no less than 300 Acres of Hop-Yard."

Farnham hops consistently fetched high prices on account of their flavour. Also light in colour, demand increased from the 1750s as paler beers grew in popularity. This was mostly thanks to the White Bine Grape hop, introduced by Peckham ☛

Farnham's Victorian Town Hall was opened in 1866 and its demolition began in 1930.

Williams, who enjoyed the trappings of a country gentleman at Badshot Place, his substantial residence at Badshot Lea.

In 1805, when a pocket (240lb/109kg) of Kentish hops cost £7 to £9, those from Sussex fetched £8.5s. (£8.25), but Farnham's commanded a price of £10.15s. (£10.75).

Local hop grounds usually varied in size from about 15 to 60 acres (6-24ha) and the plants grew up poles variously of 10, 18 and 20 feet (3, 5.5 and 6m) in height. But disease was always a problem. In 1823 William Cobbett noted at Selborne, "the bines and leaves are black, near, as soot...and covered with lice...Upon inquiry I find that the hops are equally bad at Alton, Froyle, Crondall, and even at Farnham." From the 1850s they were dusted with sulphur to help control mould. 1865 saw a soft soap solution being used a crude insecticide and after 1883 spraying became the norm.

Usually picked in Farnham on around 8th September, "hopping" lasted for about three weeks. Picking was immediately followed by drying the cones ☛

Hops represented in one of the stone reliefs on the north wall of Farnham Police Station.

remainder of the three storey building was concerned, "the mullions of the windows are of Bath stone, with carved caps and red terracotta shafts." It was destined to be as incongruous for its location as East Street's Woolmead development would be exactly 100 years later.

In the best Victorian traditions the Corn Exchange was the product of a competition, the winner being the London-based Edward Wyndham Tarn, architect to the Religious Tracts Society. He remained in the profession for only a further ten years, preferring to concentrate on authorship. His formative work, *Stability of Domes*, was published in 1866 in the same year that his Farnham building was completed. Not for the first time, an architect would inflict a building on a town which he rarely, if ever, would have to visit.

Just two years years later in 1868, and only two doors away at 75 Castle Street, the results of the work of the celebrated Victorian architect Richard Norman Shaw, who also practised in London, were clearly apparent. The bank he designed, for a princely fee of £18,000, was for the local Knight family. A massive four-storey Neo-Tudor pile, it was jettied and tile-hung and built at a scale that was wholly at odds with its surroundings.

This incongruity was probably the result of clients wishing to place their stamp on the town, being egged on by their architect, and vice versa. "When we builds, we builds," either John or James Knight is said to have remarked of the towering structure. Shaw would have required little encouragement. Many of his other commissions, because of their gigantic proportions, have been demolished in the face of the latter-day realities of practicality and maintenance.

Not all Victorian building in the town was so intrusive. In 1865, when the new Corn Exchange was under construction, work was also underway on the recently restored St Andrew's Church. The aim was to double the height of its tower. The original, rather squat, 15th-century edifice had the appearance of having been abruptly truncated at 65ft (20m) and it was surmounted by an ungainly cupola.

The extension, which took its height to 120ft (36.6m), was completed in October 1865. Dr Charles Sumner, Bishop of Winchester, who had taken the keenest interest in the project, spoke of the new tower as "a noble pile, lifting its turrets high and glorious above meaner things, giving Farnham an air of importance it never possessed before." But the bells remained situated at their original lower level for a further five years before they were raised to the present belfry.

The work cost £1686. The architect was the appropriately named Ewan Christian, who built 27 churches and restored some 350 more. He was paid £78, but most of the locally raised money went to the builder, Frank Birch, whose bill was £1591. He was having a busy

Left: A drawing by Harold Falkner of Norman Shaw's gargantuan 75 Castle Street, built in 1868 and demolished in 1931. Its ornate chimneys were reconstructed at The Bush Hotel and in the Bailiffs' Hall, The Borough.

over charcoal fires that took place in kilns, or oasts. These were square in outline until the 1840s, when round oasts were constructed under the mistaken impression that they were more efficient. Both styles continued until about 1900 when the angular style again attained ascendancy.

The decline in Farnham's hop industry began in 1885, against a background of ten years of disastrous summers. Brewers had begun to import cheaper hops from the Continent and North America where they were less vulnerable to the vagaries of climate. Paradoxically, this occurred at a time when beer consumption was at an all-time high, although the temperance movement would accelerate the closure of local public houses. And the town's hop grounds were particularly vulnerable to the twin demands of building and gravel extraction. Hops are still to be found in gardens and hedgerows throughout the Farnham area as reminders of those years when they dramatically transformed the fortunes and appearance of our town.

Right: Hop pickers enjoying the Farnham Herald *in September 1958.*

Victorian Architecture
If the 18th century represented 100 years of order as far as architecture was concerned, the Victorian era was characterized by what some might regard as disorder as a multiplicity of styles held sway.

Up until the 1850s, most houses tended to remain Classical in outline, although they were invariably rendered in stucco with slate roofs and embellishments to windows and door surrounds. Churches usually were built in the Gothic style, which followed a revival begun in the mid-18th century.

However, the publication of John Ruskin's influential trilogy, *The Stones of Venice* (1851-53), also gave a particular fillip to Italian Gothic themes which featured arches of alternating coloured stone. These initially appeared in public buildings, ☛

41 Castle Street dates from 1866.

time because he was simultaneously responsible for the new 'Exchange and, later, Knights Bank. His father, William, had established his business by the 1820s in Castle Street and subsequently moved to a yard in Downing Street where the police station now stands. But it was his son's association with Norman Shaw which proved enduring. In 1876 he built Pierrepont at Frensham. Later, in 1878, when Shaw essayed Flete, a massive Neo-Medieval pile in Devon, for Henry Bingham Milmay of Barings Bank, he took Frank Birch with him. When he died, this noted Farnham builder left an estate valued at some £150,000, which was about £30,000 more than the bequests of the prolific Victorian architect, Sir George Gilbert Scott.

In 1863 Birch had taken on an articled pupil called Gordon Tompsett. He was destined to take over the building business which was renamed Tompsett & Kingham on account of his alliance with John Kingham, architect son of Farnham grocer William Kingham. The latter invested £10,000 in the firm, but Kingham junior departed in 1896 to set up in practice, which he combined with an estate agency, at Grosvenor Road, Aldershot.

His best-known Farnham work dates from 1921 and is the reconstructed Lion and Lamb Hotel in West Street. In the meantime Tompsett remained at Longbridge until 1909, by which time he had completed the construction of the town's new Council offices in South Street.

Two of his former apprentices, Arthur Mardon and John Mills, were the new occupants of what was known as the Steam Joinery Works. Mardon & Mills, a company that built Church House in nearby Union Road, endured until 1919 when Mardon departed to the adjoining Wagon Yard, having formed a new business with George Ball. Mills had, in the interim, been joined in the business by his children. As John Mills & Sons – they had Harold Falkner's Town Hall Buildings to their credit – the firm survived until about 1954. For its part Mardon, Ball, which built Lloyds' new bank in Castle Street, lasted until 1965.

In 1958 another Farnham building institution, Goddard and Sons, based at 65 East Street, closed down after around 100 years in business. Founded by John Goddard, its commissions included over 50 churches in the district, and the firm also attained a national reputation for laying parquet flooring.

Then there were W. German and Son in West Street, Crosby, which was responsible for Farnham Grammar School, and Caesar Brothers at Hale, who built Farnham's first cinema in Bear Lane. The brothers George and Alfred Robins not only developed much of the south of the town, they also pursued another lucrative activity with the extraction of local gravel deposits.

With so much building activity, skilled workers were in great demand. Harold Falkner recalled that, in the late 19th century, Farnham had "a group of very excellent craftsmen in the carpentry and joinery trades. Not many of these were locals. I remember the tradition that if a man called in [at Tompsett's], in the evening he could have the cost of a night's lodging on the strength of his tools."

This was how the builders called Le Clerqs, who were active in the town during the interwar years, arrived in

as did elaborate, often multi-coloured, external and internal decorations featuring different building materials. The latter were all too apparent on Farnham's Corn Exchange of 1866.

A reaction to Classical designs, and what was denounced by Ruskin as a dishonest, foreign style, took root in the 1860s having been given expression in William Morris' Red House of 1859. Philip Webb's design drew on English vernacular themes of brick walls and tiled roofs in which Roman symmetry gave way to irregularity.

Late in the century Arts and Crafts architecture, as typified by Church House in Union Road, took as its inspiration the plain walls and asymmetry of the medieval cottage.

Norman Shaw, that accomplished mixer of styles, from the 1860s built a series of outstanding country houses in which tall chimney stacks with decorated caps and the tile-hanging of a Wealden cottage were successfully juxtaposed. The latter features appeared at Knight's Bank in Castle Street, demolished in 1931, although his distinctive chimneys survive (see page 114). Shaw was also a practitioner of a Queen Anne revival, begun in the 1870s.

Goddard and Sons' works at 65 East Street in 1958.

Farnham. Hailing from the Channel Islands, they landed at Southampton with the intention of walking to London. But they stopped in the town on the way and decided to stay.

Falkner had been one of Gordon Tompsett's more talented but impatient recruits. He later recalled that when he first began to take an interest in architecture in the 1880s "there were two oldish men practising – Mr Wonnacott, a prominent Free Churchman who would not build a pub; the other, Mr Stapley, had no such prejudices." Sidney Stapley was in fact Harold Falkner's next-door neighbour at 23 West Street. He was surveyor to the town's Burial Board and Inspector of Nuisances for the Local Board, while much of his work was for Farnham United Breweries. Reputedly, he designed the defunct Fox and Hounds which adjoined its West Street premises and The Albion in East Street. He died in 1900. His daughter, Jessie, married builder John Goddard.

Thomas Wonnacott's practice was at 112 West Street. A Cornish school teacher and lay preacher, he had switched careers at the age of 25 in 1859 and went to work in an architect's office. He arrived in Farnham in 1866, following attendance at University College, London. A Methodist, he is best remembered as the architect of the Congregational, now the United Reformed Church in South Street. Destined to become a familiar local figure seen astride his tricycle, by 1890 he had returned to Cornwall to continue his practice there. He retired in 1902 but by 1908 was back in Farnham, via the Isle of Wight. Stylistically both men were at odds, Stapley's work tended to be Classically inspired while, as a builder of churches, Gothic was Wonnacott's favoured style, although an example of his more conventional domestic work can be seen at 15 South Street. He is also thought to have been responsible for the semi-detached houses on the north side of Abbey Street.

Between 1877 and 1887 he was in partnership with William Wells, who had been his pupil between the years 1872 and 1876. When the Cornishman left town, Wells, who has been credited with 21 The Borough, continued with the practice. From 1911 this was based at 63 Castle Street, his home until he died in 1928.

Another of Wonnacott's pupils was J. Alfred Eggar but his architectural works in the town centre were few, 7 and 10 West Street being his best-known designs. However, he was responsible for a number of schools in the area. Like

John Kingham, he had a second string to his bow and his auctioneering and estate agency soon overshadowed his architectural practice. This was a reflection of the fact that Farnham was growing; its population doubled from 3142 in 1831 to some 7300 in 1910.

Expansion had begun in earnest in the 1870s when the first of the more easterly hop fields between East Street and Farnham Park gave way to housing. This was followed in the early 1880s by inroads made into the Waverley Estate to the south. Then the neighbouring Fir Grove Estate also began to make way for bricks and mortar. The prestigious Great Austins development followed in the leafy spirit of Letchworth Garden City of 1903 and, in due course, Farnham Lane was accorded the now familiar name of Firgrove Hill.

The hop grounds were disappearing, for the industry was, by the late 19th century, in decline. And its plight did not leave the community unscathed. Falkner remembered in his boyhood "30 empty properties in the town, 13 of them being shops in The Borough. Bankruptcies were frequent – Carr, the corn and hay factor of Willey Mill was one...Tom Mathews, the brewer, was another."

Nevertheless, the commercial accent was on growth and a contributory factor to this expansion had been the arrival in 1849 of a branch of the London and South Western Railway. In those days the journey to Waterloo was made via Guildford. The present route to the capital through Aldershot dates from 1870 and reflected the growth in importance of an erstwhile village which, following the Crimean War, was transformed into the principal camp of the British army. Farnham would soon feel the effect of thousands of thirsty soldiers on its doorstep. Beer sales rose dramatically and led in no small part to the creation in 1889 of Farnham United Breweries.

The number of public houses in the town, that existed in respectable numbers anyway thanks to the hop industry, grew in the second half of the 19th century. In 1892 there were 45 in Farnham, a state of affairs only reversed in 1902 by local magistrates who that year closed seven of them. The Justices continued with their purge until 1927, while other pubs succumbed to dwindling custom.

The arrival of the railway also spelled the end of the great era of the stagecoach. This had reached its peak in the 1830s. In Farnham Hero, Red Rover and Tally Ho used

Harold Falkner (1875–1963)
Harold Falkner's father, Charles, was a prosperous Dippenhall hop grower and farmer. However, he died aged only 37 in 1875, just five months before ☛

Harold Falkner (left) in the mid-1950s with F.A. Morgan, headmaster, between 1925 and 1954, of Farnham Grammar School. This photograph was taken by the latter's daughter, Sylvia Morgan.

to stop at The Lion and Lamb, The Goat's Head (demolished to make way for the new Corn Exchange) and The Bush. A regular train service to London sowed the seeds of Farnham becoming a commuter town but, with freight now arriving by rail rather than road, the era of the horse-drawn wagon was also beginning to pass. The demise of Wagon Yard – later occupied by Mardon, Ball – dates from this time. Building materials, namely bricks and slates, were also transported by rail with the result that yellow London stock began increasingly to be seen in the town. It is surely no coincidence that they are to be found around the area of Farnham Station?

String-straight South Street, together with Union Road, was opened in 1870 in direct response to the arrival of the railway. Previously the only way to Station Hill had been via Longbridge and the narrow, unsuitable Abbey Street. In many respects the construction of the new road marked the beginning of the modern era, although property development began slowly and continued intermittently over the next 30 or so years. Nationally, stucco had now given way to terracotta decoration and this duly enhanced the look of many of the new street's shops and offices, behind which, on its eastern side, the cattle market had found a new home. South Street's status was further

Farnham has long been a commuter town, the railway having arrived in 1849.

underpinned by the completion in 1902 of new impressive offices in the Queen Anne style for Farnham Urban District Council (UDC), created in 1895. This was the work of the latest recruit to the town's small architectural community.

In 1889 Paxton Hood Watson had established himself at 15 West Street. He had previously been articled to Charles and Septimus Searle and Edward Hayes in London's Ludgate Hill. He had also studied in Italy and was an accomplished Classicist. Architect Guy Maxwell Aylwin recalls that he was "a remarkable man…I remember him well, always in a tearing hurry and viewed by his townsfolk with feelings in which admiration and amusement competed for precedence." Watson was clearly destined for greater things. By 1900 he had gone to concentrate on his London office at 4 Adam Street, Adelphi, which he had opened in 1897. In addition to the Council's premises in South Street, soon to be outgrown by the new authority, he has left us the nearby former Central Club and 94 West Street on the corner of The Hart. However, much of the detail work of these buildings was undertaken by his able pupil, Alfred Cox.

In 1909, just seven years after the completion of the Council offices, around the corner, a still raw Union Road was to be similarly improved by the completion of a new

Harold, who was his third child, was born on 28th November. Brought up by his mother at 24 West Street, with his sisters he attended Miss Andrews' School at 89 West Street, then Churchers College, Petersfield, which he hated. So he completed his education at Farnham Grammar School, next door to his home.

After attending evening classes at the Farnham School of Art, at the age of 16 he became a full-time student there where he also studied wood carving. Exposed to the influence of W.H. Allen, he embarked on an architectural career which began with a two-year apprenticeship, during which he studied building practice, with Tompsett & Kingham. Articled to London

Harold Falkner's inspired "creative reconstruction" of the frontage of the Bailiffs' Hall dates from 1934. It replaced a Victorian front, see page 49.

architect Sir Reginald Blomfield, he qualified at the age of 21 in 1897 which was the year in which his mother died.

Commissioned that same year as honorary architect of the Farnham Swimming Pool, a subsequent association with two other architects proved to be short-lived. It dated from 1900 to 1903, although the brass plate which proclaimed the names of *Falkner, Niven and Wrigglesworth* remained a fixture outside the door of his West Street home for many years afterwards.

Initially drawn to the Arts and Crafts movement and in particular to the work of C.F.A. Voysey, for whom Tompsett had built houses, Falkner was soon swept into the Classical Revival. "Stranger's Corner", a house commissioned by his mentor Allen, was in this style, as was much of his work in the town.

During the First World War Harold Falkner joined the Royal Engineers but he badly injured his leg in a motorcycle accident near Newbury and thereafter walked with a pronounced limp.

Eccentric and articulate with a lively sense of humour, but impatient and abrupt in manner, he wore a succession of ☛

property. While so much of Farnham reflects the influence of the Classical world, Church House has the distinction of being the town centre's only Arts and Crafts building, so named because the Arts and Crafts movement reflected a revival of interest in the country's vernacular architecture. In this instance a local architect was not chosen; instead the commission went to Richard Bassnett Preston, who was Manchester-based and has many churches in the north-west to his credit. Artist-craftsman William Morris is credited with being the instigator of the movement, talents which Harold Falkner, who qualified as an architect in 1897, possessed in abundance.

Forget the latter-day image of an eccentric, sartorially indifferent "super tramp" who had apparently endless brushes with authority. In fact, Falkner was an architect of great ability and an outstanding craftsman. However, perhaps "one of the greatest handicaps he suffered", as Guy Maxwell Aylwin has suggested, was the £10,000 fortune (the equivalent of half a million pounds by today's values) that he inherited in 1896. This meant that he no longer needed to work for a living. Thankfully he did continue to do so, but he bridled at the form-filling and the bureaucracy of building regulations. His technical drawings were, by all accounts, abysmal and his disdain for clients absolute! He completed no less than 100 or so buildings in Farnham and district but, if you wish to see his qualities best exemplified, contemplate his reconstruction of the frontage of Bailiffs' Hall in The Borough which is a triumph of perception, sensitivity and proportion.

While a pupil at Farnham Grammar School, he forged a friendship with Charles Borelli, a boy two years his senior, which endured until the latter died in 1950. It was an association destined to be of incalculable worth to the town. For if the impatient, opinionated, supremely talented Falkner was the engine of the partnership, then the diplomatic, urbane Borelli provided the steering and the brakes.

Bill Ewbank-Smith, a past rating officer for Farnham UDC and the author of a splendid trilogy of books on the town, knew both men. "Together in their lifetime, they became a legend. Both unmarried, they were free to devote their abundant talents to a common cause, the preservation or restoration of Farnham's older buildings."

The individual credited with firing both men's commitment to Georgian architecture is William Herbert Allen, who became Master of Farnham School of Art in

battered green felt hats, shorn of their brims. Removal of this distinctive headgear, recalled his long-time friend, solicitor Alfred J. Stevens, "would set free a flowing mass of white hair over a high forehead…the shape of his one-time perfect aquiline nose was somewhat marred [in his later years] when he drove into the end of some scaffolding poles carried by the vehicle in front…his eyes were very striking and bright and unerringly observant and the natural dignity of the whole man was such that it would not have mattered if he wore 20 scarecrow hats; he was always entirely himself in any place and any company."

Today he is commemorated by Falkner Court, off South Street and Falkner Road, appropriately the home of the Surrey Institute of Art & Design.

Before Borelli and Falkner: 6/7 The Borough, with the advertisements that disfigured them before the First World War.

The new ground floor bow windows were the most obvious change.

Charles Ernest Borelli (1873–1950)

Mission accomplished: Charles Borelli stands amid the rubble of the demolished Corn Exchange.

Immortalized by the Wey-side Borelli Walk and Borelli Yard and Mews, Charles (although Ernest to his friends) was born on 18th August at 48 Castle Street. When he was four, the family moved to 35/36 The Borough. This shop, complete with a yard that was Farnham's finest, was to be his home for the remainder of his life. His father, Charles, had come to the town from Italy as a boy to join his uncle Clemente's jewellery, silversmith and watchmaking business. When he died in 1917, Ernest and his brother Frank, known as Leo, took over. Both were prominently associated with the Roman Catholic community.

Following education at Farnham Grammar School, Borelli studied in London at the Horological Institute where he won the Turner's Medal, given by the Lord Mayor of London, which carried with it the Freedom of the City. In 1906 he became a member of Farnham UDC and remained so for some ☛

1889, after the original appointee unexpectedly took up a position in New South Wales. An accomplished watercolourist and gifted teacher, Allen, to his eternal credit, also succeeded in convincing Falkner to take up an architectural career rather than becoming a vet as had been his original ambition.

"He transformed our outlook, which thought nothing of our Georgian past and relegated its furniture to the attics," Falkner remembered and Allen similarly motivated Charles Borelli, whose family had arrived in Farnham from Italy in the late 18th century. For him Allen's words were perhaps more of a reawakening because the architectural influences of the Renaissance were readily apparent throughout the town. Destined to spend some 40 years as a councillor, he and Falkner became a two-man planning committee and they were to have a profound impact on Farnham's appearance. Not only were numerous buildings given "the treatment", the first came in 1910, some were acquired and other owners of property in the town followed in their wake.

It was a creed also espoused by The Old Farnham Society, formed in 1911, which, in addition to Borelli and Falkner, counted W.H. Allen and George Sturt among its founding fathers. Whatever new building took place in Farnham between the wars was therefore invariably Classical in inspiration and conceived to chime with its surroundings. The Neo-Georgian style works well when executed in this context although less so when, in more recent years, it has been applied to office development.

In consequence there are very few properties in the town centre that reflect contemporary architectural thinking. The most significant of these was the Regal in East Street, the work of Harold Seymour Scott, a Birmingham architect who had designed his first cinema, The Oak at his local Selly Oak, in 1922. But even then Borelli succeeded in convincing its owners that they should build in brick, rather than opt for walls of towering stucco. Completed in 1933 in what today is known as the Art Deco style, it was summarily demolished in 1987.

The same fate befell 38 to 44 South Street in 1981, which were brick and tiled shops with flats above whose design unmistakably reflected the influence of the Modern Movement. However, Dibben's former builder's merchants showrooms and depot in East Street, designed by local architect H.Y. Margary in 1937, still survives.

Although the results of the Borelli/Falkner regime can be seen throughout the town, their influence is most apparent on the corner of Castle Street and The Borough. There, in 1930, work began on the demolition of Wyndham Tarn's Corn Exchange and Town Hall. Over the next four years, it was replaced by the range of Town Hall Buildings which sprang from Falkner's prolific pen. A great improvement on the ornate Italianate pile they replaced, despite its name, the community lost its Town Hall as the building's upper storey was given over mostly to offices.

Soon afterwards, in 1931, Norman Shaw's gargantuan Neo-Tudor timbers were also felled to be replaced by a smaller, far less dramatic building. Although its "Georgian" replacement was more in scale with its neighbours in Castle Street, it was, perhaps, a little dull by comparison.

Harold Falkner was Farnham's dominant architect until the completion of the Town Hall complex in 1934. Thereafter he began to devote much more of his time to Dippenhall where he created nine extraordinary timber-framed houses, the first of which dated from 1921.

Falkner's contemporary Arthur Stedman had also gained his practical experience with a Farnham builder. But in his case it was Goddards during the ten years between 1886 and 1896. The son of a Normandy wheelwright, Stedman attended Farnham School of Art and in 1896 opened his practice in South Street. His work included Bells Potter's nearby offices and the McDonald Almshouses at the end of West Street. He was consulting architect to the Diocese of Guildford and Farnham UDC. A near neighbour in South Street was Alfred Guyer, who in 1902 designed the local authority's first council houses which were to grow in number during the interwar years.

Farnham continued to expand to the south-east after the First World War. In 1922 the oasts at Broomfield Farm, near Farnham Station, were demolished. Their disappearance signified, if it were needed, a demonstrable end of hop-growing in the town, although the legacy lingered on until 1973 before finally being extinguished from The Hart. Such was the town's growth that in the 1930s its population exceeded the 20,000 mark for the first time. By 1959 it had grown to over 25,000.

Between the wars, the ranks of the town's practising architects were swelled by the arrival of Guy Maxwell

40 years. He was its chairman in 1911, again in 1927-29 and, although in the following year he lost his seat by one vote, he was re-elected in 1931. On his return he informed his colleagues that "on severing his connection with the Council in 1930, the rooks had departed from the trees of Station Hill, but now they were back again building their nests."*

It was his friendship with Harold Falkner, a relationship that solicitor A.J. Stevens described as a "David and Jonathan partnership", that was to prove of incalculable value to the town. "Both had keen eyes for everything that was going on in the building line, and if Falkner had the main ideas, Borelli was invaluable in helping to carry them out".

In 1944 his commitment to Farnham's architecture resulted in him being awarded honorary membership of the Georgian Group.

The *Farnham Herald's* proprietor, Ernest Langham, remembered "in scores of controversies about his beloved Town he never lost his temper; in fact he always seemed unruffled...Serene as he was, he was, however, tremendously tenacious, and never knew what defeat meant. It is really astonishing how often he turned defeat into victory."

**Farnham in War and Peace* by W. Ewbank-Smith

The first stage of Harold Falkner's Town Hall Buildings was completed in 1932. Note that the entrance to the ground floor corner site, then occupied by the National Provincial Bank, was in Castle Street, rather than The Borough as is now the case.

Aylwin. The son of John Maxwell Aylwin, a butcher of 8 West Street, after studying at Farnham Grammar School he won an architectural scholarship to King's College, London. Thanks to an introduction from Harold Falkner, he was articled to Niven and Wrigglesworth in the capital and briefly worked, before war service, on the plans for New Delhi with Sir Herbert Baker. Later, in the mid-1920s, Aylwin spent three years in Jersey as resident architect to Sir Jesse Boot, but he returned to Farnham in 1927.

There he entered into what he later described as a "rather explosive partnership" with Harold Falkner which endured until 1930. He later remembered "the inevitable 'blow up' has not prevented us remaining good friends and neighbours. We share a mutual respect which in his case is generous, in mine inevitable." The one-time Alliance public house on the corner of Downing and West Streets and The New Seven Stars were designed during this period. Aylwin was also responsible for Bush House in South Street. This was completed in 1937, the year he moved to 26 West Street which served as his home and office.

In 1929 at about the same time as the Aylwin/Falkner association was bearing fruit, Arthur Stedman was joined by his son Leonard, who had studied architecture at the Bartlett School, London University and then been a pupil of the celebrated Sir Edwin Lutyens. While in his employ, he worked on Queen Mary's famous doll's house. On joining his father's practice, Leonard Stedman essayed the Royal Deer Buildings in South Street; his many other local works included a shop and flats at 26 Downing Street, and 49 Castle Street, a fine house in a prime location. After the end of the war he was responsible for the design of over 600 council houses and eventually retired in 1969.

By this time the firm had been renamed Stedman and Blower, a name which followed the arrival in 1964 of Michael Blower. After qualification at the Architectural Association, he was project architect for the 1958 Brussels World Fair. He joined Stedman from the Guildford practice of Scott Brownrigg and Turner. Among his many local commissions, Michael Blower was responsible for The Paviors in Lower South View and Cobbetts Mews in The Hart, completed in 1976. A dedicated conservationist, he undertook the restorations of Tanyard House in Bridge Square and 30 and 31 Lower Church Lane for the Farnham (Building Preservation) Trust of which he is a member.

In 1980, as his South Street offices were due to be demolished because of the Sainsbury's redevelopment, Michael Blower moved to The Fairfield. In 1989 he transferred his practice to Runfold House, his home since the early 1970s, where his sons Damian and Robert continue the family profession. Coincidentally, Runfold Farm had been occupied by farmer and hop grower Alan Tice, who in 1929 had married Arthur Stedman's daughter, Gwen. So the property is still in the family, so to speak!

Lionel Stedman was not the only second-generation architect. John Maxwell Aylwin, who arrived in Farnham after architectural training in 1953, became a partner in his father's practice in the late 1950s and he retired in the 1980s. Of his numerous local commissions, Arundell House in West Street, today renamed Craven House, is his best-known Farnham building.

In many respects the town of the early postwar years seemed little changed from the previous decade. In 1947 the Town and Country Planning Act was passed, a development that inspired the revival of the Old Farnham

Society (although the prefix was dropped). Ever since, this body has carefully monitored development in the town. Its highest amenity award is a plaque given to those buildings which are judged to have made an environmental contribution to Farnham.

As the community thrived in the early postwar years, so the amount of traffic passing through its streets steadily grew. And, incredibly, those motorists who used the A31 main road had to contend with Abbey Street and Red Lion Lane until July 1957 when the long-awaited bypass finally opened. Work had begun on the project as early as 1938, but it ceased in 1940 following the outbreak of the war.

More car parking was needed. In 1949 the Council agreed to build what is now the Central Car Park although it was only approved by the casting vote of the chairman. Charles Borelli was outraged and in a letter to the *Farnham Herald* wrote of the decision as "a step to undo much of the work which I have been able to accomplish...it will completely alter and destroy the centre of the most ancient part of Farnham" But the scheme went ahead. The car park was further expanded ten years later and enlarged again in 1988. The Wagon Yard facility off Downing Street followed in 1966, the same year that a one-way traffic system came into operation.

The backs of buildings are often more revealing that their frontages. This photograph, taken in May 1959, shows the rear of 96 West Street, built in 1893, on the corner of The Hart, occupied for many years by butcher B.W. Toop. The adjoining older long building belonged to neighbouring 95. Both were demolished and replaced in 1967 by a Neo-Georgian office block, today named Sequel House.

Change was in the air. In the early 1960s Toop the butcher, and the adjoining Old House Bookshop, on the eastern corner of West Street and The Hart closed. Sir John Verney Bt., who made an immeasurable contribution to the town in the postwar years, spoke for many when he recalled "the shock when we learnt that [they] had been bought by a developer...Both remained empty for years, their windows plastered with fly-posters. It was as if a large crack had suddenly appeared on the serene face of Farnham. Was nothing any longer sacred? It wasn't."

Finally 96 and 97 West Street were demolished and replaced in 1967 by the impersonal Craven House, a Neo-Georgian office block by Guy Maxwell Aylwin which housed the offices of property developers Ellis Campbell. Today named Sequel House, it has visually suffered, like an increasing number of the town's offices and houses, from the fitment of plastic "sash" windows.

Craven House was in the Borelli/Falkner idiom, but Farnham's new, modern police station by County Architect John Harrison was, in retrospect, a far more satisfactory building, although it was much criticized at the time. Opened in 1963, it was well-proportioned, of good brick and just two storeys high with a roof of Roman tiles. It was built on the site of Mills & Sons' yard in Downing Street. Commended by Alec Clifton-Taylor in *County Life*, he predicted that it would "be a pleasant neighbour, and quickly settle down in its surroundings." And so it has proved.

However, 1962 had seen the draper J.E. Spencer, on the corner of The Borough and Downing Street, close its doors after an occupancy of 95 years. The demolition of its elegant early 19th-century premises soon followed. Sight lines for traffic were a problem and in 1929 the issue had been addressed on the west side of Downing and West Streets by Harold Falkner and Guy M. Aylwin's inspired Alliance public house. Sadly, its newly built opposite number was not only stark but graceless.

At least the new 51 The Borough was built of brick, but the community was already trying to adjust to modern architecture when in 1962 the five-storey, boxy, brutal Expedier House replaced Heath and Wiltshire's Edwardian garage in Union Road. It was demolished in 1987. In later years the *Farnham Herald* dubbed it the town's "most unpopular building architecturally".

Numbers 51/52 The Borough, occupied by Spencer's drapery shop from 1867 until it closed in 1962, and here pictured in January 1963, was demolished in 1964. It was replaced, below, by what was originally a Lipton's supermarket.

But there was more, much more of the same to come.

In the middle of 1962 the London-based Land and House Property Corporation acquired a substantial parcel of land on the north-west side of East Street. It then invited architects William H. Robbins of Wigmore Street, London to prepare a scheme for its redevelopment. This represented the start of The Woolmead project. It is of little comfort to Farnham that at this time many of Britain's historic towns had their centres desecrated by demolition to make way for wholly unsuitable buildings inspired by a movement that sought to expunge all stylistic links with the past. To this was coupled a disregard for architectural heritage – the word really belongs to the following decade – that reached to the very heart of government.

It should be recalled that Philip Hardwick's great Doric arch of 1834-38 at London's Euston Station was, in the face of universal protest, demolished in 1963, despite personal entreaties being made to prime minister Harold Macmillan. Architectural historian Sir John Summerson has described its destruction as "state vandalism".

When in March 1963 Robbins' plans for the as-yet-unnamed Woolmead were published, they were met by a predictable outcry in the town. It was a scheme that envisaged demolishing a swathe of what *The Architectural Review* had described as "genteelly shabby" East Street.

In its place came blocks of box-like, flat-roofed buildings of glass and concrete and some brick, a wholly alien concept which expunged all local influences and flew in the face of everything that Charles Borelli and Harold Falkner (who died in 1963) had held so dear. Some 40 years later, in 2000, Frank Cordier, who was chairman of Farnham UDC in the years between 1966 and 1969, told Monica Jones in the *Herald* that the council had spent three years discussing East Street. In all, 19 schemes had been considered.

Eventually 89 to 125 East Street was demolished; a total of 37 mostly 18th- and 19th-century shops and dwellings were lost, each of them distinctive although some were in poor condition. But the whole constituted a rich variety of building in which timber framing, brick and stucco were crowned by a busy, undulating roofscape of tiles, slates, parapets and dormer windows. The first stage of The Woolmead development was opened in July 1966 and the second phase, to the east of the central arcade, was subsequently undertaken by the Bristol and West Building Society. Alec F. French of Bristol was the architect.

Woolmead Road, opened in 1968, was built at the rear of the new complex and a further link was planned to run from East Street to South Street which would have necessitated the demolition of The Marlborough Head

New meets old. The Woolmead development of 1966 made an uneasy neighbour for the south side of East Street with Rose's garden and seed shop, now demolished, in the right foreground and the lofty Victorian frontage of draper James Smyth, now the Hogshead, beyond.

The presence of Woolmead Road at the rear of The Woolmead complex exposes the back of the premises to view.

and Montrose House, which adjoins the Council offices. Thankfully, it was never built, but Dogflud Way, opened in 1980, was.

There were also two stages involved in the development of the Farnham School of Art, which in 1969 merged with its Guildford counterpart to create the West Surrey College of Art and Design. In 1969 some 200 students moved into the initial phase of a new facility in The Hart, the work of county architect Raymond Ash. The second stage was completed in 1977, and almost 20 years later the adjoining Student Village by Nick Evans won the Royal Institute of British Architects' 1995 Housing Project Award. It was built in the shadow of Bishop Wayneflete's tower and featured red brick, pitched roofs, hand-made tiles and exposed oak.

The story was less happy in South Street which by 1981 had also felt the full effects of redevelopment. Despite another civic outcry, the construction of Sainsbury's new supermarket, by Broadway and Malyan of Reading, culminated in the demolition of much of the north-eastern side of this late Victorian road. Once again the all-important requirements of scale were ignored. Although the resulting brick structure of 1982 has been described as "barn-like", it possesses none of the dignity usually

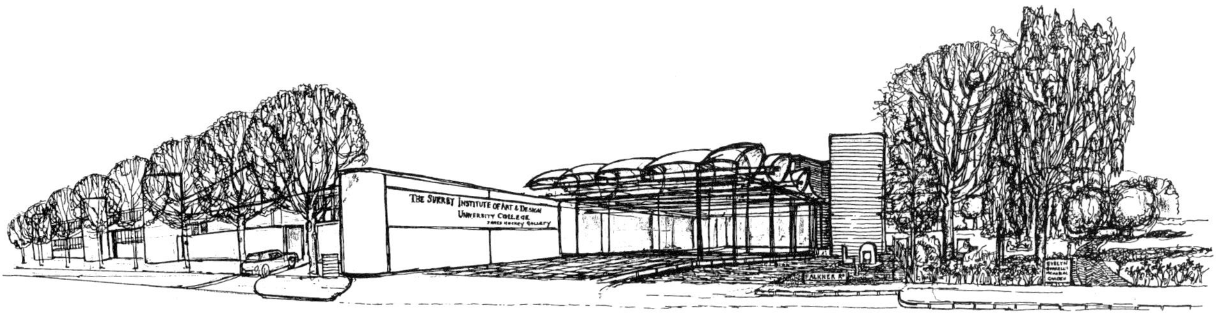

associated with such a traditional agricultural building. Even its substantial tiled roof has dulled with age. Poor South Street.

These developments took place during a time when attitudes to planning were changing. It had started in the 1960s. Former Council chairman Frank Cordier later reflected that previously it had been "very different... much simpler...All that went when Farnham came under the banner of big business. In came appeals and public enquiries with often scant regard for local opinion." As a result "East Street was bulldozed away and there was wholesale slaughter in South Street."

The structure of local government was also changing. National reorganization saw the abolition, in 1974, of Farnham Urban District Council with the town thereafter forming part of the Borough of Waverley. However, in 1984 Farnham Town Council was created. Although its powers are limited to those of a parish council, it does provide an important link between the community, now numbering some 37,000 people, and Waverley Borough Council.

It was in the 1980s that so-called backwater development emerged in Farnham. In a marked change with past practice, it sought to retain and restore the town's historic buildings rather than destroy them. Although new properties were constructed, they would echo the local themes of brick, stone, tiles, tile-hanging and weather boarding. All were united, together with ironstone setts and cobbles, in a common harmony.

The best known example and, indeed, the prototype of this approach is the Lion and Lamb Yard development, which was completed in 1986. It was initiated by Arundell House Securities, that had been established in 1977 by local developer Andrew Sturt and Ellis Campbell's Michael

The West Surrey College of Art and Design in Falkner Road is now the Surrey Institute of Art & Design, University College. Its entrance is through a Foyer Gallery which in 1999 received a Royal Institute of British Architects' Regional Architecture Award and accolades from the Civic Trust and Farnham Society.

Much of the north-eastern side of South Street is taken up by Sainsbury's development of 1982 which required the demolition of a swathe of late Victorian shops. It is scheduled for demolition if the projected East Street Regeneration Project goes ahead.

For Lion and Lamb Yard, architect Max Lyons pragmatically echoed the theme of its existing buildings. He designed new shops in brick, tile, stone and wood that were wholly in keeping with Farnham's traditions with regard to scale and the variety of natural materials employed.

Campbell. In 1980 it purchased, for £1 million, a site which included Kingham's former warehouse in The Hart and the adjoining Yard. This was an area that *The Architectural Review* had in 1961 condemned as one of "subtopian squalor of loading sheds, concrete posts and wire."

The development, which totalled 24 shops and six offices together with a Presto supermarket, won the 1987 New Centre Award organized by the British Council of Shopping Centres. Only the day before the presentation, the Prince of Wales, a committed Classicist, had spoken of the need to "create beauty in harmony with tradition," an approach the new Lion and Lamb clearly reflected.

The concept had been conceived by Max Lyons, senior partner of London-based Stevens and Partners. He moved to the town in 1973 and readily acknowledges a debt to Harold Falkner. "He was certainly a factor in my becoming an architect."

"Farnham is a town of delightful individual buildings, many of which are tucked away down alleyways and in little courtyards" observes Lyons. "One of the many reasons why The Woolmead is so unsatisfactory is that it looks as though it has been built as a single entity which is wholly at odds with this approach. Above all, the Lion and Lamb, and here Andrew Sturt was very supportive, kept the feel of Farnham." It also proved to be a turning point in Lyons' career.

This scheme and subsequent developments were made possible by a series of property deals that had taken place in the town. In 1982 the Borelli Estate, established in 1952 to incorporate the bulk of the property owned by Charles Borelli and his brother Frank, was sold for £1.5 million to Ellis Campbell. Subsequently, in September 1985, Arundell House acquired, for £3.5 million, the properties owned by the Farnham Market House and Town Hall Company, established in 1864 to build the Corn Exchange. In the previous month Mercari Holdings, which had been created by solicitor A.J. Stevens before the First World War and which owned a further tranche of town centre property, went to ASDA Holdings for £2.5 million.

The Lion and Lamb project was undertaken concurrently with Arundell House's Borelli Yard development although Sturt and Campbell went their separate ways in June 1986. The remaining shops and offices were completed by Allamanda Estates, named after the latter's yacht, which was established by Campbell and co-director Alan Taylor.

In 1988 Kents Developments, which had the Clockhouse project in East Street to its credit, completed Borelli Mews beyond the Yard. The brick and tile-hung houses had been designed by Broadway and Malyan. Offices, masquerading as domestic properties, were the work of Watts and Partners of London. Allamanda and Kents were also responsible for the St Georges Yard development, also by Broadway and Malyan. It was begun in 1988, and built in a similar spirit on back land between Castle Street and Bear Lane.

All of these schemes included business accommodation as well as shops. In 1988 the buildings on the south side of Union Road, including Expedier House, were demolished. They were replaced by an office block, Wey Court, also by Max Lyons, which turned out to be a Neo-Georgian complex complete with false chimney pots and plastic pedimented door-cases although he was not responsible for the all-important detailing. At the Downing Street end of the road, the 1991 Gostrey House by Arthur Gomez was not, for once, Georgian in style, but offices replete with Art Deco and Classical themes. The latter were also evident in The Millennium Centre in Crosby Way of 1999 by John Monk of the Farnham-based Haworth King practice. Executed in the Post-Modernist style, created in reaction to the brutalism of the 1960s, its brick walls, pitched slate roofs and 18th-century themes chime with Farnham's Georgian past.

However, the most radical scheme since the building of the now discredited Woolmead of 1966 is the East Street Regeneration Project in which Nicholson Estates and Sainsbury's Property Company emerged, in October 2002, as Waverley Borough Council's preferred development partner.

During 1963 and with the mutilation of East Street in the offing, Alec Clifton-Taylor wrote in *Country Life*: "The right answer for Farnham, surely, is an architecture which, while availing itself of modern structural techniques, continues to make full use of local materials, at least for facing. New buildings must be sensitively designed in relation to existing ones, *especially in respect of scale*" (author's italics). The Woolmead broke every rule in this fair-minded plea for pragmatism. Forty years on, are the developers, architects and planners still listening?

In Borelli Yard, Max Lyons repeated the theme, established in Lion and Lamb Yard, whereby existing buildings made of local materials were retained and converted into shops.

The East Street Regeneration Project envisages a new Town Square.

The Borough

"The best things are seen above eye level...in The Borough."

JANE BROWN, Surrey County Magazine, *1978*

Number **1** The Borough, Clinton Cards, resembles an architectural layer cake with the oldest filling in the middle. It is an indication of a building that has passed through a number of evolutionary phases.

The timber frame on the first floor gives a clue to its origins, being at least 17th century and more likely earlier. By the first half of the 18th century it was a public house, The Bear Inn. Later, in 1823, Thomas Fraser, a book-binder, owned the house and continued to do so until the 1850s. However, the outbuildings, kilns and yard were owned by hop grower James Darvill, access being through the archway to the east of the shop.

Part of the property was then taken over by Arthur J. Lucy, who in 1859 launched *The Surrey and Hampshire*

The Borough in pre-First World War days. Note number 40, just beyond Sturt's, prior to its reconstruction in 1910. The NatWest bank next door had been enlarged in 1904, although the substantial corniced chimney, one of three, was taken down in 1968.

News. It survives in the town as the county's oldest newspaper although, probably in the 1920s, it moved to Castle Street. Incorporating *The Farnham Advertiser and Aldershot Gazette*, it was during Lucy's tenure, in the late 19th century, that radical changes were made to the property's appearance.

At this time it was a two-storey structure with a rendered front, which concealed the timber framing and incorporated three sash windows. The tiled roof featured a single flat-topped dormer window but this disappeared when an extra storey was added, along with two new sashes with curved top rails and moulded architraves. The first-floor sashes were similarly replaced and the entire first- and new second-floor frontages were cement-rendered.

In 1901 the shop was occupied by milliner A. Palmer and, subsequently, motor factors Usher. Then, in 1920, it was acquired by "Lionel H. Smith (from Harrods)", a "High Class Ladies & Gentlemen's Hairdresser", late of 103 West Street. During the 1930s he retained Arthur and Leonard Stedman to convert it into "One of the Largest Salons in the South of England" which offered permanent waving and employed "the Eugene and Macdonald Systems". In mid-1954 Stedman undertook further work, this time to alter the shop's exterior by exposing the timber-framed first floor; the sashes were removed and replaced by more appropriate leaded casements. But in the 1970s Lionel H. Smith, which was by then owned by two brothers, closed its doors. Later Rumbelows, the electrical retailer, occupied the premises.

Next door, **2** and **3**, is Woolworths which has had a presence in Farnham since 1929. As at number 1, the frontages of both properties have experienced alteration since being cement-rendered in the 19th century. By the time that F.W. Woolworth Co Ltd, as it was then, arrived at number 2 in 1929, the property had been occupied by Ward the shoemaker (1901) and Carrie Tigwell's newsagents, the latter moving to South Street. While the conversion was being undertaken, a number of clay pipes were discovered embellished with a heart symbol and the initials W.R. It was to be another six years before Woolworth's frontage grew to its current size when in 1935 it took over number 3 which was occupied by Shaw's drapery. And despite Charles Borelli's entreaties, it insisted on a corporate "mass produced" shopfront.

Although many of the properties in this part of The Borough are timber-framed, the wood is hidden behind their brick frontages. Happily, that of number 1 has been exposed.

The vertical line dividing the two properties can still be clearly seen today and the second floors of both premises have retained their Victorian characters. But the first floor of number 2 originally possessed two flat-topped bays while the two adjoining windows of number 3 have lost their pediments. This alteration probably dates from the time when Woolworth acquired the latter property which received a new shopfront that sliced the bottoms off both sets of windows. However, it is possible to see what those at number 3 were like, because the one on the extreme right remains, complete with its pediment and original depth. All have been replaced by sashes but with moulded plaster architraves to harmonize with those on the floor above.

The 1901 edition of *The Farnham Directory* list no less than four occupants of 2 The Borough, namely Mrs Edwards, J. Garrood, boot- and shoemaker, C. Rose, corn stores, agent for County Fire Office, and J.A. Ward, bootmaker. Sometime earlier, number 3 had housed builder and undertaker James Parratt.

Unlike 1 The Borough, which has had its timber framing exposed, the structure of number **4**, formerly Petit

The frontages of 5, second left, 6 and 7 The Borough which were reconstructed and restored in 1915. This photograph was taken in the 1960s.

Delice, is not so apparent, but it was originally constructed in this way and was at one time jettied. After three rendered fronts, it is good to see brick, although this was also hidden until the late 19th century when the cladding was removed. When combined with its single Venetian window with rubbed brick above, and a cornice below the parapet, the flavour is distinctly 18th century.

It was owned by Henry Nicholas of Castle Street in 1839 and in the 1870s Samuel Newman and, later, Frederick Newman, both basket makers, occupied the shop. The latter was so listed at the turn of the 19th century and he was also "a dealer in brooms", the exterior of the building being festooned with his wares. In 1910 it became John Farmer's shoe shop, his second outlet since being established in Aldershot in 1907. Fifty years later, in 1960, a new shopfront was installed, at which time the Venetian window, which hitherto had a imitation semi-circular head to it, was restored. The premises continued under the Farmer name until 1991 when the business was taken over by Clarks.

The Chocolate House, number **5**, so named since the mid-1960s, along with Sketchley, **6**, and Sevens, **7**, were all, albeit indirectly, beneficiaries in 1915 of the Borelli/Falkner "treatment". Prior to that event, the two adjoining properties to the west were, at various stages of their life, in common ownership.

Another timber-framed building, in the 19th century 5 had a plain brick frontage with parapet and a single window surmounted by a substantial stone lintel. At this time the shop, and its two neighbours, were owned by the Page family. Around the 1850s, it was occupied by Jane Edwards, a milliner, subsequently by cabinet maker Henry Smither and then Davis' boot store. The latter had approximately two-thirds of the premises.

The balance, together with 6 next door, was occupied by baker and confectioner F.T. Burningham's shop. In 1906 he was advertising his bread "of High-Class quality only" and claiming a national following. "This Bread….is dispatched regularly by Rail and Parcel Post to all parts of the British Isles."

Burningham and Davis were destined to be the last occupants of these shops prior to a sensitive reworking, 5 to 7 having been acquired by Lloyds Bank. The premises as they appear today are credited to Horace Field, an appropriate choice of architect as he was the author of

Until recently, Petit Delice, 4 The Borough was for some 80 years a John Farmer shoe shop, see photograph on page 42. Originally a timber-framed building, it was refronted in brick in the 18th century.

English Domestic Architecture of the 17th and 18th centuries (1905). There was also input from Charles Borelli. The original rather plain front was replaced by the present one with its cusped parapet, complete with three blind recesses. The flat-topped bay window with three sashes was enhanced by a frieze which chimes with the original one at number 5 next door. At this point those premises were separated from its neighbour and it became a self-contained shop. Subsequently occupied by Mrs Davey Dodd (1937), in the 1950s it was the Sweet Shop and then became The Chocolate House, which changed hands in 1985 and is still going strong.

Another timber-framed building, 6 and 7 has a frontage added in the late 18th century with two first-floor sashes complete with margin panes and a blind window inbetween. There is a plain cornice to complement the obligatory parapet which partially obscures the two flat-topped dormer windows.

In the late 1790s Mary Page and Sons were running an ironmonger's business there, while the turn of the 19th century saw 7 occupied by tea and coffee dealer F. Cudby. He in turn gave way to Barrett's Stores which covered the facade with painted advertisements that proclaimed the goods available within (see page 27). This eyesore was swept away during Horace Field's renovations which mainly consisted of sprucing up the exterior and introducing three bow windows on the ground floor.

Lloyds Bank's occupancy dated from 14th February 1916 when the manager was Horace Scott Evans. However, in 1918 Lloyds amalgamated with the London and Counties Bank, which had a branch at 75 Castle Street, and in 1921 it left the Borough and moved around the corner to Norman Shaw's towering "Elizabethan" pile.

By the 1950s number 5 was occupied by Burtol Cleaners, who were followed by Flair; the present occupants are Sketchley and Supersnaps.

Seven became, between the wars, The Brown Owl tea room, so named because it contained the figure of an owl produced by the local Wrecclesham Pottery. Sir John Verney was a regular and he used to "sit in the Brown Owl sketching the customers whilst pretending to read the paper." In the '70s it was briefly The Mermaid Fish and Chip shop and in 1977, Tony Green opened a wine bar there which he named Sevens, because its address was 7

The Borough. Aided by his family, it played a significant part in Farnham's social life. Sadly he died in 1998, but Sevens Bar and Restaurant continues under new ownership. In 1986 Tony Green had enlarged Sevens to incorporate number **8** next door in premises that had hitherto been occupied by Sparrow's dress shop.

Tall and narrow, sandwiched between Sevens and The Queen's Head, and with a rendered front, 8 was occupied for nearly 100 years by Speed's tobacconists. In the 1880s G. Speed ran a cigar store there, although the front has undergone some revision since that time. A tall chimney just behind the parapet was removed in recent times and the roof has been reconstructed, while the first-floor sash window has lost its top moulding. By the 1950s this "High Class Tobacconist" was being run by Mrs Davey Dodd and there was ready custom from individuals waiting outside the Queen's Head bus stop.

The **Queen's Head** occupies number 9 and is a considerably older building than it might appear at first sight. Behind the commanding three-storey brick facade are the remains of a timber-framed two-storeyed house, jettied and infilled with brick. In the 18th century this acquired a brick facade with a central pedimented doorway with sashes either side and three more on the first floor, plus a shallow parapet and a tiled roof line which was only slightly higher than that of neighbouring 6/7. This frontage is shown in a print which depicts an omnibus standing in the foreground indicating its destination as "Aldershott" Camp. It opened in 1854 so the present Queen's Head frontage must be of a later date.

This would have been when the third storey, complete with three small sashes, was added beneath a slate roof

Below left, a lithograph by H. Prosser, probably dating from the 1860s, showing the corner of The Borough and Castle Street with an omnibus destined for "Aldershott" Camp, there being no direct rail connection between the two towns until 1870. The Queen's Head was then a two-storey building and was reconstructed, right, at some time after the drawing was completed.

Timber-framed, although it is concealed beneath the plaster, and jettied, 10 The Borough is thought to date from the early 17th century. It was re-roofed in the late 19th century.

with prominent eaves and exposed brackets. Those on the extremities of the first floor featured margin panes similar to those at 6/7. The central sash is curiously positioned, being slightly lower than its neighbours which may suggest an inheritance from the previous frontage.

Known in the 18th century as The Coffee House, the building subsequently became The Queen's Head and Coffee House, although by the 1820s the suffix had been dropped. At this time it was occupied by Jane and William Page, members of the family which owned 6/7 nearby. Soon afterwards, in the 1830s, it was acquired by the Knight family. It was owned by Barrett in 1872 and in 1888 was sold to Gale and Company of Horndean, Hampshire. It has been in this company's ownership ever since. Gale's initially placed a large oblong board above the guttering proclaiming the availability of its *Horndean Ales*. Licensees include Artaxeres Daniels (1850s) and Mrs Freeman (1877) although, by the turn of the century, T.H. Bubb was manning the beer pumps.

Unlike its neighbours to the west, **10** The Borough was never concealed behind a brick facade, probably because of its jettying. Its early 17th-century timber-framed origins are today all too obvious. Two-storeyed, with prominently scrolled ground floor brackets, the lofty first floor gives the building its height but the structural woodwork is concealed behind plaster. A steeply inclined roof meant generously proportioned attic rooms with dormers facing both The Borough and Castle Street. This is an appropriate building for a prime corner site.

It has been the subject of some changes over the years. A painting of Castle Street of 1761 (see page 80) shows the jettying and accompanying brackets bricked in. The resulting shopfronts, which faced the corner, encroached into the road and required their own tiled roofs. These extensions had been removed by the 1820s when the original structure was once more exposed. But towards the end of the 19th century, number 10 received a radical facelift which also involved The Coach and Horses, its near neighbour in Castle Street. This suggests that they were in common ownership at the time.

The latter was raised in height and rebuilt as a mirror image of number 10, imitation timbers being added to the first-floor facades of the two properties. Both buildings were re-roofed, at which point The Borough dormer acquired the pitched roof that it retains to this day. Anyone standing on the opposite side of Castle Street could not be blamed for imagining that they were facing a commodious and imposing Stuart house.

The final instalment of the story occurred in the 1920s with input from the Borelli/Falkner partnership. This resulted in the false timbering being removed from number 10. However, it was covered but subsequently revived by the 1930s around the corner on The Coach and Horses!

Ten has been a shop since at least the late 18th century and was probably one even before that. In 1782 it was owned by James Lamport and John Cook, who were described as mercers, a term which implied a dealer principally in textile fabrics. Later, in the early 1840s, came George Lamport, a corn dealer, while hop grower James Darvill was the owner in 1852. The following year the property was leased by the Mangles brothers, who opened the West Surrey Bank there, it being conveniently positioned for Farnham's cattle market in Castle Street. But the West Surrey enjoyed a relatively brief existence when, according to John Henry Knight, it "came to grief after the Gurney Overend failure." He believed that this long-forgotten financial calamity occurred in 1867.

By the turn of the 19th century the entire ground floor was occupied by Hearn's Borough Stores which also incorporated 1 and 2 Castle Street. The name was prominently proclaimed on the building's Borough frontage. It advertised gin at 12s. (60p) a gallon and whisky at 3s.6d. (17.5p) a bottle. In 1910 came news that the Stores had been purchased by the London and Midland Bank although the deal does not seem to have been finalized. What is certain is that from June 1933 until May 1970 it was Mrs Browne (Farnham) Ltd which sold "Furnishing Fabrics, Loose Covers...Upholstery, all work carried out in our own workshops". Later came Overseas Antiques, then more recently Hogg Robinson travel agents and finally, in 1993, Going Places.

When 10 The Borough was built in around 1610, just to the east at the bottom of Castle Street, Farnham's Market House had been standing for some 50 years. Destined to survive for close on 300, its demolition in December 1865 was the first link in the chain of events which lead to the construction of the present **Town Hall Buildings** that date from 1930-34.

By the 1860s, the *Old* Market House, as it had become, was looking its age and Farnham's residents began to bewail their lack of social amenities. Covered markets were gaining in popularity and there was nowhere, apart from The Bush, for social gatherings. A public meeting was duly called there on 17th March 1864 which led to the creation of the Farnham Market House and Town Hall Company. A committee of 19, under the chairmanship of Samuel Nicholson of Waverley Abbey House, was elected and the business registered some two months later on 26th May.

The net result of these proceedings was that the Old Market House was demolished and The Goat's Head Inn, which stood on the corner of The Borough and Castle Street, was purchased in 1864 for £1800. James Knight, its owner, had originally asked £3000! Another possible site, which thankfully was too expensive, was that of The Bush. Also in Knight's ownership, it was available for £6750 although the figure was subsequently reduced to £5000.

A coach, named the Alton and Farnham Machine, was advertised in 1760 as setting out "every Monday, Wednesday and Friday morning, at Six o'Clock, from the White Hart in Alton to The Goat's Head in Farnham." From there it travelled to The New Inn in the Old Bailey, Ludgate. There was room for three passengers from Alton and Farnham apiece, who respectively paid 10 shillings (50p) and 8 shillings (40p) for the privilege. Exposed outside passengers were charged half that figure.

Unfortunately The Goat's Head was badly damaged by a fire in 1796. Although it was rebuilt, the place, which behind its new exterior remained a jumble of buildings of varying ages and conditions, seems to have gone into decline. The arrival in 1849 of the railway in Farnham spelled the end of the stagecoach era, and this must have hastened The Goat's demise. When it was demolished in 1865, the licence was transferred to 40 The Borough, almost opposite, which perpetuated the name.

Wyndham Tarn's white brick and terracotta Town Hall and Corn Exchange was completed in 1866 and Harold Falkner, who designed its successor, readily conceded that, "Considering the space available [90ft x 57ft/27.5 x 17.5m], the scheme was exemplary". The 70 x 36ft (21 x 11m) Corn Exchange was capable of seating 500 people on the ground floor while the Town Hall was on the first floor. It measured 48 by 32ft (14.6 x 9.75m). There was an arcaded pedestrian way facing The Borough accommodating four shops and above were seven offices, most of which were available for hire.

One fragment of The Goat's Head Inn that survived at the easterly end of the site was an incomplete portion of the 17th-century brick **Bailiffs' Hall**, decoratively enhanced with naive Ionic pilasters and strapwork. But in order to match the building line of its new neighbour, the decorated front was demolished and the building cut back. The original was replaced by a stark brick facade which incorporated three arched windows. Its abruptly curtailed flat top was in line with the string course introduced between the second and third floor of the new 'Exchange.

An opening banquet was held on 15th March 1866, at which the building was described as "the greatest public improvement effected on Farnham". Falkner recalled that his father was present "and he came home in such a state that my mother threatened to lock him out!" But even then there were concerns about the appearance of the white-bricked structure. One critic at the banquet opined "that it was out of harmony with Georgian Farnham". Later, in 1900, Gordon Home in his guide to the town wrote disparagingly of it and Eric Parker's *Highway and Byways in Surrey* of 1908 described the 40-year-old building as "out of keeping and hideous".

The four shops provided much-needed revenue and in 1901 the *Surrey Advertiser's* advertising office was at 1 Corn Exchange, the building's overseer occupied number 2, William James, practical watch- and clockmaker, established in 1783, was at number 3 and bootmaker G.C. Morgan at number 4.

Tarn's three-storey Town Hall with its substantial corner tower was destined to occupy this prominent position for 64 years. Its location ensured that it remained a constant irritant to Charles Borelli, across the road in his shop 35/36 The Borough, who no doubt looked upon it as embodying all the excesses of Victorian vulgarity. For some years he and Harold Falkner plotted its demolition.

As it happened, the Town Hall Company's dividends had dwindled; debentures had even been issued prior to its opening. These began to come on the market in the 1920s and, says Falkner, "Borelli, who always had an itch for real estate in Farnham, began buying them...Having obtained a majority 'we decided we would rebuild'."

The Bailiffs' Hall, which dates from about the mid-17th century, was cut back and refaced circa 1866 to harmonize with the new Corn Exchange and again reconstructed by Falkner in 1934. The original frontage perpetuated the sequence of Ionic pilasters on the sides of the building; there were four in all with strapwork decoration in-between. In the mid-19th century a centrally located round-headed window, with a doorway below, was introduced.

The first outward indication of the demolition came in October 1928 when tenants of the Town Hall shops were given notice to quit, with effect from March 1929. This fired speculation that the Town Hall was going to be rebuilt but even Ernest Langham, proprietor of the *Farnham Herald*, did not know the truth. "Wait and see" was Borelli's Delphic response to his questioning. A problem then arose regarding the architect. Harold Falkner was the obvious candidate – "Borelli and I had for years agreed that I should do the job". However, Falkner's mercurial reputation had gone before him and the other directors objected. At the time Falkner was engaged in what proved to be a short-lived partnership with Guy Maxwell Aylwin and he brought in a friend, William Benslyn, who had offices at London's 5 Lancaster Place. It was his job, said Falkner, "to eat the directors' dinners and soften them up!"

So Falkner's plans, made public in 1929, were prepared by the hastily established firm of Falkner, Aylwin and Benslyn. "The first idea was to build on the first floor a much larger hall, with shops and a bank below." But after protracted negotiations, Surrey County Council turned the idea down and there was another impasse.

"However, the Inland Revenue came into the picture and offered a rent which nearly covered the whole expense but – fortunately – they wanted more floor space than was available and this necessitated the arcade, or colonnade, [a feature of Tarn's Corn Exchange] which I had always advocated but which the directors were dead against."

Harold Falkner's Town Hall Buildings under construction in 1931 with part of its Victorian predecessor in the background.

On the debit side Farnham lost its Town Hall even though the building was given this appellation.

Demolition began in 1930. The first element to succumb was the apex of the corner site which meant the Castle Street frontage, the tower and the first five bays of The Borough. A gilded weather vane, a representation in beaten copper by Thomas Elsley of Sir Francis Drake's ship *The Golden Hind*, was installed in 1931. It crowned a modest turret which at its base incorporated the clock mechanism that had previously been located in the tower of the old Corn Exchange.

While the Inland Revenue occupied the first floor, the prime ground-floor site with its entrance in Castle Street was taken by the National Provincial Bank, which marked its arrival in the town. It moved in on 17th September 1931, before this initial stage was completed in August 1932.

The balance of the work was finished by 1934 and the whole, built by John Mills & Sons, constituted a building which was much more in keeping with Farnham. Inevitably it was Neo-Georgian, or to put it more precisely, as Nigel Temple does, "English Renaissance and Jacobean Renaissance Transitional".

The long Borough frontage was designed to indicate distinct breaks in the two-storey facade that was built in no less than five clearly defined sections to eliminate any risk of monotony. Norman Shaw had adopted a similar approach with the timbered frontage of Pierrepont at Frensham. The first three sections are of a perhaps not wholly sympathetic red brick. A ground-floor arcade alternately incorporates arches, a lintel and arches again supported by unfluted columns with capitals which respectively embrace the Tuscan, Corinthian and Tuscan architectural Orders. There are sash windows above, although those in the second section have margin panes with an eaves-cornice above. The whole is crowned by a roof of Roman tiles with dormer windows projecting from the two easterly segments.

This part of the building is of orthodox design, but Falkner really let himself go with the remainder of the complex. This is Temple's "Jacobean Renaissance Transitional", a substantial structure of richer brick set back from the building line with a steeply tiled roof, two projecting asymmetric wings, a first-floor balcony with a lintel below supported by a pair of Ionic columns and

A floral decoration in cut bricks that began life on one of the chimneys of Norman Shaw's 75 Castle Street which was transplanted by Harold Falkner to the reconstructed Bailiffs' Hall, today the home of Breaking Free clothing.

a balustrade or two for good measure. As an indication of the high esteem in which he held the architect, Falkner seamlessly incorporated the remaining Norman Shaw chimney that he had saved from the demolished Lloyds Bank in Castle Street into the west wall of the Bailiffs' Hall.

This flight of architectural exuberance permitted Harold Falkner to successfully integrate the Hall into the Town Hall Buildings. The origins of the name, which is not contemporary, are obscure. It has been variously dated as anything between 1537, 1566 (which Falkner appended to the frontage) and 1657. The latter attribution features in an article on the town that Christopher Hussey wrote in 1942 for *County Life* and is endorsed by Ian Nairn in his Surrey volume of Pevsner's Buildings of England series.

However, in the mid-19th century a window with a semi-circular head had been introduced to its Borough frontage, along with a door below. It was at about this time that a Mechanics' Institute met there until it moved to what today is the Freemasons' Hall in Castle Street. It similarly played host to a Young Man's Association

which subsequently transferred to the newly opened Farnham Institute in South Street in 1891.

More significantly, the Bailiffs' Hall was the first home of the Farnham School of Art which came into being in the 1860s. Its founder was an unlikely candidate, Lt-Colonel John Luard, a veteran of the Peninsular War and Waterloo, who retired to Farnham in 1860, his 70th year. A talented artist, Colonel Luard took up sculpture in his later years and was responsible for a number of church fonts in the district. He succeeded in obtaining backing from like-minded contemporaries and began giving classes there, although he subsequently moved into a room in the Town Hall.

In the early years of the 20th century a small shop was created in the Hall's ground floor. This was occupied for many years, certainly at the time of its closure in 1929, by a glory-hole that went by the name of the Boro Bazaar Stores.

The only real problem with the completion of the work, was that the building had lost its original front in 1865/6. As Falkner recalls "we endeavoured to get photographs... and searched the museums, but at last decided to do the

Town Hall Buildings of 1930–1934 in its entirety. The Borough frontage, unlike that of its predecessor, does not overwhelm its surroundings, thanks to its scale and the clearly defined stages of the overall design which were in sympathy with the rest of the town.

A detail of the eastern wall of the Bailiffs' Hall, in part reconstructed by Harold Falkner.

best we could." He had "dispensed with his partners by this time" and designed a new gabled frontage which incorporated an arch, niches and strapwork decoration, together with side arches to complete the arcade. Despite their rift, Guy Maxwell Aylwin recollected witnessing the creation of the design, "I saw this develop on paper overnight... Here is vision, feeling for the past and design for the present."

In fact it was not until 1959 that Nigel Temple discovered, in the print room of the British Museum, a painting of the original frontage, made in 1822 by John Hassell. And while it does differ from Falkner's version in several significant respects, the way that the scale and relationship of his constituent parts, one with the other, reflects the original is a tribute to this remarkable, if controversial, figure.

In 1936 the Town Hall shops were occupied by The Milk Bar, F. Sturt, Scotch Wool and Hosiery Stores, John Farmer Shoes, Lintern and Peters, C.S. Mauld and Astaire. Their 2003 equivalents are the Nationwide Building Society, Three Cooks Bakery, Contessa, Lunn Poly, Café Rouge, which occupies two of them, and Breaking Free.

There is no 13 The Borough. W.H. Smith is at number **14**. Of three storeys in white brick (like its now absent westerly neighbour) with dressings of red brick, it has a slate roof with projecting eaves and probably dates from the 1870s. Prior to that the site may have been occupied by Charlotte Smith's ironmonger's shop. In the 1880s this was James Hewitt's "China, Glass and Earthenware Warehouse", as well as his home, although by 1901 the shop had passed to "G & A Hewitt (late James Hewitt)". Their successors, Lintern and Peters, "also at Tunbridge Wells", were in a similar line. Boots was at 14 by 1912 and it was destined to remain there until 1934 when the business moved to 41/42 The Borough. Its place was taken by W.H. Smith and Sons, late of South Street.

Numbers **15** and **16** The Borough (QS Clothing and butchers Smallbone and Sons) are united under a single tiled mansard roof, complete with three flat-topped dormers. Of brick and probably built in the early 1800s, number 16 is of a slightly later date. There are no less than six window apertures, of which three are blind, on the first floor of both buildings. Number 15 was the shop of William Jeffery, a gunmaker, who is listed as being there in

1841. It may be that he made use of the forge behind the shop run by Richard Smith and his wife Ann. The firm was still in business in 1937.

In the 1880s Samuel Jeffery, a watch- and clockmaker and jeweller, occupied the western side of the shop and R. Jeffery, the eastern one. By 1950 Mrs G.B. Loe's business, The Gift Shop, was there and remained so for the next 25 years. For a short time in the late 1970s it was a chemist, followed by Leighton's opticians and, until the early 1990s, Kitchen Showcase. In 1991, its successor, QS Clothing, applied for planning permission for a new shopfront but local historian Jean Parratt was able to produce photographic evidence that the existing front was the 19th-century original. On advice from Waverely Borough Council, the application was withdrawn and a piece of Farnham's architectural heritage was saved.

At about the same time that S. and R. Jeffery were trading from 15, next door at 16 was "Morgon, Hairdresser," who in 1895 was advertising: "Grey & White Hair Wanted. Combings etc., Bought". Subsequently, in 1901, butchers Ainslie Bros. occupied the premises which remains a butcher's shop to this day. It was later acquired by Dewhursts, which fitted a new front in 1935, and they remained there until about 1980 when the present occupants took over.

The site of the Farnham branch of Abbey National, opened in 1970, at **17** The Borough was, from the 1750s at least, The Ship Inn and later The Ship Hotel. The original, as George Sturt, who grew up in the shop next door, remembered it, was "a low half timbered building". On winter evenings his family could hear the "'clump-clump' of people dancing…and the rattle of a game of skittles." The Ship was acquired by local brewer Barrett in 1858, and in that same year Sturt's father "going out just before six o'clock in the morning to his business at the wheelwright's shop in East Street, found 'The Ship' in ashes. It had been burnt to the ground during the night; yet none of us had heard anything of the fire."

The premises were rebuilt with the facade, like 14's, fashioned of white brick with red dressings. The resulting Ship Hotel was a smarter establishment than its predecessor with "good accommodation for commercials and cyclists" and "good stabling". Barrett sold it to Farnham United Breweries but The Ship was closed by

The Card Department at 18/19 The Borough is on the site of the stationery shop in which George Sturt grew up and is immortalized in his book, A Small Boy in the Sixties.

Farnham magistrates in 1914 although the Breweries did not dispose of the property until 1928 following its takeover by Courage. It was bought for a respectable £3400 by S. Bide and Sons, established in 1854, as a flower shop. Samuel Bide had pioneered the washing of hops to prevent them from being attacked by blight.

The site of The Card Department, numbers **18/19**, is where George Sturt grew up in his father's stationery and newspaper shop. A tall, narrow, three-storey building with a cement-rendered front and slate roof, its character has been captured in his *A Small Boy in the Sixties.* He writes of its "six rooms, beside a wash-house at the back. The downstairs room on the street had a shop window its full width – ten feet or so – at one side of the street door; and on the other side of this door was 'The Shutter Hole'." This was used for storing the wooden shutters.

However, in about 1875 the family moved to 42 The Borough. Soon afterwards, this shop, along with numbers **19** and **20**, was run by the improbably named H. Kendall Bentall. He not only offered an "an immense variety of ready-made clothing" but he was also a "tailor, hatter, outfitter, and boot and shoe manufacturer". In due course, in 1933, he was replaced at 18/19 by Sainsbury's where "you will enjoy better quality and save money". This was to remain the store's home until 1966 when it moved to 7/8 The Woolmead. Its place was taken by Halfords.

This shop, along with 20 (Lucy's Lunchbox) and **21** (Alliance and Leicester), occupies part of a three-storey building opened in the 1890s. Of red brick relieved by terracotta decoration above the first- and second-floor windows, it was the work of William Wells, previously partner of Thomas Wonnacott. It was built on the site of the modest two-storey Waterloo House where draper Alfred Josiah Bentall, father of Kendall, offered "dressmaking, millinery and upholstery". He continued to occupy 21, on the corner. Harold Falkner remembered him as "a benevolent and harmless oldish man with electric whiskers like…[an] Italian general." Other members of the family left to establish Bentall's store in Kingston upon Thames, where, unlike Farnham, the name survives. Later, in the 1930s, Alfred Wyles' drapery business took over the premises, together with number 20, and continued to trade there until the 1950s. But by the 1970s it had become Courts' furniture store.

William Wells was also responsible for the design of **22** The Borough on the south side of the road, although Barclays Bank, which has been at that address since 1930, demolished the building in 1983. Owned by John and James Knight, it dated from 1872 when it was occupied by George Ransom's tea rooms. They survived until 1930 when George's son, Arthur, retired for health reasons and the bank took over. It retained Arthur Stedman to convert the premises and Stedman and Blower also made alterations in 1970. The present larger building, brick-built at least but featureless and stark, opened in 1984, and absorbed what had been 23 The Borough. It also included a shop, number **24**, which is today occupied by Workstation stationers.

The now absent 23 had been the home of F.A. Mitchell's "Borough Cigar Stores", established in 1870 and boasting "all popular brands of Havana, Mexican and Indian Cigars in stock". One regular customer in 1914 was the then editor of the *Farnham Herald*, who was pleased to endorse Mitchell's Little Gem cigar, which, he maintained, was a "splendid little smoke". The business survived into the 1950s.

What is now 24 stands on the site of a shop that in the 1890s was owned by chemist J. Griffith who also supplied "Randall's Old Fashioned Ginger Beer". He was succeeded by Alfred Dunston, who already had a chemists at 49 The Borough. By 1904 he in turn had sold to the Portsmouth-based Timothy White. It continued to run both premises, but had left 24 by 1962 and the shop was later occupied by Hall of Cards.

Its neighbour, **25**, with its colour-washed late Victorian frontage and large third-floor window, had been occupied since 1898 by George A. Hale, who sold photographic and "athletic goods" and was still there in 1909. He subsequently moved across to the Corn Exchange. Later occupants were chemist P.E. Leapman in the 1950s, then more recently Bookshelf Bargains and currently Ash Hairdressing.

Pictures & Frames, number **26**, is one of four shops built in 1931 by George Whitehead and Company which had recently acquired **The Bush Hotel**, for centuries the hub of much of the town's social life. Previously, 26 had been a single-storey off-licence, run at the turn of the 19th century by T.H. Bubb, who was licensee of the nearby Queen's Head.

By the early 1950s the adjoining numbers 1, 2, 3 Bush Hotel Shops were respectively occupied by Captain Yorke's tobacconist, County Studios and Rawlinson's. They have

The courtyard of The Bush, flanked by creeper-clad brick and enhanced by ironstone setts. The fountain is of a relatively recent date.

since been renumbered, from east to west, **27**, **27A** and **27B**, **28** The Borough, and are currently empty, with the exception of the British Heart Foundation at 28. This was where in 1901 G.C. Morgan "practical boot and shoe maker" conducted his business; in the 1950s it was occupied by Dora Grey and in the 1970s it was the Betta Wool Shop.

The Bush's facade of yellow bricks dates from the 1840s; it is a fine three-storey frontage worthy of the town's oldest hotel. With strong projecting eaves and exposed brackets, appreciation of its form is somewhat restricted by the narrowness of The Borough. The oblong first-floor windows allowed guests to walk through onto a wrought-iron balcony. However, this was removed when the shops were built and access to the courtyard was improved by splaying the entrance to improve the sight lines. Beyond the facade, by 1931 work was being undertaken – both inside and out – to designs drawn up by Falkner and Aylwin, and this included some rebuilding of the eastern end of the hotel. This South Street frontage incorporated, in a New Service Block, one of the two Norman Shaw chimneys from the recently demolished 75 Castle Street.

The Bush's charming, creeper-clad courtyard is flanked with red brick buildings of varying heights and prospects that are mostly of 18th and 19th century origins. It would appear to be the quintessential coaching inn; in fact its foundation predates the stagecoach era. Reputedly of 14th-century origin, documentary references to the premises do not appear until the 17th century. The Bush "at Farneham" is mentioned as early as 1607 in correspondence addressed to a Mr Gavell, which involved the transportation of timber from Alice Holt Forest to Reading. King Charles I nearly slept there! In 1648 a discussion took place between officers of the King's Escort about the most suitable place for their royal prisoner to spend the night in the town. And "some were for the Bush which was the best Inn..."

At this time it possessed 11 acres (4.5ha) of ground, including two meadows which constituted most of the west side of what is today South Street, and some of The Borough's frontage. It has passed through the hands of numerous owners. In 1788 it was the property of Thomas Bunch, who in turn sold to Benjamin Nicholas, while in the 19th century it became part of the substantial property interests of John and James Knight.

This partnership was dissolved in 1887 and George Trimmer acquired The Bush in December of that year at auction for £5900. It then consisted of 11 reception and sitting rooms and 25 bedrooms and thus came within the orbit of Farnham United Breweries. The hotelier at that time, Edward Bromley, briefly stayed on but was replaced in about 1890 by Charles Hart from Bromley, Kent.

In 1906 The Bush advertised the merits of its "recently enlarged and redecorated large banqueting hall capable of dining 120 persons…coffee & private sitting rooms overlook a charming old garden". There was a tennis lawn and bowling green.

The hotel was acquired by G.F.R. Smith in 1936 and in 1956 he sold it to Anchor Hotels, which was a subsidiary of Courage, Barclay. In 1986 it passed, via the Hanson Trust, to Trust House Forte and then to Macdonald Hotels, its current owner. There have, inevitably, been changes over the years and the first of two south-westerly extensions were completed in 1972. The second followed in the 1980s. Before leaving The Bush, the writer must make reference to the now defunct Vine Bar that used to be housed in the building beyond the west side of the archway. For many years, until its closure in 1991, he enjoyed, over a glass or two of beer, good conversation in an atmosphere that was seasonally enriched by the presence of a log fire. It is a much-missed Farnham institution.

Like the Bush's frontage, the next two buildings are of three storeys. Prior to the mid-19th century **29** (Toni and Guy) and **30** (Boots Opticians) were brick-faced, at which point they received fashionable stucco fronts and bracketed cornices over first-floor sashes. Number 29 was, in the 1890s, the home of Brinkworth, which offered tomatoes at 3d. (*c.*1p), melons at 4d. (1.5p) each and white grapes at the same price per pound. S. Sawyer (1901) and later S. Bates were in the same businesses. In the 1950s the shop was occupied by radio and sports stockist Clark and Co.

Number 30 The Borough was where tea dealer John Price proclaimed in 1892 that "there is nothing more refreshing than a cup of Price's tea". From 1909 it was the home of Joseph Frisby which moved its Great Leicester Boot store from two doors away at 32. It was then noted for its "very large and very extensive stock of good and cheap" boots and shoes with "gentleman's walking, shooting and football…always in stock". Later the firm had little compunction in describing its boots as "England's Best". Frisby survived at 30 The Borough until the 1980s.

Its neighbour, **31**, accommodates Dorothy Perkins which has been at this address since the late 1960s. Brick with a gable, together with a solitary leaded window on its eastern side, might suggest 17th century. It was built in front of a surviving timber-framed structure. In the early 1900s it was the shop of J.T. Fountain, who was a saddler and harness maker, and later came hosier, hatter and shirt maker Hamilton-Jones. In the late 1930s he advertised himself as being "Outfitters to Gentleman and their Sons" and the business remained there well into the postwar years.

Moben Bathrooms now occupy number **32** which is of a similar age to its neighbour, although it has two flat-topped dormers and was stuccoed in the 19th century. Its shopfront is one of the town's older frontages. Frisby arrived at 32 in 1882 and departed for number 30 in 1909 after which the shop was better known as the home of electrical goods supplier Hale Ltd., who had started at 25 and arrived via the Corn Exchange. It closed in 1994 to be replaced by the present occupant.

The Midland Bank, now HSBC, has had a presence in Farnham since 1921. Then, as the London Joint City and Midland Bank, it opened for business at **33/34**. A three-storey timbered building, of which 34 next door was a part, the frame was just visible through the rendering. The shop at 33 had been previously occupied by draper A.J. Bentall, also of 21 The Borough. Thirty four was occupied by Farnham brewer Alfred Barling, who since 1857 had run a grocery and wines and spirits store founded by his father, Thomas, in 1819. It closed in 1925 although an off-licence, opened in 1872, continued to trade.

Midland demolished the old three-storey building in 1925 and replaced it with the present Neo-Georgian front with its large sashes. It was a single-storey structure. The off-licence at 34A survived at its west extremity and was briefly succeeded by estate agents Cubitt and West in the early '50s. The bank's occupancy was extended to annex the site which is when the last two sashes were added. The second storey only dates from 1965 but you can't see the join!

Hair Colours Works hairdressing, now The Retreat Hair and Beauty, has occupied **35/36** since 1997, having taken over from estate agents Cubitt and West. But for 107 years

it was the premises of Charles Borelli and Sons, "watch and clock maker, jeweller, silversmith and optician". The firm was also a royal warrant holder and Queen Victoria's coat of arms can be seen in the fanlight above the front door.

Borelli Yard after the closure in 1973 of the Borelli business in The Borough and prior to its redevelopment in the mid-1980s.

Guiseppe Borelli, one of 30 children of the four-times-married Pasquale Domenico Borelli, a miller from Germasino, Italy, arrived in Farnham in about 1797 from Sicily where he had served an apprenticeship in watch and jewellery making. Subsequently joined by his nephews, Donato (1804–1861) and Clemente (1810–1877), who may have fled from the Austrian army, in 1828 the men opened a jewellery business at 111 West Street under the name of D. and C. Borelli. In the 1860s four further nephews emigrated to England of whom two, Gaetano (1842–1921) and Charles (1843–1917), joined Clemente in Farnham. Donato had died in 1861.

By this point the business had moved to 11 East Street, although in 1866 it found a new home at 36 The Borough, which in the late 17th century had been part of The Bush estate. By 1901 Borelli had expanded to absorb number 35, previously occupied by Mason's coal merchants. When Clemente died in 1877, Charles took over the shop and the business was renamed Charles Borelli and Sons, following the birth, in 1873, of Charles Ernest. Frank Leonard, known as Leo, followed in 1881. Charles was unmarried but Leo was the father of a Roman Catholic priest, Father Charles Vincent Borelli, who was ordained in 1939.

In many respects the building, said to date from 1615, with its first-floor flat-topped bay windows and fine 19th-century shopfront, encapsulated everything that Charles Borelli attempted to achieve in Farnham between the wars.

To the east of the shop is the archway to **Borelli Yard**, so named in the late 19th century when it was occupied by the St John Ambulance Association and J. Hall, a shoemaker, although they subsequently departed. A medley of stone flags, mellowed creeper-clad brick, tile hanging and leaded lights, it provided a glimpse from the busy, bustling Borough into the quieter world of the 18th century and earlier.

Following the closure of the Borelli business on 10th March 1973, the yard remained empty and it eventually became overgrown. In 1982 the Ellis Campbell Group acquired the Borelli estate. Planning approval to develop the yard, adopting a similar approach to the Lion and Lamb, was gained in December 1984. Work, to the design of Max Lyons, began in 1985 and the site soon began to yield some important archaeological finds. In September a tile kiln was discovered, which has subsequently been dated between 1180 and 1215.

An even more exciting development occurred in November when a section of the town ditch was uncovered. Although mentioned in the Bishop of Winchester's pipe rolls (accounts), archaeologist Nicholas Riall's excavations confirmed its long-suspected existence.

The first of the Borelli Yard shops, Bluebells which sold dried and artificial flowers, had opened in September 1987. This was followed by Breeze, a hairdressers, and in January 1988 Borelli's wine bar opened in what had been an old bakery at the rear of the complex.

The second phase of the yard development followed which required the construction of new buildings, rather than the renovation of existing ones. Five office suites, set in a walled garden with trees, were designed by Watts and Partners. The area is enhanced by the presence of a bronze sculpture, entitled Matriarch, by Ben Franklin, who was head of sculpture at West Surrey College of Art and Design from 1970 to 1981.

Beyond, **Borelli Mews**, completed in 1988, comprise 17 housing units which consist of flats and town houses with walled gardens, together with a paved and landscaped courtyard. Their construction required the demolition of Merton House, latterly marooned within the Central Car Park, and hitherto occupied by solicitors Gregsons. It had previously been the head office of the Victoria Transport Company, "steam wagons & petrol lorries for hire by day or job" established in pre-First World War days by Alfred Robins.

Hagreaves Sports is the present occupant of **37** which from 1896 was Rogers and Sons' bakery. Although now with a two-storey timbered facade, a painting by John Hassell in 1822 showed a plastered frontage with slightly different windows. There was a large yard behind, part of which disappeared when the adjoining bank was built. It had contained a ten-oast kiln. It continued as a bakery, subsequently run by Mills and Company and later Brooker, up until the early 1980s. Then it became a branch of Kentucky Fried Chicken. By the early 1990s it was a Benetton fashion shop, prior to the present occupancy.

The National Westminster Bank, now NatWest, has

Borelli Mews of 1988, designed by Broadway and Malyan, which combined the convenience of town centre housing with what Kents Developments described as "traditional construction using quality clay facing bricks and clay roof and vertical tiling."

occupied the site of number **38** since 1865. It replaced a two-storey house of late 17th-century appearance which had been owned by Thomas Eyre, a chandler. Indeed his family had pursued this trade since the early 17th century. Originally it was hoped that what became South Street would begin there, but Eyre would not sell.

The London and County Bank, as it was then named, was originally located at 11 West Street. But as the branch flourished, new premises were needed and the prime site of 37 The Borough, with its view directly up Castle Street, was acquired. It was built in 1865, the same year in which the Corn Exchange opposite was being constructed. The original bank building, the architect is not known, was Italianate in style, of colour-washed brick and stuccoed, three storeys with a prominent, decorated cornice but just three bays wide, with the door in the most westerly arch. It was tall and narrow, like a doll's house.

However, in 1901 the opportunity arose for the bank to acquire the vacant shop to the west, namely **39**, that was also owned by the Eyre family. A deed of 1764 relating to

Borelli Yard *35/36* *37* *38/39*

both properties referred to "shops, corn lofts, Brew house, stable yard and garden." The last occupant of the two-storey premises in the 1890s had been the International Tea Company which in 1900 had moved to 116 West Street. Prior to that the building had been the office of auctioneer John Nash, who left for new premises in South Street.

The additional frontage and two extra bays transformed the proportions of the building, imbuing it with a dignity which is readily apparent from Castle Street to which it provides a focal point. The architect was Horace Cheston of Old Broad Street, London and the work was completed by Tompsett in February 1904. Stand in the Central Car Park and you can see, by the changes in the roofscape, where the extension has been added.

But if the authors of the Farnham Town Plan of 1947 had had their ways, the then unfashionable Victorian bank would not have survived. They wrote that it was "the most unfortunate in the town…should be demolished…to make way for a smaller building." This was "on account of its poor design, bad scale and extra height…"

Goat's Head Passage **40** **41/42**

Above: Goat's Head Passage, although lacking a name plate, is the alleyway that runs between The Spinning Wheel and the NatWest bank. It has changed little over the years, as this photograph, taken prior to the former property's reconstruction in 1910, indicates. Now there is paving in the middle of the path. Unfortunately, in recent years some of the bricks in the left-hand wall have been painted.

Above right: The former Goat's Head Inn being transformed in 1910. During the work the initials G.I.W. were found on a corbel which may relate to George Wroth, a draper, but his association with the house has not been confirmed. The building has been variously dated at circa 1600 (Ian Nairn) whilst Nigel Temple quotes c. 1660.

In 1909 the London and County Bank merged with the London and Westminster, which led to it being renamed The Westminster Bank. In 1970 came a change to National Westminster Bank, following an alliance with the National Provincial, and the latter bank, an occupier of Town Hall Buildings since its inception, soon afterwards closed.

The building changed little over the years, although in 1968 its handsome but heavy three corniced chimneys were demolished when they were found to be unsafe. By this time a two-storey extension with mansard roof had been completed at the rear in 1965 and further sympathetic brick and tile-hung offices by Max Lyons date from 1986.

In 1959 a major part of the rear garden had been leased to Farnham UDC for an extension to the Central Car Park. Pedestrian access from The Borough was by a walkway to the west of the Bank, named Goat's Head Passage. This takes us to number **40**, which was the first building in Farnham to receive the Borelli/Falkner "treatment".

Dating from the 17th century, this three-storey, timber-framed building is shown in a drawing by John Hassell in 1828 with its timber exposed, decorative barge-boards and a substantial chimney. During the previous year John Nichols had established a post office there, along with a printing and bookbinding business next door. Since 1866 it was The Goat's Head Inn, owned by Thomas Mathews, the licence having been transferred when the building opposite was demolished for the construction of the Corn Exchange. It was during this time that it suffered, the barge-boards were removed and plaster was applied between the timbers which remained exposed.

In 1909 Farnham Magistrates closed The Goat's Head. At this point it was owned by Hodgson's Brewery at Kingston, which received £660 while the licensee James Holmes got £75. This was when it was acquired by Charles Borelli. Restoration work was completed by the end of 1910. In its issue of 28th December of that year *The Times* reported that "underneath some modern lathe and plaster work was another covering of old rough cast and when this was removed, evidence was found of much earlier framework."

The present interior mostly dates from the 1910 reconstruction, the staircase having come from Leigh House in West Street following that property's conversion into the town's Post Office. Beams were courtesy of The Bell and Crown in Castle Street, demolished in the same year of 1910.

The appearance of the building was much improved by its re-roofing and the fitment of barge-boards, albeit not the decorated originals. An oriel window was introduced on the first floor, along with two on the second which, perversely, did not appear on Hassell's 1828 drawing! No matter. The Victorian ugly duckling had been transformed into a fine Elizabethan swan.

Borelli's first tenant gave the building the name which it retains to this day – The Spinning Wheel. She was Miss Florence Paget, whose family owned Brightwell House and her shop, at 17 East Street, was then in its grounds. From there she ran an antiques and bookbinding business and she was particularly adept at carding and spinning wool. She pursued this business at 40 The Borough in company with her lifelong friend, Mrs Gerald Streatfield, daughter of Richard Combe of Pierrepont, Frensham. Miss Paget retired in 1920 when the shop was taken over by

Before: *41/42 The Borough, then Sturt's stationery shop, undergoing reconstruction in the early 1920s. It was roomier than 18 The Borough, recalled George Sturt, "and the shop, too, would admit [an] extension of business which had been beyond my mother's reach before."*

H.M. Philipson-Stow, who continued to sell antiques until 1940 when Wilfred Gosling took over, offering "English and French period furniture and works of art". But when he ceased trading in 1958, it marked the end of The Spinning Wheel's association with antiques. Since then it has been a shoe shop, first that of T. Elliott and Sons while the current occupant is Bowleys Shoes which arrived in 2000.

The restoration of The Spinning Wheel was to influence the owner of the next-door property and soon after the end of the First World War, numbers **41/42** were radically altered in appearance. Like 40, this had been occupied by the Nichols family but George Sturt recalled that "my mother and father gladly accepted the tenancy of an old family book and stationery shop Mr Nichols owned... In short whilst 18 had been only a little poky tenement, on the other hand, 42 The Borough was an opening to considerable middle class comfort."

This was in about 1875 and the business was subsequently managed by George's brother, Frank. In addition to stationery, he ran a library, and published books and postcards.

At this time it was a double-fronted, three-storeyed shop, stuccoed with a slate roof and three sashes on the first floor and the same number of blind apertures on the second. The "new" premises bore little visual relationship to this structure although, reputedly, evidence of the shape adopted was found during the rebuilding in about 1922. This was timber-framed and dominated by a single large

After: *41/42 following its transformation by Crosby into 20th-century Tudor. The Sturt shop, selling books, stationery and newspapers, was run by George's brother Frank until his death in October 1930. It subsequently, in 1934, became the Farnham branch of Boots and is today occupied by Next.*

jettied gable. The similarly extended first floor contained an oriel window which echoed that of The Spinning Wheel next door.

Frank Sturt died in 1930 but the business was subsequently transferred to 1 Town Hall Buildings and traces of the Sturt name can still be seen on the lintel. In July 1934 the property was taken over by Boots which had previously been at 14 The Borough, the new building having been converted by corporate architect P.J. Bartlett.

Boots was destined to remain there until the mid-1970s. Thereafter the building became a charity shop and a temporary home for Barclays Bank while 22 The Borough was being rebuilt. The Jewellers Guild took over the premises soon afterwards and in November 1985 it caused local outrage when it removed the bow windows without planning consent and replaced them with flat plate glass. The Guild was subsequently ordered to replace them but decided instead to leave the premises which were taken over by Next, the current occupant, which reinstated the bows. These were clearly in keeping with those of **43** next door, even if they only dated from 1932!

Now occupied by Zikomo, this had been best-known as the shop run by the Misses L. and E. Williamson, who by 1906 combined a newsagent's business with "wools and silks of every description" and a circulating library. Subsequently taken over by tailor John Silver, in June 1932 plans were submitted to Farnham UDC for a remodelled shop in which the steadying hands of Borelli and Falkner are immediately apparent. The alterations involved the removal of the Victorian front and its replacement with a copy of Fribourg and Treyer's original double-bowed frontage at 34 The Haymarket. The two bay windows above had their single-pane sashes removed and replaced with multi-paned glazing, a favourite Falkner feature. Silver's continued to occupy the premises until 1995 when it was replaced by Table Top, which sold china and glass.

By contrast, **44** next door, now Thornton's chocolate shop, displays a less elaborate frontage, being rendered with a single sash window with margin panes on the first floor. In the 1890s this was Holden's Boot Store, established in 1873, although by 1906 it was Holden Brothers with branches at Godalming High Street and 223 Regent Street in London. By 1905 it had moved next door to 45. Its place was taken by J.E. Spencer, also at 51.

Clarks shoe shop, number **45**, brick, late Victorian, was in 1901 Mrs Stovold's "grocer and dealer in game." From 1974 until 1991 it was a John Farmer shoe shop, which had transferred from Town Hall Buildings. It had previously been occupied by Holden's, which was in the same business and was there until the 1950s. For many years it was in competition with Stead and Simpson, which also sold shoes, next door at **46**. Today it is Mister Minit. At the turn of the 19th century, 44 to 46 was occupied by Bond and Jerome who were grocers and butchers, but in the 1950s it was A. Lewis and Co (Westminster). A three-storey building, the top storey has the appearance of being a later addition.

Mann estate agents are next door at number **47**, which is a three-storey building in yellow brick and clearly built to harmonize with its larger westerly neighbour. In the 1880s it was occupied by solicitors Potter and Crundwell, who in 1892 moved to new offices in South Street. Their

Numbers 46, 47, 48/49 and 50 The Borough: Victorian, mostly yellow brick but in the Classical tradition.

place was taken by fruiterer, florist and greengrocer J.A. Absalom, although S.H. Hume was there in 1909 and then it was greengrocer F. Meyers's shop until the 1970s.

Boots has been at 48/49 The Borough since 1968 having in that year taken over Timothy White. Up until the mid-1970s Boots also continued to occupy **41/42**. Of three storeys, yellow brick with a slate roof, Whites occupied the mid(dish)-Victorian number 49 in about 1904, premises that had been home to at least four chemists: William Portello, strictly an apothecary, William Higgins, Louis Cullingford in the 1890s, and Alfred Dunston, who sold to the Hampshire business.

A chemist as well as a hardware shop, in 1913 Timothy White's absorbed number **50** next door, previously H. Pullen's hairdressers. This has been occupied since 1998 by estate agents Carson and Co. Back in 1913 it had a brick, rather than its present rendered, frontage. But Timothy White's later vacated 50 and, by the mid-1930s its address was 48/49.The former property had, by 1912, been Miss T.F. Wilson's millinery store.

In 1973 Boots embarked on a scheme to enlarge the shop to the rear. Sixteen years later, in 1989, the store was

The clunch barn that abuts the rear of the easterly wing of Ivy House was in 1989 incorporated into Boots' extended store. Only the replacement tiles jar a little.

effectively doubled in size when it was extended behind its easterly neighbours by means of a wing which imaginatively incorporated an existing barn, clunch with brick dressings, which abutted the rear of Ivy House, off Downing Street. Customers were therefore able to walk through a new, paved courtyard to the Central Car Park.

The prime corner site of **51/52** The Borough was occupied for 95 years, from 1867 to 1962, by draper J.E. Spencer. This elegant, early 19th-century, three-storey building was stuccoed with a slate roof (see page 34). Initially John Spencer had opened a shop at 7 East Street in 1860, having earlier worked for a draper in Midhurst. In 1867 Spencer moved to 51 The Borough and by 1901 the firm had consolidated its position by taking over 52, the corner shop which also faced Downing Street.

In 1904 a new front was fitted which apparently excited much local comment because "the window glass extended down much nearer to the ground than was then customary". Soon afterwards, in 1908, the new type of window was introduced to the Downing Street frontage but the exterior changed little thereafter. But after over a century in the town, in February 1962 news broke that Spencer was to close that June. Its former shop was demolished in 1964 to be replaced by the present corner premises. Developed by Liptons, which opened a supermarket there, this closed in 1969 and the Southern Electricity Board, previously at 18 West Street, moved in and remained there until the mid-1990s. It was replaced by the current occupant, the Age of Elegance gift shop.

Falkner's Fireplaces: I
Harold Falkner lived for practically all of his life at 24 West Street and one of the many desirable features of the house is the variety of its fireplaces. In later years his childhood memory was one of them being "immense...which took a whole scuttle of coal at a time – at 25s (£1.25) per ton." This is a hob grate, designed for coal rather than wood, which was popular in the late 18th century.

Bridge Square

"Bridge Square, potentially one of Farnham's more attractive features, has its promise, seventy years later, of achieving that distinction..."

Bill Ewbank-Smith, Victorian Farnham, *1971*

The junction of Longbridge with Firgrove Hill and Abbey Street has, since the mid-19th century, been dignified with the name of Bridge Square. It has been variously known both as Downing Street and Longbridge, after the bridge which spans the River Wey. This extended from what is now Bridge Square to where the road takes a right-hand turn into Downing Street.

The Bishop of Winchester's pipe rolls (accounts) refer to Longbridge in 1265, its name deriving from the fact that the marshy ground required an elongated wooden structure spread over many arches. Erected just to the east of an ancient ford, it was the only way out of the town to the south. This bridge and its successors survived until 1853 when an iron bridge, the girders having been cast in London, was installed at a cost of £334. Its successor, the present reinforced concrete structure, dates from 1971.

The **Bridge House,** on the south-east side of the bridge, still sports the painted sign on the river frontage of *Reid & Co's Ales and Stout*. The property, of colour-washed brick, consists of a three-storey building, possibly of medieval origin, adjoining the pavement with a later 19th-century addition overlooking the river. It comes as no surprise to find that the pub was named The Bridge House. It was owned by the Knights from the 1850s, although by the time it closed in 1902 ownership had passed to Reid. The property subsequently became a private house and was owned by the Cranstone family for over 80 years.

Its neighbour, **2A**, now the premises of The Farnham Bathroom Company, dates from 1901. The site was redeveloped by G.J. Stacey, who had taken over the

Prior to 1969 the William Cobbett pub was named the Jolly Farmer. This photograph was probably taken in the interwar years before the colour-wash was removed in 1947. It then included this shop, Bridge Stores, which was subsequently incorporated into the public bar.

grocery shop on the corner which was flanked by run-down cottages, brick-faced to the left and timber-framed to the right.

Fortunately we have been able to delight in the fine brick frontage of the **William Cobbett** pub opposite since 1947 when colour-wash, applied during the 19th century, was removed. In the same year the reformed Farnham Society presented the terracotta plaque which graces the front of the building and indicates that "William Cobbett was born here on March 9th 1763".

It was an inn even then, for his father, George, was not only the landlord of what was named the Jolly Farmer, but also a farmer and surveyor. Although William attended a dame's school, "in the winter evening my father learnt us all to read and write...". And write he did with a simplicity of style, directness and power which still resonates today. Cobbett was destined to become the greatest of the English radicals who exposed corruption and spoke for those who lacked the articulation and social status to make their voices heard.

Driven by a consuming sense of justice, in 1803 he established *Cobbett's Parliamentary Debates*, the precursor of Hansard. His most famous work, *Rural Rides*, was published in 1830. "No man," wrote the historian A.J.P. Taylor, "has used the English language to greater effect. His writings remain the perfect model both for those who seek to persuade and those who wish to denounce." Cobbett died at Ash in 1835 and is buried by the north doorway in Farnham churchyard.

His birthplace, with a commanding view over the bridge and into the town, dates from the late 17th century and incorporates a cottage at its western end. This is 16th century, being timber-framed, and it once contained living quarters and a shop. Later incorporated into the pub, between the wars it had been Rose's Stores and, later, Bridge Stores, by which time the frontal timbers had been exposed. It continued as the Jolly Farmer until December 1969 when it was renamed in memory of Farnham's most famous son.

An imaginative reconstruction of William Cobbett about to embark on one of his Rural Rides, *outside his birthplace. Writing in 1796, he recalled: "My father, when I was born, was a farmer...My first occupation was driving the small birds from the turnip-seed, and the rooks from the peas."*

The western frontage of the Maltings, as it appeared, derelict and neglected, prior to its transformation into a community and arts centre. This process began soon after its sale by Courage in 1969.

By 1802, the year in which Cobbett founded his famous *Political Register*, brewing had begun in part of what today is known as the **Farnham Maltings**. With its plain but dignified frontage and an irregular roof line of tiles and slates surmounted by distinctive cooling ducts, this impressive, functional range of industrial buildings came close to being demolished in the 1960s.

The oldest surviving part of the complex is the timber-framed, two-storey 13 Bridge Square, better known as **Tanyard House**, that was restored in 1984. It is all that remains of a larger T-shaped property built in the 1480s for a wealthy and influential citizen. Originally jettied, the brick infilling may have replaced wattle and daub when the ground floor was bricked in to make it flush with the projection above. It contains the solar – in modern parlance a first-floor drawing room – that was originally open to the roof timbers. There is structural evidence to suggest that an adjoining hall, now lost, continued westwards. By contrast, the easterly annex appears to be an afterthought.

Stanley Bolen, a tanner, purchased Tanyard House in 1770, along with the adjoining and probably old established Tannery on the south-west part of the site. In 1802 it was acquired by Farnham brewers Michael and James Page, who converted it into a brewery. It was bought in 1845 by John Barrett and George Beldham, who by 1826 had been running a small brewery across the river in Upper Church Lane. The Barrett family lived nearby at what is now known as **The Old Malthouse** in Firgrove Hill, but was then called Elm Grove. It is an 18th-century house with Victorian embellishments. Tunnels under its back garden were used as cool vaults for beer barrels. Barrett's hop kilns, now Castle House, were in Bear Lane.

Later, in 1839, Barrett acquired the Maltings, which is where barley is converted into malt. This was at the eastern end of the complex which had been established early in the 19th century by Robert Sampson, who also grew hops. In 1841 his son Sampson took over the business and the family home at **18** Bridge Square, where his name can still be seen on its eastern wall. In 1881 he sold to Barrett, by which time he had moved to the more genteel surroundings of Wickham House in West Street.

Robert Barrett, with public houses in both Farnham and for soldiers in Aldershot, developed the site to the river. What had become the Red Lion Brewery also had its own pub, the appropriately named Red Lion at 2 Red Lion Lane. Opened in 1859, it survived until 1920.

In 1889 George Trimmer, of the Lion Brewery in West Street, acquired Barrett's business. This created, on 22nd October, Farnham United Breweries with capital of £417,000 and 91 public houses and eight off-licences on its books. Brewing was concentrated at Trimmer's facility and the Bridge Square/Red Lion Lane premises became its maltings which were further developed. The present Wey-side frontage dates from 1903.

When Courage purchased Farnham United Breweries in 1927, brewing soon ceased in West Street but the Maltings continued to function until 1956. For five years it was used for storage. Then, in February 1964, what had become Courage, Barclay and Simonds submitted a planning application to redevelop the site which involved retaining two of the empty buildings and converting them into dwellings. However, the remainder of the Maltings would have been demolished to make way for 23 flats, houses and garages. Five residences in Bridge Square would have been retained. However, although the plan received conditional approval, the brewery decided not to proceed. Instead in December 1967 it submitted a new application for the erection of 20 houses.

The Maltings as it is today. In 1978 it received second prize in a competition organized by the Royal Institute of British Architects and The Times *newspaper for the best use of an industrial building for community purposes.*

Alan Fluck, head of music at Farnham Grammar School and a regular visitor to the Maltings at Snape, near Aldeburgh in Suffolk, which had been converted into an arts centre, believed that the redundant buildings could fulfil a similar purpose. The Farnham Society convened a public meeting, held on 27th February 1968, and a 12-strong action committee, inspired by Sir John Verney, and under the chairmanship of solicitor Raymond Krish, was established.

Courage generously agreed to a selling price of £30,000, provided that the building was to be used for civic purposes. A six-week deadline expired on 25th March 1969; £18,000 was raised by public subscription with a further £12,000 coming from the Farnham (Building Preservation) Trust which acquired the adjoining houses, namely 2 and 4 Red Lion Lane and 12 to 18 Bridge Square. The Farnham Maltings Association was incorporated in May 1969 and the council of management, under the chairmanship of Colonel Peter Drake-Wilkes, adopted a three-phase plan submitted by Kenneth Adams and Partners of Guildford. At its heart the old two-tier No 5 Working Floor would be transformed into a Great Hall.

Since then the Barley Room, Malt Room, Tannery, Main Bar, Forum, Maltings Gallery and Studio, Long Kiln Room, Dance Studio, South West Kiln, the East Wing Studios, Dressing Room and Play Group Studio have been completed. Some 300,000 people visit the Farnham Maltings every year, thanks to the foresight and imagination of the few, the generosity of the many and the untiring volunteer effort that has helped to turn a dream into reality.

Castle Street

"...a street, indeed, which for sheer visual delight has few equals in all England."

ALEC CLIFTON-TAYLOR, Country Life, *1963*

In the 1890s 1 and 2 Castle Street, which included **The Coach and Horses**, was part of Hearn's Stores that also occupied 10 The Borough next door. Today there is no number 1 but the public house is 2. Although its northerly section appears to be an old one, it actually dates from the late 19th century. This was when it was rebuilt to match 10, which dates from the early 1600s (see page 46). Both buildings were clad with imitation Tudoresque timbering on their respective first storeys, but this was painted over in the 1920s although it was still discernible through the

This photograph was taken at some time between 1853 and about 1867 when the West Surrey Bank (the name is discernible on the window glass) occupied 10 The Borough. On the extreme right is what today is part of The Coach and Horses, of just two storeys, before this modest building was raised to echo its near neighbour, a genuine 17th-century structure.

Above: A watercolour dated 1761 showing 10 The Borough in the left foreground with the western side of Castle Street behind. It reveals that, although today regarded as a Georgian street, many of the houses were then gabled, with only the occasional 18th-century parapeted frontage intruding. The Old Market House is the right foreground.

Above right: Castle Street in the later 19th century with the towering frontage of Norman Shaw's Knight's Bank on the extreme right. The Bell and Crown Inn beyond at 73, demolished in 1910 and now the entrance to St Georges Yard, can also be seen.

colour-wash. This was removed from the pub in the 1930s and the woodwork has remained exposed ever since.

There has probably been an inn on the site since the mid-18th century. In 1839 Francis White was named as landlord of The Coach and Horses at a time when coaches were still arriving at The Goat's Head Inn opposite, but it seems likely that this was a new name for The Golden Horseshoe. This name appears in 1775 and refers to a two-storey house built on the site of two dwellings nearest to The Borough. It also features in a painting of Castle Street of 1761 and although the inn sign seems to show three cups, rather than horseshoes, this may be a drafting error on the part of the artist.

A Barrett house by 1872, as rebuilt The Coach and Horses was known as the Borough Arms between 1891 and 1904. It was fitted with oblong ground-floor windows, the lower half of which featured decorated glass, although these were removed in 1962 and replaced by the present bow windows. In 1969 the *Farnham Herald* reported that the Coach attracted a varied clientele of "local journalists and junk dealers…to meet their friends from the Art School, both staff and students, who in turn make contact with actors and technicians from the Castle Theatre just up the street."

The 1761 painting depicts the neighbouring **3** as a house with a prominent single gable of the type current in the 17th century and the alleyway on the south of the property, which is still there, is clearly visible. However, the "Aldershott" print of the 1860s (page 45) shows the house as a two-storey Georgian-style structure with a flat-roofed dormer window.

The present mid-Victorian building was built soon after that and it is at least the third to occupy the site. It is of three storeys with a stuccoed facade, round-headed windows on the first floor and sashes with curved top rails on the second. It has been a shop for many years. Once owned by Thomas Falkner, in 1839 Ann Falkner was listed as a tallow chandler. By the mid-19th century it was the home of William Vine's Wine Stores although he subsequently moved across the road to 3 The Corn Exchange.

In 1886 grocer John Povey took over, and he was still there in 1901. By 1912 George Ransom, with tea rooms at 22 The Borough, occupied it. Between the wars E. Kimber ran a fruiterer and florist's, their motto was "we serve ourselves best by serving others better". However, in 1934 the rear of the premises was badly damaged in a fire. Alexanders the jewellers arrived in 1946 and is still there. On the top floor was Miss B.J. Bridgeman's "Swift Typewriting & Duplicating Bureau…Duplicating in three colours, Black, Red and Blue".

Its neighbour to the north and once 4A, now incorporated as part of number **4**, is deceptive. Originally featuring, like 3, a single gable, this timber-framed and brick house was reconstructed, along with its neighbour, early in the 19th century. And although apparently of three storeys, it is actually two-storeyed with the top half-sashes introduced into a deep parapet which conceals the presence of a tiled roof. It was the offices in the 1950s of coal merchants Corralls, and prior to that Eric Lowe who was in the same line, and it is now part of the offices of estate agents Hamptons.

Next door, also occupied by Hamptons, there can be little doubt that this Regency face conceals an older building. The door at the north end of the property is

2 3 4

4 5 5A 6/7

usually opened and the timber-framed wall of the earlier building, which was gabled, can be seen. Inside more beams are in evidence. Jack Wing of Godalming-based estate agents H.B. Baverstock opened its office there in 1938. It merged with Messenger, Morgan and May of Guildford in 1965 with Hampton taking over in 1986.

In the 1820s the freehold of this house had been owned by Henry Nichols, a member of a prominent Farnham family, who was a wine merchant. One of his sons, also called Henry, was a hop planter and his other son, Benjamin, at one time owned The Bush Hotel. Henry may have been responsible for the conversion and the architect charged with the job undertook his work with great skill and sensitivity.

Although this is a three-storey stuccoed frontage, no less than three of the six sashes – the southerly one on the top floor and those directly above the north door – were blind and included to provide an element of Classical symmetry. However, today they are all functional. In its original form the ground-floor sash window with margin panes was essentially the same as the two directly above it. But it was removed in the late 1950s and replaced by the present shopfront. The southerly door with its pillared supports and fanlight are noteworthy features.

After stucco, brick. Number **5**, three storey with slate roof and open eaves, is Victorian in proportion but Georgian in detail, with the wide offset doorway giving an indication that this property dates from the early to mid-19th century. It may be that John Leadbeater (or Lidbitter), who died in 1843, was responsible for building this house on the site of an earlier timber-framed and gabled property. In 1831 he acquired a business owned by John Stevens, who had brought his loom from Reading in 1827, to continue his trade of making wagon cloths in premises behind the Bell and Crown Inn in Castle Street, almost opposite to Leadbeater's house. In 1831 he transferred this business to Factory Yard, off West Street, (see page 207) where he continued to produce wagon and rick cloths as well as sarplices for the local hop industry. His products were dispatched, twice a week, for sale in London.

Subsequently a doctor, Edmund Yalden Knowles, occupied 5 Castle Street and later James Stevens, a solicitor, worked there. But in 1884 Stevens submitted plans for new offices in South Street and soon afterwards moved. At the turn of the century it was the home of Dr Hugh Ealand. His partner at that time was Dr Coad although by 1913 it was Dr H. Sloman, who was local Medical Officer of Health.

During the Second World War the house was occupied by the Red Cross and, after hostilities, it became the Regency House (sic) Restaurant and Club. However, by 1950 it was the offices of solicitors Stevens and Bolton, who remained there until the late 1990s before removing to Guildford. It is now occupied by the Harley Street Hearing Aid Centre.

The small adjoining two-storey property, **5A**, similarly dates from the first half of the 19th century. It has a parapet and an Adamesque fanlight on the first floor which looks as though it might have originally been destined to go above a front door. On the ground floor is a shop window with glazing bars and a curved top rail. It is best remembered in the 1950s and 1960s as the booking office of the Lower Bourne-based Comfy Coaches. This firm offered "Daily excursions and tours throughout the season… 26-41 seater coaches available for Private Party Hire". But this office removed to The Woolmead in the late 1960s. Photographer Michael Sargent was there in the 1970s and antiquarian books were briefly sold. It is currently vacant.

It was built in front of the southern end of **6** Castle Street and, indeed, is attached to the latter. This fine frontage dates from about 1820 and, happily, retains its later Victorian shopfront. Like the many of its southerly neighbours, it is also timber-framed, although in 1958 much of the interior was radically altered. In the 18th century it housed a pub, The Fleur de Lys, and until the interior alterations were made, a mural was visible in an upper room, reputedly the work of a monk in return for board and lodging. If so, this would mean that the inn dated from at least the 16th century and probably before that.

However, the name most associated with this building is that of Tily & Brown and the legend *Cocoa Mat, Matting, Rope, Line & Twine Warehouse* can still be seen on the frontage. John Tily was listed in 1826 as a patten- (wooden shoe) and brush maker and later he and his family occupied both 6 and 7 which in 1868 was converted into a single building.

M. & J. Tily, the initials stood for Mary and James, were not only ironmongers but also dealt in agricultural implements. In 1896 the company applied to the year-old Farnham UDC to build a workshop in nearby Long Garden Walk. Permission was refused but they built it anyway…and, rather than demolish it, were permitted to retain it for ten years. It has been assumed that is where the Tilys produced their rope with the appropriately named Long Garden Walk doubling as a rope walk. Back in 1909 John Henry Knight recalled: "String was made at Tily's in Castle Street. I remember seeing the man with his bag of tow [the unworked stem of fibre or flax before it was heckled] walking slowly backwards across Castle Street, the wheel being somewhere up Long Garden Walk. There was not much traffic in Castle Street in those days."

By 1906 the company had added bicycles to their growing range of products and advertised as makers of the "Beau Ideal". It was also sole agents for the superlative Sunbeam two-wheeler.

Between the wars the business branched out to 117 West Street, having taken over Harts ironmonger there, but this closed in 1933. By this time the business had become Tily & Brown. Later, it expanded to Guildford and in the 1950s was referring to its outlet there at 185 High Street.

Although the town was beginning to change, the Castle Street shop remained much as it had been in prewar days. Sir John Verney, who was an accomplished artist, later remembered Tily & Brown as "the perfect ironmongers. You could also buy pure powder colour scooped from little wooden drawers by charming elderly assistants. An ounce of Prussian Blue weighed out into a spill of brown paper. However, I soon became reconciled to, and a regular customer of Robert Dyas."

This change took place in 1958 and Dyas was destined to remain there until 1996 when it moved to 42 Downing

Street. At this point the premises were divided into two with Café Uno in what had been 6 and Oddbins wine merchants at 7.

Number **8**, its rather grand neighbour, dates from 1870 and was built for Charles Hazell, who was one of Farnham's leading hop planters and maltsters. Constructed for him by Goddards, the date is indisputable because Nigel Temple was able to examine the builder's day book for that year and it contained a reference to "meeting Mr Hazell to discuss the new house in Castle Street."

Of three stuccoed storeys with a large archway, it was built on the site of an earlier house which in the 1830s was occupied by William Lockerbie. He was also a hop planter and maltster with a malt house behind the garden of number 7 next door who sold to Charles Hazell in 1858. Although he died in 1894, Hazell's unmarried daughter, Carrie, continued to live in the house until 1927, by which time it was clearly in need of a coat of paint! It remained a private dwelling for some years, although is currently occupied by interior designers Connaught Mason.

After stucco, it's back to brick again for **9** and **9A**, which is one of those properties which makes Castle Street so special. Of two storeys, five bays with parapet, tiled roof and two flat-topped dormers in the attic storey, the fanlight of the pedimented doorway incorporates a lantern.

This is a brick refronting of an earlier building which by 1730 had been converted into two dwellings. Owned in that year by Anna Child, a widow of John, it was sold to John Leigh, a surgeon, for a not inconsiderable £1300. It was subsequently owned by solicitor John Hollest and,

8 *9* *9A* *10*

in 1797, he passed it on to James Moore Molyneux of Loseley Hall, by which time it had reverted to being a single house as it was to remain for the next 160 or so years. Subsequently, in the mid-19th century, it was owned by William Crump, who was a linen draper.

In about 1960 it was again divided with the southerly portion retaining the number 9 and the northerly half becoming 9A with street access through the one-time side entrance. However, since 1987 the entire house, although still separated, has reverted to common ownership.

All of these Castle Street houses have retained a more or less regular building line but number **10** is set back from the road and its owners thus have the benefit of a front garden. Fortunately it is possible to view the property through the fine wrought-iron gates which are reputed to have come from Moor Park House, outside the town. Dating from the early 18th century, more Queen Anne than Georgian, this impressive house was built by London grocer Thomas Piggott, who hailed from Kingston. This was not the refacing of an older dwelling but a property built on a site that had hitherto been occupied by The Corn Rooms. They reflected Farnham's booming corn market which was at its height in the late 17th century.

Piggott was in occupation by 1730, so the house had been completed by then, being of five bays, the central three slightly projecting, with sash windows and a string course in between. There was a tiled roof and the porch is of the balcony style supported on Corinthian columns. Inside is a magnificent oak staircase.

By 1763 Piggott had sold his house to John Randall, who was a cheesemonger, and it was then let. Later it was bought by one John Bradley and passed to his son, Bristow.

The Hop Blossom, on the corner of Long Garden Walk and Long Garden West, was so named because of the hop fields that were once almost adjacent to its doorstep. An alehouse licence was granted in 1864. It was originally owned by George Trimmer, and thus passed to Farnham United Breweries. Since 1984 it has been a Fuller's house. The author and the artist often met there to discuss this book.

It was sold, following his bankruptcy, in 1814. Then it was acquired by William Samways Oke, a surgeon, so triggering an association with the medical profession that was to endure for much of the 19th century. Among the medicos who practised from there were John Drinkwater and Robert Oke Clarke. But by the turn of the 19th century, it was occupied by Ernest Jackson, who was a solicitor.

Sadly by this time, Thomas Piggott's house had been "modernized". The original tile roof had been replaced with slates, the glazing bars removed from the windows and the bricks colour-washed. Considerable changes were wrought inside which upset the symmetry of the rooms.

It is to the great credit of dental surgeon John Gilbert and his wife, who bought the property in 1972, that they have reversed all of these Victorian alterations. So outwardly 10 Castle Street has, in most essentials, reverted to its original, inspiring, early 18th-century appearance.

John Gilbert conducted his dental practice from 10 but in 1992 he purchased **11** and **12** next door, and in 1993 this became his surgery. Dating from the first half of the 19th century, a stone bearing the date *1826* was discovered during the conversion. With three storeys, it was for at least 100 years commercial premises. By the early 1900s it housed J.S. Giles' Old Curiosity Shop "where something interesting, that is quaint and rare, will be found". He also undertook upholstery, cabinet and picture frame manufacture and in 1906 was advertising "new extensive showrooms" at 26 and 28 East Street.

The shop subsequently became the second home of the Farnham Co-operative Society, which had been formed in September 1907, its first commercial outlet being at 68 Castle Street, opposite. But by 1909 it had moved across the road to 11/12 although it soon outgrew these premises and in 1912 moved to a permanent home in Union Road.

Between the wars it became Davies Bros' newsagents business while in 1969 it was taken over by the Woking-based NSS Newsagents. The shop window was removed during the 1993 conversion, being replaced by a rendered wall which sensitively incorporates four-pane sash windows which match those on the first floor.

The rendering on the ground floor chimes with the pebble dash of **13** which adjoins it and shares the same slate roof line, although it may be of a slightly earlier date. Its next door neighbour, number **14**, three storeys, of two

One of the stone reliefs on the north wall of Farnham Police Station which features the origins of the town's past prosperity, namely corn and wool.

bays with rendering and a pedimented door in the second, was one of 11 houses for sale in 1809, six of which were sold to Joseph Hart. It was at 14 that, around the turn of the 19th century, Mrs Swayne, who had moved from 74, Castle Street, ran her Modern Commercial School & Kindergarten. In 1906 she would advertise a curriculum that included "French, Science, Drawing, Painting, Singing Music…Fees very moderate…A limited number of boarders taken."

Next door number **15** is effectively what 14 would have looked like before it was rendered, although it may be late 18th century on account of its three-pane sashes on its two upper storeys. In the late 1890s it was occupied by a Miss Mayhew and in the 1950s by G.R. Burningham.

From three to two storeys, **16**, **17** and **18** are believed to have formed a single hall house in the late Middle Ages. This conclusion followed investigations by The Surrey Domestic Buildings Research Group which determined that it dated from the 16th century and possibly earlier. A substantial inglenook fireplace was added to what today is 16 at some time in the following 100 years, and the property was divided soon afterwards. Its frontage, with the sashes flush with the brickwork, dates from the 18th century.

In 1891 number 16 was occupied by Crookham postman C.F. Pierce. Later, in 1930, its then owner offered it to Farnham UDC as a public convenience. Happily, this initiative was not taken up. Another postman, one

11/12 ***13*** ***14*** ***15*** ***16***

T. Mathews, lived next door at 17. There are few shops in this part of Castle Street but this has such a front and, for many years, from 1899 at least, it was an old fashioned, crowded draper's shop run by the Misses Kelley who moved there from a few doors down at 28. From 1947 until 1970 it was P. & G. Wells' bookshop and you can still see the iron support projecting from the wall where their sign once hung. With a head office at 11 College Street, Winchester, they were booksellers "to Winchester College and Charterhouse" with another branch at the latter establishment. Wells' also offered a bookbinding service and "stationery of every description" was in stock.

Next door, tall and slim and three storeys high, **19** with its three-pane sashes flush with the walls suggests the early 18th century. In 1891 it was occupied by one T. Streeton and in the 1950s by a Mrs J. Jarvis.

Number **20** is a three-bay, two-storey structure which Nigel Temple dated at about 1820 rather than as 18th century as it might otherwise appear. The evidence are the four-, rather than three-pane sashes and slim pillars to the pedimented doorway, although a slate roof might be expected by this date. A Victorian double shopfront was fitted at some time although the brickwork has been scrupulously restored. Like some of the properties further down Castle Street, this is a refronted timber-framed building.

17 *18* *19* *20*

It was the home of Joseph Hart, who bought the six houses in 1809 (see number 14). Following his death it was sold in 1832 to John McDonald, a well-heeled gardener, and it later passed in 1871 to his son George, who is best remembered for endowing the McDonald almshouses in West Street. In 1891 no less than four maiden ladies, the Misses Lynes-Clinton and the Misses Hastings, lived here. By the 1950s it was the home of Group-Captain Sydney Smith D.S.O., A.F.C.

Twenty one and **22** are also of two storeys but roofed with slate rather than tile, which might suggest early 19th century rather than 18th. Number 22 retains a shopfront and during the 1880s it was occupied by George Chuter and Son, bakers, who offered "genuine wholemeal bread made from stone-ground wheat meal".

It is back to three storeys for **23** and **24**. Probably dating from the early 19th century, like 15 they have four-pane sashes on the ground floor and three-pane ones on the two above. They were respectively occupied at the turn of the 19th century by one C. Bradford and Mrs Williams.

21 **22** **23** **24**

The adjoining two-storey numbers **25** and **26** are older, with brick beneath the rendering, and are said to date from the 17th century. Reputedly once a single property owned by the Bishops of Winchester, it was apparently divided to house respectively their graces' butler and cook.

The imposing numbers **27** and **28** are on three floors with an archway between, of colour-washed brick and middlish Victorian. Today the former, which consists of two-thirds of the building, is four flats. The Henley Veterinary Practice is at 28. This is the successor to Underwood and Croxon which was established there for some 20 years.

Back in the 1890s James Tily, who had a shop at 6/7, lived at 27 while his neighbour was Miss Kelley, a "dress and mantle maker". In the 1930s number 27 became the practice of husband and wife vets Everett and Lock and they continued there until the mid-1970s. The premises successively became a pet shop, poodle parlour and hairdresser, prior to its present status.

In 1886 Miss Kelley, later of 28, was listed as running a dress-making business at the neighbouring **29**, a two-

25 26 27/28 29

storey property with a five-pane sash on the ground floor to let the light in. It is quite like a cottage in character with a rendered front, a tiled roof and clearly pre-18th century.

Between the wars **30** and **31** were Fisher's Private Hotel, proprietor Mrs W.H. Fisher, although by 1946 number 31 had been converted into four flats. The former, three-storey and rendered, is of Georgian character, probably early 19th century. By 1891 it was the home of W.H. Allen, the accomplished watercolour painter who so inspired Harold Falkner. The double-fronted, stuccoed, three-storey number 31 with its grand entrance with bracketed cornices on the ground and first floors was the home in 1877 of Sir Fothergill Cook. Ten years later E. Jackson lived there.

Also Classical in inspiration, three-storeyed and stuccoed, numbers **32** and **33** were built by Farnham builder William Birch, who died in 1863. The former property was, in the 1880s, the home of Miss Josephine

30 *31* *32*

Reynard's School for Ladies, which moved there from 38. Next door number 33 was in the 1870s the home of Lt-Colonel John Luard, founder of the Farnham School of Art. By the 1890s surgeon J.A. Lorimer was in residence.

Lowndes' Buildings are entered through the alleyway between numbers 33 and 34 and were named after Thomas Lowndes, who on his death in 1833 left land and these nine houses in his will. He also owned numbers 34, 35, 36, 37 Castle Street. It's back to brick for the first of these, numbers **34** and **35**. These are two-storey properties, slate-roofed with a flat-topped dormer window apiece, three-pane sashes and dating from maybe the late 18th century. In 1891 the latter was the home of G.W.H. May, a postman and numismatologist, in other words a collector of coins and medals.

The frontages of the three-storey, rendered numbers **36** and **37** are older, probably early 18th century on account of their exposed three-pane sashes.

Lowndes' Buildings

33 34 35

The southerly bay of **38**, there is a join in the chimney, may date from the 1830s; it fronts a timber-framed house. The two northerly bays could be 30 or so years later. The house is washed in a plum red colour. In 1879 Miss Reynard moved the school from here to number 32.

When Nigel Temple wrote *Farnham Buildings and People*, published in 1963, he described **39**, **40** and **41** Castle Street as being "grey-brick-fronted houses under slate roofs". Today they have been colour-washed and arguably look the better for it. All were built in the 1860s for Thomas Ainsley, the Bishop's steward, by Frank, son of William Birch, a one-time resident of Castle Street, who was Farnham's leading builder of the day.

A watercolour by George Shepherd of the northern end of Castle Street, which is dated 1818, clearly shows the building that occupied the site prior to the construction of

36 *37* *38*

Ainsley's houses. Endowed with three distinctive gables, perhaps dating from the 17th century, this made way for 39 and 40 that were conceived as an entity. Number 41, the last of the trio, was completed a little later in 1866. All are essentially the same, although 41 is slightly taller, three-storeyed with moulded architraves and cast-iron balconies on the two first-floor windows. Local auctioneer A.J. Nash was living at 40 in 1891 and in the 1950s number 39 was used by surgeons Mrs C.E. Philips and Mr G.E. Green as a surgery.

The last building on the west side of Castle Street, which by 1952 was named the **Freemasons' Hall**, is brick, nicely proportioned. It is of five bays of which the projecting centre three are surmounted by a pediment. Dating from the third quarter of the 18th century, by 1822 it was described as "The School, Castle Street".

39 **40** **41**

Subsequently named the National Schoolrooms, it fulfilled this function until St Andrew's Church of England School was built in 1860.

It later became known as the Farnham Working Men's Institute which in 1864 held an exhibition of "works of art and industry" there. The *Surrey and Hants News* reported that it included "a painting by Elmer of Farnham Castle and…the Bishop lent the Bible on which Queen Victoria took her Coronation oath." Subsequently, in 1909, the trustees offered "The Castle Street Institute" for sale on 28th May. Auctioneer J. Alfred Eggar suggested that it might be suitable for "a Museum, Furniture Warehouse or *Motor Garage*" (author's italics).

Whatever the outcome, the building continued to have a scholastic role. After the Second World War, in 1946, Charles Borelli undertook negotiations in the hope that the Institute might indeed be acquired as a museum for the town. But he then heard that the building had been sold to someone else.

Further up Castle Hill, in Old Park Lane, stands **The Grange**, a medium-sized early 18th-century house which

Freemasons' Hall

contains a sumptuous interior of a quality that is unmatched in the town. Tantalisingly, the date of its construction, information regarding the first owner and even the circumstances that prompted its building are unknown. It is surrounded by a large walled garden with fine wrought-iron gateways. Until it was "disparked" in 1710, the land on which it stands was the property of the Bishops of Winchester. It is believed to have been built in the early 18th century by the shadowy Edward Forbes, who was woodward, or forester-cum-secretary, to Sir Jonathan Trelawny Bt., who had become Bishop of Winchester in 1707. Confirmation of Forbes' association with The Grange comes from Senex's map of Surrey, published in 1729, which marks the house and indicates "Mr Forbes" as the owner.

This is a property created for an individual of taste and probably one who was accustomed to wealth. The most outstanding feature of The Grange is its painted stairwell and ceiling, depicting scenes from Classical mythology which has been attributed to Sir James Thornhill. However Sir George Bellew, a recent owner, would go no further than stating that the artist "might have had an influence on the staircase painting…" The landing is panelled in pine, as are all the principal rooms.

Outside, each elevation differs from its neighbour with the west and south fronts featuring canopy-type door-cases. One of these may have featured in the original southern aspect but it subsequently featured in a carefully executed three-floor extension, which dates from about 1909.

This later addition is less apparent on the east front and its door-case is outstanding (see frontispiece) with Corinthian pilasters supporting an elliptical pediment. Sir George believed that it may have been the work of William Emmett, a master carver and colleague of Sir Christopher Wren, who undertook work at the College of Arms. Or, he mused, was it an instance of different craftsmen using the same pattern book?

The windows are mainly sash, with the exception of the more recent southern elevation which features leaded casements.The entire exterior is topped by a parapet which may be of a later date, as such a feature is not usually seen on Queen Anne houses.

The Grange passed, in 1730, to Forbes Fisher, its builder's nephew. Following his death in 1760 the house

A Bishop of Winchester with his Farnham Park and Castle, as depicted in the stone relief on the Police Station.

Wealthy hop planter Charles Andrews (left) in 1905 with the eastern frontage of his house, The Grange, in the background. He died there in 1906, his 90th year. In its obituary the Farnham Herald *wrote of a man "very careful of his appearance, and invariably wearing a silk hat and frock coat."*

was leased to tenants and, on the demise of John Knowles in 1831, it was sold by his widow in 1837 to Samuel Andrews, a member of an affluent hop-growing family with a large kiln in Potters Gate. After he died in 1842 it was owned for the next 64 years by his son, Charles Andrews, who was Farnham's largest hop grower, with a farm and kilns nearby. At the time of his death in 1906, and despite leaving an estate worth £417,266, the house was in a poor state of repair. It passed to Mrs Bertha Gough, a relative, and she sold in 1907 to her cousins, Howard and Emily Johnson. Much restorative work was undertaken by Major-General Sir Edward Perceval, previously of nearby Guildford House, who acquired The Grange from Emily for £5000 in 1919 and he remained there for the next 36 years. It was inherited in 1955 by his son Max and was bought in 1970 by Sir George Bellew, who was Garter King of Arms. On his death it passed to his son and since 2000 it has been the home of architect Max Lyons and his family.

The Tudor-style **Cedar Court**, the first property on the eastern side of Castle Street, is secluded yet accessible to the town. Built by Lt-Colonel Marsden, the plans were submitted to the Council in August 1891. It was constructed on the site of an 18th-century-style house named The Cedars which was occupied in the early 1800s by Elizabeth Penfold, who later lived at Guildford House nearby.

Just above Cedar Court was a small reservoir which filled the town's conduit at the bottom of Castle Street.

Albert Winslade, a tailor from East Street who was born in 1864, recalled that in his youth "an old chap named Wells" used to fill "a wooden barrel on wheels" from this source with a scoop on the end of a pole and then "sold the water house to house. He had to make a good many journeys, for the boys often turned the tap of his barrel and he would have to go back and fill up again."

In 1872, Charles Andrews, in addition to owning The Grange, also acquired **Castle Hill House**. A two-storey property, parapeted and constructed of high quality brick with five bays and three-pane sashes, it is thought to date from the mid-18th century and has a fine mahogany and oak staircase. The gabled northerly extension is of a later date. The original owner may have been Thomas Baker, who was a hop planter, solicitor and Justice of the Peace. Following Andrews' death, Mrs Gough also inherited Castle Hill, it then passed to Howard Jackson and in the 1950s was the home of Commander F. Cartwright, RN.

Guildford House next door is at heart a late 18th-century house although its appearance has been enhanced by the playful presence of mid-19th-century additions. Back in 1824 the property, in its original form, belonged to Miles Penford and it passed on his death in 1837 to his wife Elizabeth. When she died in 1842 she was one of Farnham's largest landowners, with over 300 acres (121ha) to her name. Her father, Peckham Williams, was a successful hop grower.

The property was acquired in 1853 by the Reverend J.S. Utterton, who was responsible for effecting changes

Castle Hill House *Guildford House*

to what was then named Castle Hill House. These were completed by 1856. At the front the alterations consisted of grafting on two bays with a covered porch inbetween surmounted by a balustrade which matched the one on the main body of the house. In addition, a gothick oriel window with ogee roof was built in the centre of the rather formal facade. Bays were added at the rear with a gazebo, echoing the oriel at the front, introduced on the first floor.

Mr Utterton's architectural sensibilities speak for themselves and he was in the forefront of initiating the extension of St Andrew's Church tower in 1865. He was also chairman, from its inception in 1855, of the Farnham Burial Board and in 1862 was made Archdeacon of Surrey. Interestingly, at its meeting on 8th June 1874, he signed the minutes "J.S. Guildford", on becoming Suffragan Bishop of Guildford. It seems that he was responsible for changing his residence's name to Guildford House.

By the early 1950s it had become the Farnham Hospital Nurses' Home, but in 1961 it was in the private ownership of architect C.V. Tillett who undertook a sensitive restoration, which included the demolition of two flanking blocks at the rear and replacing the glazing window bars.

Its neighbour to the south, **45** has an dignified facade dating from about 1720 and possesses, along with the neighbouring 46, a small front garden, a luxury denied to

45 **46** **47**

all of its more southerly neighbours. It features five bays with a centrally located pedimented doorway and a tiled roof, although this lacks the expected parapet. In 1839 it was owned, along with number **46** next door, by Sarah Williams. In 1867 the family sold to James Burningham and it changed hands again in 1905, together with 46. This property, which does have a parapet, complete with three blind recesses, is an early 18th-century brick refronting of a timber-framed building which may date from the 1590s.

The same applies to **47**, which along with the adjoining **48**, were refronted in the early 19th century with margin pane sashes. Prior to that they were one house that was divided when owned by one Lowe in 1746. Later, in 1810-1812, they again passed to a single owner, John Newell, who may well have been responsible for the present frontages. He went on to sell them separately. In 1891 a Mr Gibbons, who was a painter and plumber, lived at 47.

Charles Borelli was born at 48 in 1873, prior to moving to 36 The Borough, but the house remained in the family's ownership and Father Charles Borelli lived there until shortly before his death in the 1990s. The first-floor window above the porch was introduced relatively recently, although the neighbouring one at 47 appears original.

Next door, number **49**, is described by Ian Nairn as "a trap for the unwary; a very good imitation". Dating from

48 *49* *The Nelson Arms*

1929, this Georgian town house is the work of Leonard Stedman and worthy of a pupil of Sir Edwin Lutyens. It was built for Dr Hugh Ealand, then of 5 Castle Street, and his unmarried daughter Beth was still living there in the mid-1950s.

Its frontage reveals clear echoes of 45, a few doors away and replaces a two-storey, timber-framed building with a prominent gable and a roof line shared with The Nelson Arms next door. These are probably one of "three cottages…adjoining the Nelson's Arms", which produced an aggregate rental of £23.8s. (£22.40p) when they were offered for auction in 1888.

Now **The Nelson Arms**, 50/52 housed a pub in the early 18th century when it was named The Hand and Pen, which was a scrivener's (scribe's) sign. It was owned by John Tanner of Haselmere and occupied by Francis Parker. At the time the inn occupied the northern part of the present structure. It has progressively absorbed the two adjoining cottages and thus the corner of what is now Park Row. In 1739 the name was changed to The Baker's Arms and this persisted into the 19th century. But by 1839 it had been altered again, this time to Nelson's Arms, with

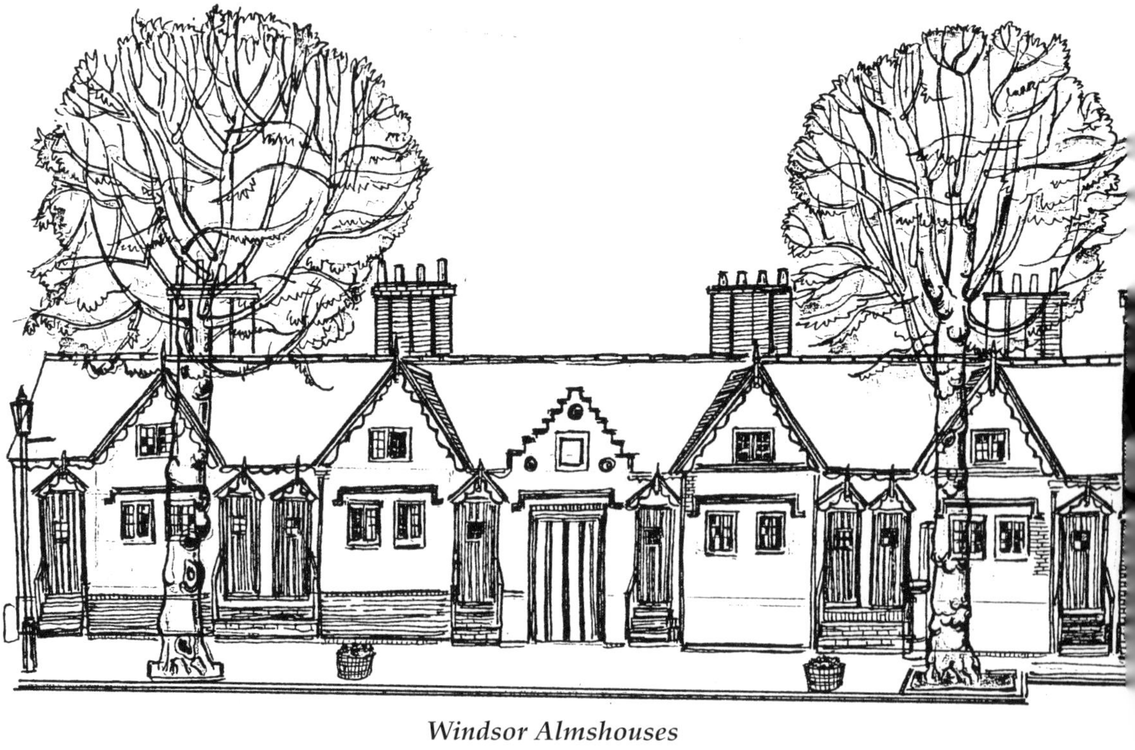

Windsor Almshouses

Edward Elliott as licensee. This may have been because of a connection between Admiral Nelson and Firgrove House, Firgrove Hill, which was demolished and replaced in 1965 by the Trafalgar Court flats. Although it was owned by Sir William Hamilton, husband of Emma, he never lived there but he generously left the property to Horatia Ward (née Nelson) who was the daughter of Horatio Nelson and his former wife. On the other hand, many public houses throughout Britain were named after Nelson at around this time…

By 1872 The Nelson Arms was a Knight house, then it passed to Barrett and so to Farnham United Breweries. In 1910 the brewery applied to build a club room at the Nelson and maintained that it would not change the exterior and turn it into a "gin palace". The application was rejected with the Board pointing out that the Garabaldi, around the corner in Park Row, had been closed and that the Nelson's future also looked vulnerable. Happily it survived. Alterations were undertaken in 1925 when 11 ornamental fish carved from ivory were found on a rafter. The "Tudor" windows are of a later date. The interior succumbed in 2002 to an insensitive minimalist-theme

61 **62**

A resident of the Windsor Almshouses, which were then colour-washed, apprehensively views the camera on a summer's day before the First World War. The three plane trees were planted in 1897 to commemorate Queen Victoria's Diamond Jubilee.

makeover, both bars being decked out in stark white paint.

The Nelson was at least convenient for occupants of the **Windsor Almshouses**, 53-60, on the south side of Park Row which date from 1619. Brick built with timber interior framing, the properties are of one and a half storeys, the top window being an attic, and there are five gables with barge-boards. On the stepped central gable is the oft-quoted legend: "The habitation and relief of eight poor honest old impotent persons." They were endowed by Andrew Windsor of Bentley who died in September 1620, the year after their completion. Occupants were to benefit from 1s.8d. (9p) a week income from land at Buscot, although in 1621 his brother Peter defaulted on this agreement and was found guilty.

The buildings remained essentially unchanged, apart from having three plane trees planted in front of them in 1897 to commemorate the Diamond Jubilee of Queen Victoria. However, in 1983 the accommodation was altered from eight rather cramped self-contained flats to one for a single occupant and four further units. A single-storey extension was also added at the rear. In 1995 it was recognized that further restorative work was required, due to "serious structural cracking of the walls, particularly in the gables" and repairs were duly undertaken.

The almshouses' southerly neighbour, number **61**, has a fine late 18th-century facade with some controlled vitality introduced by the ground-floor arched recesses, complete with four-pane sashes. These are on either side of the pedimented front door and the central bay which stands proud. Of five bays with three-pane sashes on the first floor, above the door is a window with a curved top, a configuration that the house shares with 90 West Street.

In the early 19th century much of this part of Castle Street was owned by hop planter James Stevens and many of the hop fields on the land between East Street and Farnham Park belonged to him. He also owned number **62** and it may well have been occupied up until the 1850s by Elizabeth Stevens, who was unmarried, and her niece Louisa. Two ladies, plus servants, this is a big house! However, by the second half of the century it was the home of Alfred Henry Stevens, who was a member of the Farnham Burial Board.

A little earlier than its neighbour, the two-storey, mid-18th-century frontage has five bays while the flatness of the parapet is relieved by the presence of five blind recesses rather than a cornice. The fine pedimented doorway is approached by steps.

There is an architectural association with number **63** because, from 1911 until his death in 1928, this was the home of William John Wells, Thomas Wonnacott's erstwhile business partner. Of two storeys, the three-pane exposed sashes with curved top rails suggest the early 18th century. The central window on the first floor, which was once blind, has been added in recent years.

The neighbouring 64 and **65**, are now one house. It is probably later Georgian with three-pane recessed sashes, two floors plus a tile-hung attic storey. In 1891 Mrs Dunford, a milliner and dressmaker, was the occupant of 64, while J. Hoptoff, perhaps a relative of Downing Street tea merchant I. Hoptoff, lived at 65 in 1877.

Although Classical in spirit, the frontage of **66** – two storey with parapet and four-pane sashes – is probably late Georgian. In 1877 one C. Smither, who may have been the cabinet maker of 42 Downing Street, lived there, although by 1891 the Misses Warner were in residence. But by 1976 the property had become badly dilapidated and it was sold to Mr and Mrs Fletcher who undertook the extensive restoration.

Ian Nairn dated numbers **67** and **68** as 17th century, "tile hung like a Wealden cottage". Number 67 is now the Crafty Kid toy shop, but in 1901 it was the town's "Telephone Office" manned by one S. Hunt. Its present ground-floor bow window is a postwar addition and replaced an earlier sash. From 1967 until 1972 it was Catherine Fenez's ladies' dress shop.

In the mid-1930s The Castle Café occupied 68 and it was to annex 67. Mrs Skidmore's tea shop was just the type of establishment you would expect to find in a Home Counties market town of the interwar years. It continued to occupy 68 until the 1970s, but this is now The Colony Chinese restaurant with a first-floor dining room complete with an oriel window with fine views of Castle Street. This property and its outbuildings have experienced much entrepreneurial activity over the past 100 or so years.

In the 1880s number 68 was occupied by a builder's merchant J. Diamond. This was followed by Hickley and Company, also a builder and coal merchant, founded in Aldershot in 1845. It soon moved to its new purpose-built

63 **65**

premises on the corner of South Street and Abbey Street. Hickley was replaced in 1901 by Arthur Mardon, who had been one of Diamond's employees. He was later to forge a partnership with John Mills to form Mardon & Mills, based at Longbridge.

In December 1909 Mardon applied to Farnham UDC to transform his old workshop at the rear of 68 into a skating rink, a facility then enjoyed by both Aldershot and Alton. The Farnham Rink and Recreation Co Ltd duly came into existence and the *Farnham Herald* commented that the promoters were the entire Council...The following year it was enlarged and fives and squash courts were opened in May. But all these facilities were destined to enjoy only a brief two-year existence. On 15th May 1911 Caesar Brothers began work demolishing the rink and its ancillaries. They were replaced by Farnham's first cinema, the Picture Palace, with its entrance in Bear Lane. It opened in June of the same year.

This was not the only business being undertaken there. In 1900 Olive Edis, just 24 years old, embarked on a career as a photographer. In addition to a presence in Norfolk, she spent four months of the year at 68 Castle Street, where her Farnham studio was located with "sittings given daily". Later, in November 1907, it briefly became the Farnham

66 67 68

The fanlight of 70 Castle Street incorporates two hearts at its centre and shares some similarity with that of 104 West Street, see page 207.

Co-operative Society's first shop. Although the cinema only survived until November 1913, it took over the rival Electric Theatre in East Street. The Picture Palace building was then used as a delousing station for soldiers returning from the First World War.

It subsequently became the premises of Quinette Crushes which made soft drinks there. The business was owned by Mr Palin-Evans in conjunction with his mother and local businessman Dick Martin. Its timber-framed offices were decorated in shades of orange, lemon and green to represent the company's most popular lines of beverages. The corporate logo was a roundel which featured three owls head of Quizzit, Quoffit and Quenchit. In the late 1930s the business was acquired by Kia-Ora.

Then, in September 1939, a theatrical touring company named the English Classical Players arrived unexpectedly in the town. They had been touring French schools but this activity was cut short by the outbreak of the Second World War. Arriving in Southampton, complete with scenery, they only intended to stay in Farnham overnight. By chance the director, Laurence Ray, encountered Charles Borelli and he suggested that the one-time cinema might be converted into a temporary theatre. The rest is history. The first production, Bernard Shaw's *You Never Can Tell*, took place on 5th December 1939. What was now known as the Castle Theatre was able to seat 167. It was, for licensing reasons, a theatre club with, eventually, an accumulated membership of some 6500 and it remained there until 30th March 1974, when a move was made to the newly-built Redgrave in East Street. Subsequently, in about the mid-1980s, the current occupant, Pizza Piazza, arrived.

On the south side of the entrance stands Catherine Fenez ladies' dress shop which has occupied **69** since 1972. In the early 18th century the site played host to The Bull and Butcher public house, owned by Robert Knight. His father, an enterprising carpenter, also owned, in 1739, The Hand and Pen, now The Nelson Arms, further up Castle Street.

The property subsequently passed to the Knight brothers' Farnham Brewery and it was offered for sale in 1891 as a going concern, its facilities including a skittle alley and market room. By the time it came on the market again in 1901, it had closed. It was described as a public house "...recently known as The Bull and Butcher".
By then it had a stuccoed exterior with a single ground-

floor window and three first-floor ones with a moulded string course inbetween. There were open eaves with decorated brackets. Soon afterwards, in 1903, it became the Farnham Steam Bakery, jointly run by Ransom and Rogers who were well-established bakers in the town, although the latter soon dropped out. A sign was painted on its south-facing wall which was then exposed to view.

In 1929 further changes were effected when the frontage of the building was radically altered in the Borelli/Falkner spirit to do away with its Victorian embellishments. Brick now replaced stucco, there were multi-paned double fronted shop windows and the first floor now had two sashes, complete with margin panes. The only indication of the previous facade can be seen on the exposed north wall where the Victorian quoins can still be seen.

Ransom's claimed that its coffee was "roasted by experts" and encouraged passers-by to "Try Our Noted Sausages". In 1945 the business was acquired by W.H. Cullen, also of 30 South Street, although it continued to trade under the Ransom name until 1955 and survived in Castle Street until 1972.

Agreeably understated, number **70** has five bays with a parapet, flush-fitting three-pane sashes and a centrally positioned pedimented door. It was built in about 1780 on the site of the early 17th-century inn, The Rose and Crown, later The White Hart, another of the street's lost public houses. Acquired in 1721 by Dr Thomas Leigh, it consisted of three houses. He sold these to George West the elder, who was founder of the Farnham Friendly Society. West demolished the two most northerly properties and built 70 in its place. The third became 71.

In pre-1914 days there was gated access to the rear of the adjoining number 70 although this space was filled in about 1930 by a carefully matched extension. This is now separated from its neighbour and is numbered 70A. In 1891 number 70 was the home of Captain Lancelot Austwick and 50 years later, in 1941, Mrs Fillery's St George's preparatory school opened there. It moved to Frensham in 1989 and survives today in Rowledge.

Like 70, number **71** next door was built where part of The White Hart once stood. Perhaps the presence of the alleyway to the south prevented the builder from repeating the three-pane sashes on the first floor of both properties on the ground floor. Instead 71's is a four-pane example because the presence of the door meant that there was only room for one window rather than two! It is currently occupied by solicitors Draper and Company.

Thresher Wine Shop, **72**, is another example of a timber-framed, jettied building that has been refronted. However, the pebble-dash of the facade is all too 20th century. It is also the site, or part of, a public house which possessed at least three names: The Lamb, The Lamb and Flag and, later, The Bell and Crown.

The house was also used as a day school and in 1839 the "Misses Stratford", Jane and Louisa by name, were listed as running such an establishment. Coming into the ownership of the Knights, in 1887 the premises, described as a "brick built and tiled house and shop", were sold to saddler and harness maker Charles Smith for £700. He had been renting them for £40 a year. In 1906 he was advertising "a good assortment of hunting crops, riding and driving whips" and describing himself as "dealer in corn, hay, and straw". In 1911 Smith moved to South Street and his place was taken by H.H. Ayerst, who was in the same business.

In 1950 the shop became The Westminster Wine Company off-licence, a subsidiary of Watney's, which from 1898 until the mid-1950s occupied a site to the rear which extended east to Bear Lane. In 1839 John and James Knight's brewery was there and following the death of James Knight in 1869, his son, James Junior, carried on the

69 ***70A*** ***70*** ***71***

business until May 1888 when it evolved into the Farnham Brewery Company.

In 1891 it was put up for sale, together with 13 fully licensed houses and four leasehold properties, although it was not until 1896 that it was taken over by the London-based Reid and Company, a business that in 1898 became Watney, Combe, Reid. It closed the brewery and the facility became a bottling plant for beer brewed at Mortlake.
In 1947 Watney's absorbed Crowley of Alton and in about 1954 transferred its Farnham operations to those premises. The site was then variously occupied by Coca-Cola and Southern Egg and Poultry Producers.

Access to Knight's brewery had been via the archway located in the frontage of its rebuilt Knight's Bank at number 75. But this was too restricted for the new owner's needs and in 1910 it demolished number **73**, at one time The Bell and Crown public house, to improve access to its bottling facility.

These premises had been rebuilt in the late 18th century, having a three-storeyed, stuccoed frontage with slate roof that was the same height as the neighbouring 72. There were two bay windows on the first floor. The pub was so named from then until its closure by Farnham Magistrates in 1902 and its demolition came eight years later.

The entrance to St Georges Yard now occupies the site and the *Watney, Combe, Reid & Co Ltd* legend is still just discernible on the wooden beam above the entrance. Work on this project began in 1988. The office development was by Allamanda Estates and the houses by Kents. Broadway and Malyan were the architects and its flint-faced properties off Bear Lane won praise from the Georgian Group. But some were still for sale in recession-hit 1991.

The entrance is flanked to the south by an extension for Pizza Express which has occupied number **74** since 1996. The house was built in the late 18th century and is of five bays, parapeted with three-pane recessed sashes, a pedimented central doorway and a shopfront incorporated in the northerly aspect. Incorporating parts of an earlier timber-framed dwelling, customers who opt for a table in the south-eastern section of the first-floor restaurant will see evidence aplenty of this earlier building.

Brewer Andrew Bristow lived there in the late 18th century and he could have been responsible for the house's

The fanlight of 74 Castle Street. The distinctive scalloped tracery was inspired by the work of architects Robert and James Adam.

construction. By 1839 a currier, William Wilkins, was in occupancy and he may well have had his shop here. He was followed by John Baker, who was in a similar line of business and he displayed his wares in the shop window fitted to the north of the front door. Mrs Emma Swayne's Middle Class School was there by 1891 and it was the starting point for Farnham Grammar School for Girls. At the instigation of Surrey County Council's Education Committee, it bought out Mrs Swayne and appointed Miss A.J. Case as headmistress. Opening on 23rd September 1901, it soon outgrew the house and briefly moved to the National School in East Street. It soon found a more permanent home, in 1906, at 25 West Street, recently vacated by Farnham Grammar School.

Mrs Swayne, however, retained the freehold of 74 which in 1909 she sold to the neighbouring Watney, Combe, Reid. Now bereft of potential pupils, she had reinvented herself and her new Modern Commercial School & Kindergarten at 14 Castle Street was aimed at a clientele not catered for by the new Grammar School.

Soon after the girls school's departure, in 1906 auctioneer and estate agent J. Alfred Eggar, previously of 10/11 West Street, moved in. Eggar, a local councillor and architect, opened a sale room at the premises, his auctions having previously taken place at The Bush Hotel. The company, which in 1963 became Weller Eggar following its merger with Weller, Son and Grinstead, was acquired by the Leeds Permanent Building Society in 1987. In the years between 1868 and 1931, this house was overshadowed by the towering tile-hung wall of Norman Shaw's four-storey

72 *St Georges Yard* **74** **75**

Part of the St Georges Yard development, begun in 1988, in which flint, brick and wood harmonize well with nearby Castle House to the right, previously Barrett's hop kilns, in Bear Lane.

bank building next door. It was a gargantuan, twin-gabled, triple-jettied, Tudoresque structure, replete with timber, leaded lights and stone-hewed Gothic entrance doors.

Number 75 was one of the tallest buildings in Farnham and was only exceeded by the recently completed nearby Corn Exchange and the extended tower of St Andrew's Church. Significantly, its lofty chimneys outshone the pinnacle of the nearby new Corn Exchange, whose existence it mirrored, almost to the year. Perversely, the building it replaced was a modest structure that had been dwarfed, to some extent, by its neighbours. It was a white, two-storey house with a colour-washed frontage and parapet which concealed an earlier timber-framed building. Its off-centre front door provided the evidence.

This was Stevens Bank, established by hop grower James Stevens, who used to attend the annual Weyhill Fair to sell his crop. Like his local contemporaries, he would return to Farnham with pockets full of gold but, following a robbery, he took the precaution of employing an armed servant to keep highwaymen at bay. In consequence, other growers availed themselves of this service which was formalized with the creation in 1806 of the bank, located at 75 Castle Street, that bore his name.

The demolition of Norman Shaw's Lloyds Bank building at 75 Castle Street in 1931. By this time one of its two towering ornate chimneys had been carefully dismantled.

In 1828-30 it passed, after some close financial calls, as John Henry Knight later remembered, "into the hands of my grandfather, my father and my uncle. It used to issue its own notes…" Trading as Jenner, Knight and Co, it became James Knight and Co. In due course, perhaps prompted by the opening of the new Corn Exchange in 1866, Knight recognized that the bank premises, were "by no means suited to modern requirements". The old premises, recalled Alfred Eggar, "were low buildings, with a step down into them."

But in 1884 the Knights sold out for £9000 to Capital and Counties Bank, itself only established in 1877, with deposits of a mere £27,000 and owing its London agents £42,000! James Knight was retained to manage it for £400 per annum. In 1918 Capital and Counties amalgamated with Lloyds Bank, which already had a branch at 5-7 The Borough, and in July 1919 this moved to Castle Street.

The demolition of the nearby Corn Exchange had been mooted, to the public at least, since 1928. Was the hand of Charles Borelli apparent in the fact that Lloyds decided to demolish its Elizabethan edifice, which would rid Farnham of two Victorian monstrosities in a single year?

Harold Falkner was not so minded. He venerated Shaw and regarded him as "the greatest architect of his time". As a consolation, the bank's two substantial brick chimneys at either end of the building were carefully dismantled, only to rise again successfully integrated into a brace of Falkner projects. One reappeared at The Bush's South Street frontage with its companion re-erected in The Borough and incorporated into the Bailiffs' Hall.

On 21st February 1931 Lloyds' staff had moved to temporary premises in the doomed Corn Exchange. Demolition of Shaw's folly followed. A casualty was the *Surrey and Hants News*, which, it is thought, had moved there from 1 The Borough and transferred to 10 Downing Street. Rebuilding was rapidly undertaken and the new building was opened seven months later, on 26th November. "It will do," sniffed the *Farnham Herald*, but the newspaper went on to confess that it suited Castle Street better than its predecessor. It was safe, of conventional proportions with just two storeys, pedimented, predictable and, inevitably, Neo-Georgian. Built by Mardon & Mills, it was designed by London architect Sir Guy Dawber, who made a speciality of designing banks and country houses.

The scale of the Shaw building would have probably not worried John "Jacky" Andrews, who ran the neighbouring butcher's shop on the ground floor of number **76**. He was no doubt delighted to see the demolition in 1865 of the Old Market House which had always completely overshadowed his premises. As John Henry Knight recalled, apart from its intrusion into Castle Street, "there was only a space of 10 to 12 feet between…" it and the butcher's premises. A shop window was introduced on the southern side of the centrally located pedimented front door. The three-storey frontage dates from the late 18th century and replaced a two-storey building complete with two dormer windows.

76 ***Town Hall Buildings***

Jacky Andrews was clearly a man of independent thought and was renowned for a spirited exchange with Bishop Charles Sumner, who resided at Farnham Castle between 1827 and 1869. The Bishop always drove to St Andrew's Church for Sunday service, remembered Albert Winslade, "in his robes, sitting inside a 'chariot' suspended by leather straps, with two coachmen on the box and two footmen in blue plush breeches and white stocking behind." Unlike many of his contemporaries, Andrews opened his shop on a Sunday and, Alfred Eggar recalled, he "always served in the shop himself in his blue smock". This had not escaped the Bishop's attention and he "sent word saying he would be glad if Mr Andrews would close his shop on Sunday. The butcher replied 'You tell the Bishop that when he walks to church I will close my shop'."

These premises, recalled Winslade in the 1930s, "would have given any modern medical officer a fit. Gas pipes were black with fly blows and the butcher kept a switch handy and smashed the bluebottles on the meat as it hung." The remainder of the house had been occupied by a lady named Sister Bessie, a keen supporter of the Farnham Division of the St John Ambulance Association. From its formation in 1881 she offered her rooms for training purposes.

The next commercial occupant of 76 was a world away from Andrews' shop. Harry Bodkin's trade was as a "tailor and habit maker". His business was established in 1885, he moved to Farnham from Canterbury in 1889 and acquired his Castle Street shop for £600. In 1892 he was clearly in tune with the times as he offered "Waterproof but not Airproof Cycling Suits". In 1906 he was selling "a carefully selected stock of coatings, suitings, and trouserings," as well as providing a "Ladies' tailoring department". And by the late 1930s he could claim to be "patronised by Royalty" which might suggest a European regal customer as, unlike the Borellis, he was not a royal warrant holder.

But Bodkin was gone by 1946 and Edward LeRoy Ltd was the occupant of 76. Later, a second shopfront, complete with two sashes with gothick tracery above and a glazed door inbetween, was introduced on the north side of the central doorway. For the last 30 or so years it has been occupied by Bateman Opticians while estate agents John D. Wood is in the shop where Jacky Andrews once pioneered Sunday trading.

Falkner's Fireplaces: 2

The hob grate and fireplace in the first-floor drawing room of 24 West Street. The style is late 18th century and the quality of the fireplace is a reflection of the room's status. The detail shows the three festoons, a common feature in antiquity and popular in the Georgian period, which was revived in the early 20th century. The use of tiles as a surround grew in popularity from the 17th century and they remain so to the present day.

Lower, Middle and Upper Church Lanes

"Lower and Middle Church Lanes are the best in Farnham to see unrestored cottage architecture…"

IAN NAIRN, Pevsner's The Buildings of England, Surrey, *1962*

Located in the shadow of St Andrew's Church, these quiet backwaters provide a welcome retreat from the bustle of nearby Downing Street. But it has not always been so! In pre-First World War days, George Hopkins, who later ran a hairdressing business at 17 Downing Street, grew up in Middle Church Lane. In later years he recalled that his mother "didn't like living where we were; she could remember as a girl how it was regarded as a noisy slum…"

St Andrew's Church is predominantly 15th century and was extensively restored by Benjamin Ferrey in 1855. The tower – the original was in a central position – was left in an unfinished state at the time of the Reformation and a cupola was added in the 18th century. It was extended to its present height by Ewan Christian, the work being completed in October 1865.

Today the Lanes' ironstone setts are a delight to the eye, but not the feet, and its architecture is agreeable but deceptive. Although the brick frontages of the cottages date mostly from the 17th to 19th centuries, they invariably conceal much older properties for these are some of the oldest parts of the town. This is very apparent at numbers **30** and **31** Lower Church Lane where the eastern wall of the latter building not only reveals the timber frame but also its jetty concealed behind a later brick facade (see page 9). It was originally one house which was divided in the 1890s. The easterly portion has been extended to the rear and the site is considerably older than the present building. A stone floor in the main room of the rear wing has been dated to the 13th century but the house it served later burned down. The present frontage dates from the 17th century and the rear is possibly late 16th century.

In 1899 the Trusler family occupied 31, the frontage of which was covered with cement rendering. They opened a hardware shop there which survived until the 1960s. The property was acquired by Farnham UDC in 1965, along with 25 to 28 Lower Church Lane, when it was developing the Wagon Yard car park.

Passing to Waverley Borough Council, ownership was transferred to the Farnham Trust which in June 1994 began a restoration which was completed in July 1995. The property has been converted into two two-bedroomed houses with 31 at the front of the building while 31A, at the rear, has

24 23 22 19

Variety in Lower Church Lane where properties often conceal timber framing behind their brick frontages. The gap between 22 and 19 was once occupied by a house that was destroyed by fire at some time between 1900 and 1915.

been named Dufty Cottage in memory of Richard Dufty, co-founder of the Trust.

This can be clearly seen from the **Wagon Yard** car park which from 1919 until 1965 was occupied by Mardon, Ball's builder's yard. It was inhabited by a variety of brick and weather-boarded buildings of agricultural and hop growing ancestry, by then in varying stages of splendid dereliction. They had been built when what had been Lamport's Wagon Yard ceased to function in the 1850s.

Mardon, Ball's old office was redeveloped and occupied by the Ashgate art gallery with Dennis Collett's Old House Bookshop, so converted in 1969, which had moved from 86/87 East Street, in the western section. This shop, in which the author spent many a happy hour, closed in May 1985 and what had become the **New Ashgate Gallery** in 1976 was extended into these premises. They had once housed The Feathers pub, which closed in 1904, and the wrought-iron support for its sign can still be seen in Lower Church Lane.

The Old Vicarage in the churchyard with its expanse of mellow tiled roof and prominent north gable, complete with fine barge-boards, is in such harmony with its surroundings that it appears to have sprung from the very ground on which it stands. The present building dates from the 14th century with 16th-, 17th-, 18th- and 19th-century additions. In the 1830s John Barrett, who had a brewery in Church Lane, was a tenant, prior to his move to Red Lion Lane.

On the northern side of the churchyard **The Rectory** incorporates parts of a timber-framed building at its north-western corner. The brick frontage is 18th century but the porch and dormer windows date from the early 1800s. The extension at its eastern end is Victorian.

Middle Church Lane, which faces the churchyard, presents an inspiring combination of brick, tile hanging and plaster. It includes a sympathetic rebuilding in 1980 of a property, **13**, into flats, the original warehouse on the site having succumbed to fire in 1974. Farnham's old Workhouse, built in 1727, is now **6** and **9.** Numbers **1** and **2** are of particularly interest because what appear to be brick facades are in fact faced with so-called mathematical tiles, hung on battens and mortared, to avoid an 18th-century brick tax (see page 13).

Around the corner is **5** Upper Church Lane. This was a

blacksmith's forge which dated from 1825. It so functioned until blacksmith Arthur Trussler, who took over in the 1970s, retired in 1998. Since then it has been occupied by Food Features, which specializes in the photography of food.

The forge had been run from 1935 by Walter Moulsley, who had worked there since 1926, and the last horses he shod were those working for Farnham United Dairies at the end of the Second World War. A Victorian predecessor had taken the sensible precaution of making an aperture in the wall of the forge through to the pub next door for the passage of refreshment! Named The Baker's Arms, before 1847 it had been called The Valiant Solider. A Barrett, then a Farnham United Breweries house, it was closed in 1909 and in 1928 the building was offered for sale by Courage.

The frontage of the present building on the site, number 4, is of more recent date. From the 1960s until 1985 it was occupied by antiquarian bookseller Henry Stevens. He was followed by Downing Street Studios, the present occupants, which moved there from the corner of the Lane.

On the north side is **11** and **12** Upper Church Lane, now respectively occupied by Curb Surfers and Thomas Ingram. This property was built on the site of Worsam's old bakery by H.C. Webb Estates, which in 1983 acquired its shop at 24/25 Downing Street. Completed in 1985, this Neo-Georgian development, designed by Max Lyons, consists of two shops, together with their fronts, with two floors of office accommodation above. The third occupies the roof space and the building is crowned by hand-made tiles with the lead flashing making its own visual contribution.

An imaginative reconstruction of Arthur Trussler's blacksmith's forge at 5 Upper Church Lane which closed in 1998.

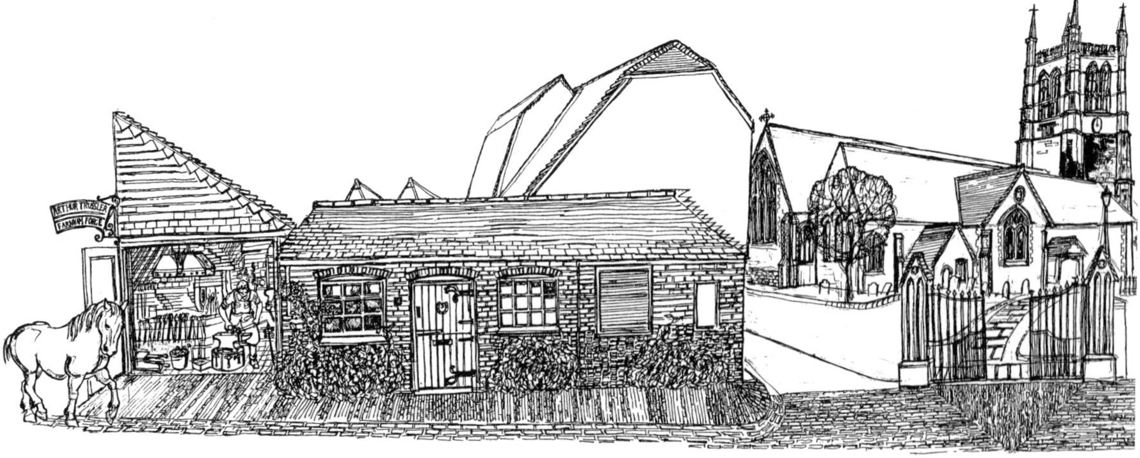

Downing Street

"Downing Street was already an old road at the beginning of the 16th century..."

ETIENNE ROBO, Medieval Farnham, *1935*

Unexpectedly, the **Police Station** turns out to be 1 Downing Street. Built by Messrs Humphreys, it was opened in July 1963 and its size, occupying the entire length of this part of Downing Street, reflected the fact that it was designed as a divisional headquarters covering an area that stretched from Hindhead, via Frimley and Camberley, to Bagshot. The work of Surrey County Council architect John Harrison, with a long, two-storey, brick frontage and Roman tiled roof, the northern end wall was imaginatively embellished with relief stone carvings undertaken by Rachel Brown and Carole Hodgson, who were students at Wimbledon School of Art. It was not, wrote architectural historian Alec Clifton-Taylor later in the same year in *County Life*, "an exciting achievement, but what is certain is that in Farnham excitement is not what is wanted".

Farnham Police Station, which dates from 1963, was built on the site of a yard that for about 100 years played host to some of the town's best builders.

Built in 1717, number 3 Downing Street is probably the earliest significant Farnham property to feature a parapet as part of its original design.

For about 100 years up until the mid-1950s most of the site was a builders' yard (see page 20). In 1951 the land was acquired for the new police station and it remained in a state of semi-dereliction for much of the decade.

A further casualty was the original 1 Downing Street at its northern end. The two-storey, stuccoed, bay-windowed Longbridge House with its tall chimneys dated from the 1860s and was probably built by Frank Birch. It was the home of his pupil Gordon Tompsett.

What is now **2** and **2A**, has been variously named Rhama House and Morley House. It is also not quite what it appears, because while the yellow-grey brick front, perhaps by Frank Birch, could date from the 1860s, it conceals a red-brick building of much greater age, possibly one of medieval origin. Despite its date, the frontage is in the Classical spirit. Considerable changes have been made at the back. In 1986 a long single-storey extension was demolished and replaced by a new two-storey one.

One of Farnham's architecturally significant houses, **3** Downing Street became Longbridge House following the demolition of the original. Of five bays, on two storeys, with a projecting central bay surmounted by a pediment, the date of 1717 is incised within. It is thought that the initials *JC*, or are they *IC*?, which appear above the door with its fine cut brick decoration, are those of John Chitty, who may have been a hop grower. He was responsible for the encasement of an earlier timber-framed building, much of which survived until a 1948 rebuild.

In December 1902, following a visit to the town earlier in the year, a Mme Desmaret was encouraged by Father Matthieu Gerin of St Polycarps Catholic Church in Bear Lane to establish St Joseph's Convent there. But it closed in 1920.

In about 1930 it nearly became a cinema and, later, a dental surgery. Between 1949 and 1969 it was the headquarters of the Wey Valley Water Company. In 1971 it was acquired by the Equity and Law Life Assurance Company and is now the home of chartered accountants Menzies.

With a commanding view of Downing Street, **4** is an imposing three-storey house of five bays with a slate roof, open eaves and long three-pane sash windows. It is enhanced by a formal porch, supported on Doric columns, and approached by three steps. Ian Nairn describes it as being early 19th century. Two-storey blocks, each with their own first-floor sashes, have been added to the east and west.

In the mid-18th century the site was known as Bartlett's Garden and, along with a hop field, had once been owned by Farnham Manor. The property was sold in 1889 to Thomas Eyre of 38 and 39 The Borough, who famously prevented South Street from starting there. In later years it was occupied by medics and Drs Tanner and Hussey are listed as occupants in 1901. The former was responsible for Farnham's swimming pool. The house is currently occupied by the Downing Street Doctors' Group Practice.

Number **4A**, the shop on the corner of Downing Street and Lower Church Lane, used to be in the latter, but in the mid-1950s a second first-floor window was added along with a door. Dating from the 1850s and built on the site of a malt house, it was subsequently known as Gostrey Cottage but was converted into a shop and is currently occupied by Lalys the Chemist.

Although The Toy Shop, number **5**, and Lloyd and Keyworth, **6** and **7**, are timber-framed and jettied, they actually date from 1932. The work of Mardon, Ball, the bricks used for the infilling were apparently purloined from a stock designated for repair work at Farnham Castle! Originally 5 could have been a recased timber-framed house while the genuine jettied article was next door. Toys were sold from the outset, first by Len Swayne, while the tradition is maintained by Andy Williams, the present proprietor, who has been doing so since 1995.

By contrast, Blindspot, number **8**, is a 19th-century house with mansard roof and flat-topped dormer.

The style is Tudor but 5, 6 and 7 Downing Street date from 1932. They were built by Mardon, Ball whose yard was nearby in Lower Church Lane, today the Wagon Yard car park.

The shop was occupied in the 1950s by Premier Cleaners. It is very similar to Autobits, which arrived in 1970, two doors up at **11**. At the turn of the 19th century, it was occupied by I. Hoptroff, a tea merchant, who had been previously based at 51. By 1952 it was a branch of the Farnham Co-op and later Guildford Glass and Metalwork.

Grant and Company hairdressing, **9**, and S2, formerly Morgana women's fashions, number **10**, dates from the early 19th century. In the 1890s the property was still a private house with separate arched front doorways. By 1937 number 9 was the premises of P.D. Lock, fishmonger, which closed in 1961. Later, by 1971, it was the home of Beyond the Fringe hairdressers. From the early 1930s until 1952, neighbouring 10 was the home of the *Surrey and Hants News*.

Eureka Jewellery, number **12**, and Brush and Bisque-it, number **13**, occupy a Neo-Georgian building, complete with the obligatory blind recess indicative of window tax. It was built on the site of two run-down cottages, one of which, 13, was where grocers E. Bailey and Son traded in the 1900s. However, in 1931, when owned by B.C.N. Giles, they were condemned as unfit for human habitation and the present shops were built in their places.

The three-storeyed, slate-roofed **14**, occupied since 1989 by Mulberry Silks, has a late 18th-century frontage. The top central window is blind. By the 1970s it was Presents gift shop.

The white colour-washed numbers **15** and **16**, occupied by estate agents Keats and Fearn since 1989, and The Seafood Store, have been commercial premises for well over a 100 years. Again there are blind middle windows on the second and top floors. In the late 19th century 15 was A. Ransom's plumbing works, followed by A.W. Lee's ladies' and gentlemen's tailor. At the same time 16 was occupied by draper, outfitter and tailor J. Stevenson. He not only sold sewing machines but also wringers, mangles and even gramophone records.

The pseudo-Tudor building, dating from the late 1930s, which houses Caroline B, number **17**, and The Framing Centre, **17A**, was built on the site of The Sun Inn, supposed in 1786 to have been named The Valiant Solider. The Sun had arisen by the 1820s but magistrates had concerns about it in the 1890s, as well as with The Bird in Hand opposite. Variously a Knight, Barrett and Farnham United Breweries house, it was closed in 1902.

Left: The former Sun Inn, which closed in 1902. In 1896 its landlord Charles Mills was convicted of permitting drunkenness and fined £2. This early 19th-century brick frontage probably concealed a timber-framed building while the archway provided access to stabling and extensive outbuildings. Beyond is the bay window of 18 Downing Street which, happily, survives. In the left foreground is Stevenson's shop at 16 that sold a variety of goods, including gramophone records.

Hairdresser George Hopkins was at 17 from 1920 until the late 1950s. He was replaced by Lloyd and Keyworth, while fishmonger John Eighteen was at 17A until the 1960s. His business was taken over by Charlie Barnes, who had worked there for many years, and he ran it until his retirement in 1977. An archway, which once led to a yard, now gives access to Clayton Court, which was completed in the mid-1980s.

Farnham Photo-Video, **18**, is noteworthy for the fact that, unlike many similar multi-paned bay windows in Farnham, this one is original although it has been modified over the years. As such, it may well have served as a pattern for others throughout the town. Now rendered, re-roofed and with leaded-light casement windows, although once a house, it was for over 100 years Baker's butcher's

Built on the site of The Sun in the late 1930s, the Tudoresque 17 and 17A Downing Street retained the archway, now providing access to Clayton Court, at its northern end.

shop. William Baker was listed in 1845 as a sausage maker. In the 1870s it was Alfred, and in 1901 Harry, who supplied "dairy-fed pork and noted Farnham sausages".

George Hopkins at 17 remembered them as "the finest pork sausages I have ever tasted. We always had them for dinner on Saturdays. I used to look forward to Saturdays." Baker was still there in the 1950s, but in 1960 the premises became the Little Soho delicatessen owned by Charles Walsh, who ran the Farnham Motor Company opposite.

Numbers **19** and **20** are of three storeys, in colour-washed brick and date from the second half of the 19th century. Now Rowlands ladies' wear, 19 was for many years the shop of electrical engineer Thomas Hill, who established his business in 1912. Although now colour-washed, in his day it was brick with the front door alongside the shopfront. Mr Hill lived above his business and was thus able to claim "electrician always in residence". In his early years he was responsible for installing electric light in many shops and houses in and around Farnham. He continued well into the 1970s. Later linen draper Lasletts occupied the premises.

In 1901 Mrs W. Chuter was the occupant of number 20, now Pilot ladies' wear. She was listed as undertaking watch and clock repairs and she also maintained a servants' registry. In the 1970s estate agent Whiteheads was based here.

Number **21**, now occupied by frozen food outlet Cook, is a Victorian, two-storey, property of colour-washed brick with a slate roof. It has retained its original first-floor sash window. In the early 1900s photographer Frank Spencer undertook "Enlargements in permanent pigments finished in black and white and water colour" there.

The shop on the corner of Upper Church Lane, **22**, was until recently occupied by tailor A.W. Pearce. Back in 1901 J. Bartholomew, a chimney sweep, lived there. It was converted from a private house in 1949 by Guy Maxwell Aylwin, who added the parapet, oriel window and shopfront. In the 1950s Sarah Stuart was there and in 2003 it was occupied by Ordri ladies boutique.

Sykes & Steel's menswear shop at **23** is mostly in Upper Church Lane and therefore lies at right angles to Downing Street. Of good brick with casements on the first floor and dormer windows, at the turn of the 19th century shoemaker R. Lowman's occupied the site.

W.R. Worsam's was one of Downing Street's longest established occupants, the shop having been a bakery since the 1780s. Henry Worsam married into the family in the 1840s and the business occupied numbers **24** and **25** which were two cottages with plastered frontages. The latter possessed a multi-paned bay window, similar to that which is still visible at 18. The premises were rebuilt in 1896 as a single property in brick with a tiled roof and open eaves. It still retains its sash windows although, intriguingly, the most northerly one is irregularly positioned. Worsam's closed in August 1983, by which time the premises had been acquired by H.C. Webb Estates. It rebuilt the old bakery at the rear with a frontage in Upper Church Lane (see page 120) and the Downing Street shop is now occupied by Walton Clothing.

The three-storey, Neo-Georgian property, Cancer Research UK, number **26/27**, was built in 1929, as indicated by the date on the rainwater head, and is the work of Leonard Stedman. By 1950 it was Lloyd and Keyworth's photography and record shop. However, the cameras later moved down the road to 17 and 26 became, in the 1970s, the business's "radio, TV, record and music shop". The premises incorporate an archway at the northern end to provide access to a yard at the back.

Estate agent Andrew Lodge has been the occupant of number **28** since 1993, and Sultan's takeaway, at **28B**, is part of the same two-storey building which is of 18th-century appearance. In 1901 number 28 was occupied by Balchin and Sons, described as "provision merchants, pork butchers". Between the wars and into the early 1960s this

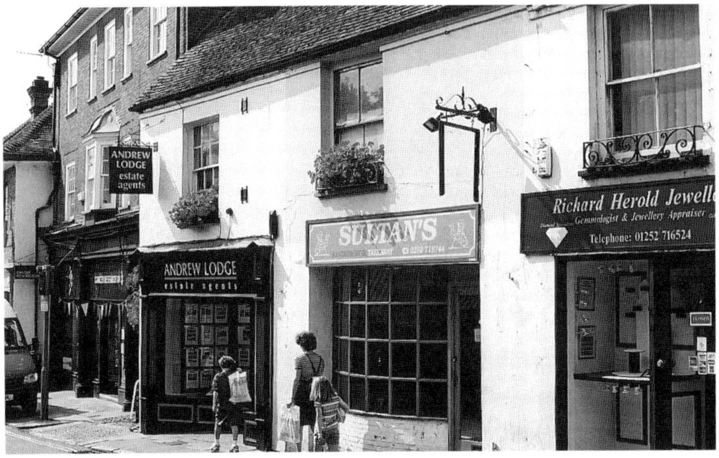

Variety in Downing Street: estate agency (28), takeaway food (28B) and jeweller (28C).

was Lionel "Fishy" Stevens fish and chip shop and café. Next door at number **28C**, now Richard Herold Jewellers, you can still see the steel support for his *Fish and Chips* sign. By the 1970s it was the office of coal merchants E. Comley and Sons.

The three-storey premises next door, **29** and now housing Coral the bookmakers, was occupied by the International Meat Company for many years. This concern was there by 1937 but had departed by 1963.

The Woolwich bank is the occupant of number **32** on the eastern side of Downing Street, a two-storey building with tiled roof and tile-hung southern elevation. Steel-framed windows have been fitted. Number 33 was, in the 1890s, home to one of Downing Street's many fish shops, in this instance it was John Lord's business. Its neighbour, Tread shoes, at number **34**, was the property from which A. Sawyer conducted his business as a harness maker in the early 1900s. More recently, in the 1970s, it was a branch of Meon Travel.

John Goodridge's Neo-Elizabethan, timber-framed and jettied menswear shop, a business still run by the third generation of the Goodridge family at numbers **35/36**, dates from 1930. Built by Mardon, Ball, it predates the not dissimilar 5/6 at the other end of the street. It replaced The Cricketers pub, a cottage-type dwelling with low browed tiled roof and frontage possibly concealing a timber frame. It seems to have had a butcher's shop attached to it. By 1877 both businesses were being run by Mrs Louisa Windibank and in 1901 by William Smart. By then a Farnham United Breweries house, it was among a clutch of inns closed down by Farnham Magistrates in 1902. It was subsequently reprieved but eventually closed in 1927.

Ivy Lane leads to **Ivy House**, the home since 1894 of the Farnham Conservative Club. Built in about 1700 on elevated ground that was not liable to flooding, it was one of Farnham's largest houses, built of brick with eight bays and two storeys. The eaves-cornice, sash boxes and tiled roof, complete with dormer windows, add to a charm which is only mildly marred by the presence of a later conservatory located between its two shallow wings. The westerly one has, at some time, been rebuilt.

The original owner was George Mill but in the 1750s it was the property of the Hay family. It subsequently passed to Thomas Beddus Mill, John Grant and James Darvill.

In 1855 it was acquired by local draper William Hazell, who ran a stay factory, which employed 40 to 50 women, making ladies' corsets in an adjoining building. This was badly damaged by a fire in 1890 and may well have later housed the Arabic-sounding Al Arak Works which briefly produced "Dr Horsey's Oriental Fibre Tooth Brush".

Returning to Downing Street, number **37/38**, occupied since 1999 by Masterpiece Lighting, has a stuccoed frontage which seems more Regency in spirit than Victorian. It is replete with Classical themes. Faced with five Ionic pilasters, the central three originally flanked a pair of Venetian windows and there were sashes at either end. These were all capped with a balustrade surmounted by three pineapples. Built on the site of a hop kiln, from the late 19th century fishmonger Edwin Clarke occupied the northern end and he was still there in 1952. Back in 1899, a petition signed by 26 ratepayers, complained about the nuisance caused by fish frying for which he was fined 10s. (50p).

One of them may have been W. Cleeves, Farnham's Parish Clerk, who occupied the adjoining number 38. He also ran a Coffee and Dining Rooms, the door of which replaced the Venetian window. "Hot joints daily from 12 to 2" were on offer, along with "beds". Dinner cost 9d. (4p). In the 1950s it reverted to being a single building and Guy Maxwell Aylwin was responsible for reviving the frontage. He replaced what was left of the original central windows with bows and added medallions above them imbuing the building with the Regency air it still possesses. By 1954 it was solely occupied by the Farnham Coffee House.

Ivy House was built in about 1700 in the Classical spirit. But it is an architectural Janus which looked back to an earlier tradition as it is not wholly symmetrical. The door-case is offset in bay five and the property is gabled at the rear.

The frontage of 37/38 was revived in 1950 by Guy Maxwell Aylwin, although Harold Falkner had also prepared a design which was not adopted. By the late 19th century it had been divided into two when the southerly portion became Cleeves' Coffee and Dining Rooms. In later years Mrs L. Smither, of nearby number 42, remembered going there as a small child with her parents and "sitting on a settle with a very high back, so that you could not see who was sitting at the next table."

Thirty-nine, now Halifax Property Services and The Banaras Indian restaurant at **40** were once occupied by a single shop, Supply Stores. Later it was Walker's Stores, which rebuilt the property in 1931, and it survived until the early 1960s when it was occupied by estate agents Hoar, Sanderson and Spooner. The three-storey stuccoed building, which happily retains its original sashes on both floors, dates from the mid-19th century when the window architraves were painted a contrasting colour to the walls.

The occupant in 1901 of number **41**, now jeweller John R. Fox, was P. Soper, who was described a marine store dealer. In those days the two-storey brick frontage was exposed; today it has been cement-rendered and colour-washed.

Robert Dyas at number **42** moved from 6/7 Castle Street into this Neo-Georgian building in April 1996. It has many windows: there are no less than seven sashes on the first floor and six dormers on the second. It was built on the site of what had been two properties. Number 42 had a three-bay brick frontage with a parapet which concealed a tiled roof. It was occupied in the latter half of the 19th century by upholsterer and cabinet maker Harry Smither. His business of C. Smither had in 1847 been established at 5 The Borough but it moved to Downing Street soon afterwards. The firm occupied the shop until its demolition in 1956, although prior to that the contents of the window may have had more to do with The Central Garage, at number 43 next door.

It had been built on the site of The Bird in Hand pub which was almost opposite the similarly absent Sun. Brick, with a tiled roof of five bays, the off-centre door indicated that this had originally been a timber-framed building refronted in the 18th century. The end came in 1927 and it was offered for sale in 1928 when it was bought by Jimmy Corps, who turned it into a garage. This survived until late in 1955 when the property was acquired by the Farnham Motor Company, which demolished it in 1956 and absorbed the adjacent 42. It was a Jaguar and Ford agency. In April 1961 news broke that it had sold the site to World Stores, which owned Walker's Stores at 39/40. Originally Key Markets supermarket, it was trading as Gateway when it closed in October 1995.

Although the frontage of Accent shoes, number **44**, dates from the early 19th century, a section of timber framing can be seen from the pathway which leads to the Central Car Park. In the early 1900s this was the site of a smithy which belonged to George Elliott, who ran the Reliance Works in West Street. It subsequently became the home of Vincent Trimarco's Maison Radio, which remained there until the 1970s.

Forty five, vacant at the time of writing, is a four-bay, three-storey Victorian shop that in the 1890s was occupied by E. Coxe, "dairyman and fruiterer". By 1912 it was the Downing Street Dairy, G. Taphouse advertising that he delivered milk "direct from the Farm twice daily to all parts". It was produced "under perfect sanitary conditions at the Red House Farm, Wrecclesham." Sixty years later, by the 1970s, it had become Popp-Ins café.

Numbers **46** and **47**, which has five bays, three storeys with three-pane sashes and a tiled roof, is suggestive of the late 18th century. The door, consisting of two Doric columns with a central one dividing the two houses, is an

The Farnham Motor Company's garage undergoing construction at 42/43 Downing Street in 1957. Today Robert Dyas occupies the site. The demolition work clearly reveals the mansard roof and parapet of the adjoining number 41. Next door at 39/40 was Walker's Stores with Farnham Coffee House just visible at 37/38.

unusual feature. One of the first owners was auctioneer Thomas Baker, who owned both properties. The initials and date – *J.N.B May 1st 1843* – have been found carved in a wall. Farnham Excise Officer William Blake bought 46 in 1876, reputedly from the Nash family who were solicitors and hop growers.

It was occupied in 1901 by his son W.H. Blake, a signwriter, who continued to occupy it until the mid-1950s. In recent times it is best known as the home of Charles Hammick's first bookshop, which opened at 46 in November 1968. This followed market research which pinpointed the fact that, apart from Wells bookshop in Castle Street and a small section in W.H. Smith, there was no other establishment in the town catering for the requirements of the local reading public.

In August 1987 Hammicks moved to Lion and Lamb Yard, having outgrown its Downing Street shop. In due course it got even bigger, expanding throughout the country to occupy over 25 outlets although in 2003 it was acquired by Ottakar's plc. Leighton Opticians replaced Hammicks and it built an appropriate extension at the rear with a red-tiled pitched roof.

Farnham Ceramic Tiles at 47 was, between the wars, a gown shop owned by Mrs W.H. Blake, who lived next door. But by 1947 it was occupied by F.W. Trusler, while Joanna Harding's dress shop was there in the 1970s.

Number **48** (Cruze mens and ladies' wear), a two-storey, late Georgian house, soon converted to a shop, has a single sash window with margin panes on the first floor. Its door is distinguished by the presence of a circular fanlight.

Like 46/47, number **49**, The Young Ones, and **49A**, The Stirling Sandwich shop, also belonged to the Nash family in the 19th century. It is of a similar size to 46/47, being a five-bay, three-storey house with three-pane sashes and a tiled roof, and is also likely to be late 18th century. It is enhanced by a fine pedimented central doorway. In the interwar years this was Mrs Chrimes' Carlton Hotel, which had closed by 1954. The property had been divided into two and shopfronts introduced. By the 1970s they were respectively occupied by the Miss Mandry boutique and Lugsdin's dry cleaners.

If appearances are anything to go by, number **50**, The Traditional Plaice Fish and Chip Shop, was built at about the same time as 48. In the 1890s it was the shop of

A.J. Mallam, "trousers and pantaloon maker" although W.J. Wilkinson "builder and decorator", who was also an undertaker, was there in 1912. By the 1950s it was used by greengrocers G. Hone and Sons, also at number 52, and in the 1980s by Farnham Office Supplies.

Number **51** and **52** provide an idea of the type of properties that existed in Downing Street before smart houses such as 46/47 and 49/49A were built in the late 18th and early 19th centuries. A low, two-storey property with a Georgian brick frontage, timber-framed behind the facade, with twin sashes on the first floor, it was reputedly once a farmhouse. The smaller shop, 51, was the place where in the 1880s I. Hoptroff "established upwards of 40 years" ran his tea-dealing business. He took over from Charles May who was similarly employed. Previously both properties had belonged to John Nash.

In 1911 greengrocer George Hone acquired the premises and the adjoining 52 and he fitted the shopfronts which still grace both buildings. Today it is occupied by Fosters shoe repair shop which moved there in 1984, Raymond Foster having established his business at 41 The Fairfield in 1952.

What is today G. Hone and Sons at number 52 is owned by Jonathan Durham, who is Hone's grandson. In 1983, when an attic was being converted to a bedroom at 51, a beam was uncovered and once the wattle and daub infill had been removed, the initials J.N. and date 1611 were discovered. They were "pecked out", that is to say punched with a nail. At the rear is Nash's circular hop kiln which bears the date of 1851. Its conical top was removed when it became unsafe in the 1920s. Opposite it is a rectangular kiln constructed of ironstone that has recently been sympathetically converted by Jonathan Durham into a private house.

The Carlton Hotel existed in this form at 49 Downing Street until 1954, when this photograph was taken, and mainly catered for commercial travellers. It had continued for a time after shops had been introduced on the ground floor. Today Young Ones is at 49, the Stirling Sandwich Shop at 49A with The Traditional Plaice next door at 50. The second and fourth top-floor windows of number 49 are blind.

50 ***51*** ***52*** ***53*** ***54***

Numbers 66 and 67 Downing Street were demolished in 1958 to allow Victoria Road, hitherto a cul-de-sac, to join with Downing Street to provide access to the Central Car Park. The adjoining Co-Op in Union Road followed in 1989.

The corner block, from number **53** to **56**, was in 1839 four cottages owned by James Darvill. Now there are small-paned, white-painted windows and shopfronts with Jan Lowen Interiors at 53; in the 1970s this was Marica boutiques. La Femme beauty salon at **54** occupies the corner site which by the 1970s was The Corner Cake Shop offering "everything that is good in handmade cakes and fancies". Later it was home of the Security Centre. Number 56, which dates from the 16th century, was for many years Service Cleaners, and is now occupied by Pastiche Lingerie. When it was still a private house, this had an arched front door, like the one to the west.

Number **57A** was where A.W. Lee carried out his business as a tailor at the turn of the 19th century, when it was just number 57. Today it is the Phyllis Tuckwell Hospice Shop. It was previously Anthony's Antiques. The John McCarthy Hair Company at **57** was once a double-fronted, colour-washed house. There was a pedimented centrally located front door with sashes either side which dated from the 17th century or possibly earlier.

The Downing Street Charity Shop, numbers **58/59**, was from at least the mid-1930s until the 1970s W.G. Williamson's newsagents. Number **60**, now Financial Profile, was for many years P. and M. Putnam's Antiques Shop. **61A**, now Jocasta Innes' Paint Magic which arrived in 1998, was previously 61. It features an Art Deco-style shopfront and replaced a shop occupied in 1901 by J. Baker, a shoemaker. Previously it was Farnham Antiques Centre and before that the Freezer and Food shop. In the 1950s it was the Co-op butchery.

Number 62 next door was, in the 1950s, Mrs Lloyd's Workman's Café. The premises was demolished early in 1990, along with The Downing Street Club, previously The Hop Bag public house built in 1906 They were replaced by **Clarendon House**, 63, being in part two-storey brick with the corner tile-hung and of three storeys. Since June 1991 it has been the headquarters of Leighton Opticians, a business that has been variously located throughout the town since H.O. Leighton arrived in Farnham from Southampton in 1928.

It was built on the site of a pub that has been known by at least four different names. In 1755 it was the Adam and Eve, by 1794 the King of Prussia but this soon changed to The Hop Bag, a variation being The Pocket of Hops.

Falkner's Fireplaces: 3

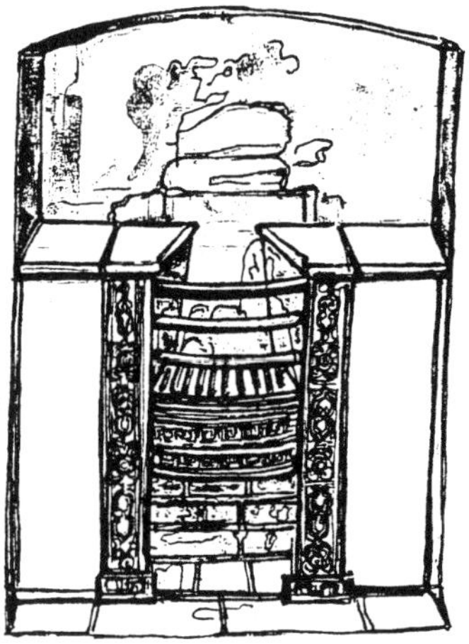

Another of the hob grates at 24 West Street. With this type no attempt was made to control the passage of air to the fire. But by the 1820s it began to be overtaken by the register grate, see page 150, which did incorporate such a facility.

East Street

"Looking back through the branches of the elm or past the huddle of carts in front of the wheelwright's shop, you saw the quiet provincial traffic...and the dingy old street, grey at dusk or in rainy weather, but scintillating and fresh-looking on bright days."

GEORGE STURT, A Small Boy in the Sixties, 1927

The **Royal Deer** has been 4 East Street since 1869 because 1, 2 and 3 were demolished for the construction of South Street. Although no longer a pub, there can be no doubt that The 'Deer was one once, thanks to the inscribed plaque which faces the road junction. It ceased to trade in 1990 after a life of about 150 years.

The original Royal Deer dated from the mid-19th century. By 1872 it was owned by George Trimmer, and subsequently by Farnham United Breweries. It was one of the few surviving inns of the many that used to flank East Street. Originally rendered and colour-washed, its business no doubt benefited from the arrival of South Street.

Rebuilt in about 1929, following the takeover by Courage, architect Leonard Stedman's 1928 design remained faithful to the layout of the original frontage,

A fragment of East Street in 1956 with the entrance to Bear Lane, left foreground, which abuts Burnett's shoe repair shop, once The Queen Street Tavern, at 125. The other half of the building (124) was occupied by Miss Baker's Babyland shop with the part timber-framed Farnham Gas and Electricity Company at 121-122-123. These were the first buildings to be demolished in 1965 to make way for The Woolmead development.

even down to the blind recesses in the parapet. It looked all the better for the absence of rendering, while plain bricks and three-pane sashes meant a Neo-Georgian rather the Victorian look.

Some 60 years later, in November 1990, The Deer was put on the market for £650,000. It became for a time the offices of Mid Southern Water. Estate agent Kelway Law opened its corner office in 2003 and Starlet took over the eastern sector in the same year.

A Georgian-effect block of four shops next door accommodating Just Pets and Eukanuba, also number **4**, Mobile Phone Centre, **5**, and Solent Cleaners, **6**, dates from 1972. The roof is tiled and the frontage brick but the 18th-century theme is not carried through to the windows which, inevitably, lack glazing bars.

It was built on the site of two shops. Number 5 was for a long time a butcher's premises. W. Legg was there in 1892, G.W. Hawkins in 1912 while J. Smith in the 1950s made a speciality of home-made sausages. To the east was M.A. Rose and Son's garden and seed shop at 6, which was there by 1874. But by the 1960s the business was no longer locally owned. It had passed to Grimsdale and Son of London's Mark Lane and the centre of the corn trade.

Despite a seeming air of permanence, Rose's closed in June 1971 and its premises were demolished. Located in a house with a Queen Anne frontage of exposed eaves, west-facing dormer windows projecting from a rippling tiled roof, it was built at right angles to the road and faced an alleyway named Cambridge Place. The disappearance

M.A. Rose and Son's garden and seed shop at 6 East Street in 1971, the year of its demolition, was located in this Queen Anne house which faced the original Cambridge Place. Today 4, 5 and 6 East Street occupies part of Rose's old site.

of this fine building was mourned by many. M.A. Rose, latterly J. Ellis and Sons, continued to trade until 1997 in the nearby throughway which had been renamed Cambridge Place in 1972.

Entrance to its shops is gained via what was once the ground floor of **8** East Street. This was a cement-rendered private house which in 1878 was the home of Miss Louisa Stratford's Ladies' Boarding School. This radical surgery was required to provide pedestrian access to The Electric Cinema, designed by Harold Falkner and built by Mardon & Mills, which opened in March 1913. Subsequently renamed The County, and featuring a brick and sash-windowed facade, it survived until its closure in 1956. It stood derelict until 1963, when it, as well as the shop which had once housed the County Hairdressing Saloon at 8 East Street, now McArthurs estate agents, were acquired by Farnham UDC for £25,000 for "highway and car parking purposes". Demolition of the cinema followed in 1971.

The **Hogshead** at numbers 9-11 occupies another of the town's fine mid-Victorian buildings. Still in the Classical idiom and well executed in brick with stone dressing and open eaves, the windows have moulded architraves. It would look even better if the glazing bars, which were removed at some time from the first-floor sash windows, were replaced. When the Hogshead opened in 1996 it was the first new public house in Farnham for many years. The town's youngsters now enjoy pints of lager where James Smyth drapers and outfitters began trading in about 1910. Extended in 1929, this respected family business survived for some 80 years before closing in 1989.

Number **12**, now occupied by chemist J.A. Hainstock, was in 1891 the premises of the Savings Bank with R.D. Mason named as actuary. In later years it became the home of the Trustee Savings Bank until the late 1960s when it moved across the road to The Woolmead.

Wimpy, **13,** has all the appearance of a three-storey, slate-roofed, 18th-century property that was refaced in the later 19th century with a brick front and windows with moulded architraves.

Next door the Tudoresque, three-storeyed, gabled and heavily beamed pub **The Marlborough Head**, designed by John Howard of Haselmere, dates from 1929. There has been a public house on the site since the 1750s although its predecessor was more modest in size with two storeys, and a colour-washed brick front. It was part timbered inside. Like The Plough in West Street, it was a Crowley and Sons of Alton house and accordingly became a Watneys pub when that brewery acquired Crowley in 1947. It was threatened with demolition in the early 1990s, but fortunately this did not occur when an expected road scheme failed to materialize.

The Marlborough benefited from the opening, in March 1933, of the Regal Cinema next door which was located well behind the building line. Designed by the Birmingham-based Harold Scott, this well-appointed establishment clearly represented a challenge to the 20-year-old County, only a few doors away. Its construction required the demolition of premises previously occupied by Heath and Wiltshire and A. Robins and Son. The latter had operated its Farnham Dairy from number 16 from 1902 until it moved to 12 West Street in 1908. One of Farnham's few Art Deco buildings and brick-built, the Regal incorporated a café on its first floor with an entrance at its eastern end. Originally it possessed an attractive canopy.

In 1971 what had become The Odeon was renamed Studios 1 and 2, it having passed into the ownership of Leeds-based Star Group, pioneers of the practice of dividing cinemas to accommodate two or even three screens. In Farnham these were on the first floor with a bingo facility operating on the ground floor. Taken over by Canon Classic in August 1985, the town was taken by surprise when Studios 1 and 2 suddenly closed on the evening of 12th September. For the first time since 1913 Farnham was without a cinema. It remained empty for two years. In 1987, by then owned by Bass plc, it was demolished. It has been an empty building plot ever since, an open wound on the face of East Street.

Its absence currently exposes the northern brick wall of the **Redgrave Theatre**, which closed in 1998. It had opened with high hopes in 1974 when it replaced the cramped Castle Theatre in Castle Street (see page 108). Local Surrey architect Frank Rutter of Milford was retained to design the building which is of brick with exposed concrete roof beams ends. Inside there was auditorium seating for 356, a bar and licensed restaurant, The Castle Room, which occupied part of Brightwell House that it abuts. Built at a cost of £260,000, it opened with a deficit of £35,000. Financial problems of varying degrees of severity would plague the Redgrave

during its 24-year life. Its first director was Ian Mullins, who had fulfilled a similar role since 1971 at the Castle.

The first production, staged in May 1974, was *Romeo and Juliet* and theatrical performances continued at regular intervals until 1991 when, between May and September, there was an ominous break. Although production of plays restarted, closure eventually followed in January 1995. The Redgrave reopened in November 1996 equipped to do double duty as a cinema, but the end came in 1998. Since then the building has remained empty, threatened with demolition and awaiting the redevelopment of East Street.

Happier days! The entrance to the foyer of the Redgrave Theatre, which opened in 1974. It closed in 1998.

Its frontage faces Brightwells Road, which at one time was the drive to the now Grade II-listed **Brightwell House** which was incorporated into the theatre. Built between 1792 and 1795, stuccoed, with a southerly frontage possessing a pair of solid bay windows and all capped with a hipped slate roof, it was the work of Thomas Turner, a local builder, who was also responsible for the adjoining (but demolished in the interwar years) substantial huddle of hop kilns. Built on a field accorded the name of Timberclose, which the house inherited, in 1816 it was leased by William Lowndes Stone from Brightwell Baldwin, Oxfordshire. In 1821 he acquired the

The eastern entrance to the late 18th-century Brightwell House. Now Grade II listed, it is envisaged that it will play a significant role in the projected East Street Regeneration scheme.

property for £900. In 1852 his son Richard, who was required to change his surname to his mother's maiden name of Garth, purchase the adjoining field of Canterburies for £300 and added a west wing to the house.

His daughter Frances Garth married Lt-Colonel Patrick Paget and the property was renamed Lowlands. It retained this name until 1905 when the widowed Frances Paget renamed it Brightwell in memory of her grandfather's birthplace. Following her death in 1912 the property passed to her unmarried daughter Florence, who ran The Spinning Wheel at 40 The Borough (see page 67). In 1919 Miss Paget offered Brightwell House and its grounds to Farnham UDC which acquired them for £3750. It took possession of the property on 24th June 1920.

What became Brightwell Gardens proved to be place of tranquillity that seemed a world away from the traffic of East Street. Tennis courts were constructed and additions made to the bowling green. The house was refurbished by Crosbys at a cost of £422, and the County Library arrived in 1929. It remained there until 1949 when it moved to Vernon House in West Street. Books were replaced by a clinic, but in 1968 this was transferred to the nearby new Health Centre. Brightwell House was now bereft of a role and its incorporation within the structure of the Redgrave Theatre seemed to offer the chance of a new chapter in its history...

The nearby **Health Centre** is the work of County Architect Raymond Ash. It looks very 1960s, although the

The south front of Brightwell House with the redundant Redgrave Theatre still visible at its western end.

harshness of its angularity is mitigated by a frontage which incorporates large areas of curved tiles. Its neighbour, the Gostrey Club, now the **WRVS Gostrey Centre**, was opened in 1964 and is the work of Leonard Stedman.

Both buildings occupied what had once been the back garden of **The Chestnuts** which is 18 East Street. Dating from 1881, it is of Georgian character with an unfussy brick parapeted facade. Build for William Higgins, who had a shop at 49 The Borough, his son, later Air-Marshal Sir John Higgins, grew up in the house.

It was acquired in 1921 by Vice-Admiral Vincent Molteno, who renamed it Goldhill. He retained Harold Falkner to remove the front door and reposition it at the side of the building. The Admiral remained here until 1935 when, after two years, he succumbed to the proximity of the Regal. The house was acquired by the Council for £2500 and renamed The Chestnuts. Although it would have made a fine library or museum, in the event it became the town's employment exchange. Two houses for council employees were built behind.

And so it remained until the Thatcher government of the 1980s purged the Department of Health and Social Security and the 'Exchange. The Chestnuts, by then in a neglected state, was closed and sold to Kents Developments. In 1988 this company sensitively converted it into offices and a second storey was added to the rear of the premises. Sadly, the sashes were subsequently replaced by pvc units. A paved area in front of the building was relaid and two trees, appropriately chestnuts, were planted.

At the turn of the 19th century number **19** was Dr Edward Reay Coffey's residence, and it was still a doctor's surgery in the 1950s. Another instance of an older building refaced in the mid-19th century with a stucco frontage, now nicely restored, it is occupied from 2003 by The French Trading Company.

With a lower roof line of slate, the adjoining **20**, **21** and **22** was in 1891 occupied by G. Beesley, who was a baker, grocer and butcher. Today number 21 is the home of the Farnham Dental Centre, it having earlier been occupied by the Farnham Kitchen Design Studio.

Number **23**, with a first- and second-floor facade dating from the second half of the 19th century which remains thankfully intact, was the home of James Lee, who in the 1870s was a collector of taxes and a stationer. By the 1950s it had become Mrs Earle's Snack Bar and later, in the 1980s, the Viceroy Indian restaurant. The all too appropriate ground-floor windows date from the early 1990s.

Twenty four next door is of 18th-century appearance and was occupied in the late 1890s by J. Duke who was a plumber. His neighbour at **25** was W. & G. Bunday, pork butchers. Part of his one-time shop is now on the corner of Dogflud Way.

Ken Kent's **Clockhouse** development of 1986 in Dogflud Way was so named because it featured a clock on its south-eastern elevation. Motorists approaching Farnham from the east would thus be able to see a clock which gave the *correct* time, then something of a rarity in the town! Constructed in red brick, tile hung with wood-framed windows, it consists of offices and four flats. Private pedestrian access from East Street is via a paved area which incorporated the rear of The Chestnuts. **Eastgate**, its immediate neighbour to the north, which are colour-washed brick offices, followed in 1995. Both are by Broadway and Malyan. They were predated by Waverley Borough Council's brick **Sports Centre** of 1981 by Arthur Gomez.

To the east of Dogflud Way, happily **29** East Street survives. Although it might outwardly appear to be a late Georgian house, it does in fact date from the mid-19th century. Perhaps the central window with its curved top rail on the first floor is the only give-away. In 1818 James Elliott opened a brewery on the site; he was bankrupt by the following year. Then John Peacock acquired the property, but he died in 1843. The business was inherited by his son George, who may have built the present house. In 1869 it was leased by Alfred Barling and in 1901 he was listed as the occupant of both 28 and 29 East Street. Brewing ceased in 1923 when Thomas Barling sold off the business. The name Still House has no alcoholic connotations. It was the choice of Desmond Taylor who acquired the property at auction in 1956 for £1475 and restored it. An osteopath, he named it after Andrew Taylor Still, the founder of his profession.

Next door but one, on the site of Avis Rent A Car, number **32** was The White Swan public house which was owned by John Peacock of 29. In more recent years it was better known as E. and C. Taddell's fish and chip shop.

This part of East Street is dominated on both sides of the road by **Swain & Jones's** showrooms and workshops which will be considered as an entity. John "Jack" Lewis-Jones and Frank Swain had originally met at the prestigious Napier and Sons motor manufacturers of Acton. Although their respective paths then diverged, the association was revived at Talbot's London factory.

In 1908 they opened as "motor agents" at 38 East Street in premises once occupied by a coachbuilder, William Keen, who had started in business there in 1826. Later, in the 1880s, the firm became Keen and Heath, George Heath having begun his career as a coachbuilder at Alton. He was gone by 1897 and soon afterwards the premises housed the coach, cart and van works of Sturt and Goatcher, which had expanded from 84 East Street on the other side of the road. The wooden weather-boarded shop with its high, tile-hung roof and distinctive turret remained part of Swain & Jones's showroom complex until 1976. But the company soon outgrew these premises and in 1913 four adjoining cottages to the east, numbers 39, 40, 41 and 42, were demolished to make way for new workshops.

In 1919 Swain & Jones was appointed Austin agents and their association with that company's Longbridge factory endures to this day. But burgeoning sales and repair work meant that space was once again a problem and in 1927 the company expanded to the north side of East Street where a new paint shop and a filling station was established at 74-78. This adjoined the Surrey Knitting Factory at number 80 which in 1960 was also taken over by Swain & Jones and converted into a showroom.

Numbers 35 to 37 East Street were demolished in 1955 to make way for Swain & Jones's expansion. Behind them is the turret which crowned the front of the one-time Keen coachworks that was destroyed by fire in 1976.

Originally this had been the Ebenezer Chapel, built by Congregationalists in 1793; later it became The British Schools, created in the 1830s for nonconformists who did not wish their children to attend a Church of England establishment. Vacated as a place of worship in 1873 when the Congregationalist's Church in South Street was completed, they continued to own the property until 1926. It was demolished in 1989.

The accent was also on expansion on the south side of the Street in the postwar years. In 1955 a new workshop was built there and an expanded showroom facility opened in 1957. However, in 1976 the buildings, that had grown piecemeal over the years and still incorporated Keen's old coachbuilding shop, were destroyed by fire. It was replaced by a new purpose-designed showroom which opened in 1978.

Yet another development of the mid-1960s was the purchase of the nearby Dogflud House which became offices. This was sold in 1995 and demolished for Lidl's store which opened in the following year.

By this time Swain & Jones had expanded on the north side of East Street. This involved acquiring number 84 which had attained celebrity by having been immortalized in George Sturt's well-known book *The Wheelwright's Shop.* Built in about 1795 of local ironstone by wheelwright William Grover, the two-storey building was acquired in 1810 by Sturt's grandfather, also named George. The business passed to the latter's son, Francis, on his death in 1884, Sturt took over and in the 1890s William Goatcher became his business partner.

Old and new: George Sturt's reconstructed wheelwright's shop on the extreme left successfully coexists with Swain & Jones's Jaguar showrooms, opened in 1989, thanks to its scale and sympathetic use of materials.

In 1899 Sturt and Goatcher expanded into new workshops in South View and the Council took the opportunity to improve access to the housing development that was taking place between East Street and Farnham Park. The lane on the west side of Sturt's property, which had hitherto provided gated access to the hopfields beyond, was widened, this being made possible by the demolition of a pair of semi-detached cottages, numbers 84 and 85 East Street. Originally to have been known as Sturts Road, this designation never progressed beyond the planning stage and on completion the new highway was named St Cross Road.

Sturt and Goatcher also built bodies for "horseless carriages". Goatcher died in 1911 and Sturt suffered a stroke in 1916. He sold the business to his manager William Arnold in 1920. Arnold and his partner V. H. Comben decided to enter the motor trade and they built a showroom, with windows flanked by wooden Tuscan columns, in front of the old shop and the adjoining house, number 83, where George Sturt's father and his uncle John had once lived.

Arnold & Comben continued as coachbuilders and they built bodies for, among others, the Aldershot and District bus company. In 1936 the premises were acquired by brothers Len and Joe Heath, later with shops at 119 and 120 East Street. Arnold & Comben moved to West Street. The Heaths sold motorcycles until 1976 and their successor, Tony West, maintained this two-wheeled tradition.

By the 1980s Swain & Jones, now main distributors for Jaguar/Daimler, redeveloped the entire site for a new

Jaguar showroom with a parking area for cars and they dispensed with the filling station. The work of local architects Hugh Harwood and Graham Swan and completed in 1989, it incorporated Sturt's rebuilt shop. Thanks to the use of good bricks and tiles, it exists in easy juxtaposition with the angularity of the Post-Modernist building which constitutes the main part of the complex.

In the 1950s Swain & Jones had been overlooked from the rear on the south side of East Street by the gas works and one of two gasometers. Gas lighting had arrived in the town in 1835. Located to the east was the power station built by Goddard's in 1912; it supplied the town with current until the 1954. The former gasworks site is now occupied by the 24-unit Riverside Industrial Park, a joint development between Waverley Borough Council and Kents Developments, which dates from 1984.

The block of Victorian cottage-style properties that adjoin Swain & Jones to the east are **43** to **51** East Street. These are currently occupied by Gristwood Pine (43), Farnham Cycles is at 44/45 and 48 is the Kar Ling Kwong, one of Surrey's oldest Chinese restaurants.

Numbers 52 to 56 were demolished to make way for Dogflud Way and the arrival of the road exposes the western wall of the Neo-Georgian St James's House, built 1834 and rebuilt in 1927, that was once the headquarters of the Farnham Gas and Electricity Company. Its original tiny gasometer was located nearby.

A noteworthy casualty of the construction of the new road was the demolition of the timber-framed 55 which

Fifty-five East Street was once The White Hart pub. In 1886 its landlord James Snowden was convicted of selling adulterated whisky and fined 10s. (50p), plus costs. It closed in 1928 but the building survived into the 1970s when it was demolished to make way for the construction of Dogflud Way.

was once John Peacock's pub The White Hart. It closed in 1928. Very much in existence is the **Duke of Cambridge**, probably constructed by Harding of West Street. In 1855 Thomas Mathews of the Lion and Lamb acquired the property. One regular at The Duke was Mike Hawthorn, the "Farnham Flyer" who in 1958 became Britain's first world motor racing champion. His father, Leslie, was a straight-talking Yorkshireman who wanted to tune and race motorcycles and be in reasonable proximity to Brooklands track.

In 1931 he had established the Tourist Trophy Garage, little more than a wooden shed at a former builder's yard, close to where Farnham Hospital is situated today. The business was so named because of Hawthorn's partnership with former Isle of Man TT motorcyclist Paddy Johnstone. However, they subsequently moved to a site occupied by redundant hop kilns in East Street. It is still a garage and today is appropriately named **Hawthorns**.

Adjoining is the substantial **Satelliet** showrooms, the town's only significant Art Deco building, completed in 1939 by J. Chuter for builder's merchants William Dibben and Sons. Threatened with demolition in the early 1990s, thankfully wiser counsels prevailed.

Like The Duke of Cambridge, **The Albion**, which stands at a commanding position at the junction of the Guildford and Hale Roads, has survived the purges of East Street's pubs. It dates from about 1886 and Sidney Stapley is the most likely architect. Although there was talk of closure late in 1998, happily it is still in business.

The Barbican building on the north side of East Street, occupied by Advantage, originally to have been called Mornington House, took its Art Deco theme from the Dibben building opposite. It was built in 1984. Although it courted some controversy, its two storeys and brick frontage do not detract from the three-storey **Zingari Terrace**, its westerly neighbour. This was built on land acquired by William Birch, a local builder, from George

Hawthorns, named in memory of Mike Hawthorn (inset), who in 1958 became Britain's first world motor racing champion. He was managing director of the Tourist Trophy Garage, established by his father, which occupied the site. Today he is remembered by Mike Hawthorn Way.

Although the proportions are Classical, Zingari Terrace with its Regency flavour dates from the early 1860s. It appearance was much improved when in 1960 the cement rendering was painted.

Trimmer in 1861 and is a further example of how long Farnham espoused the Classical style, although its fine decorative cast-iron veranda is more usually associated with the Regency period.

Further down, **Farthingfield House** by local architect Michael O'Leary is similarly of 18th-century inspiration and dates from 1986. Next door is the former St James' Church, completed in 1877, and now named **St James Court**. It was constructed to cater for the needs of a growing population. There was seating for 500 and it occupied an elevated position because it was built on a bank. The work of Guildford-born Henry Woodyer, it was constructed of local ironstone with Bath stone dressings in the Early English style but was declared redundant in 1974.

The intention of the Church Commissioners was to demolish the building and release the site for development. Fortunately, in 1979 Waverley Borough Council acquired it for £20,000. Its architect Ray Toms succeeded in converting St James' into 16 flats without undue alterations to the exterior. In 1981 this project was a worthy recipient of a Housing Design Award.

When the church was built it was located between two public houses, the original Albion was just to the east while immediately adjacent to the west was the Surrey Arms. This was in the building, number **62A**, that is now occupied by the Sinuessa pizza restaurant. Dating from 1856, the pub was closed in 1922.

There was clearly no shortage of hostelries in East Street

which may have provided comfort for those men working at Goddard and Sons building contractors at number **65**. With its three-storey, weather-boarded frontage lying parallel with, but set back from, the road, this was also a joinery works. It closed in 1958 and remained derelict and neglected into the 1970s. Now Wisteria Court occupies the site.

And just eight doors down stood The Eagle, at **73**. Probably dating from the second half of the 19th century, this Farnham United Breweries house was shut in 1910.

Funeral directors H.C. Patrick have occupied the Victorian three-storey gabled shop at **86/87** since the early 1960s. Established by builder William Patrick in the 1840s, its premises were originally at 94/95 East Street although they were demolished to make way for The Woolmead.

By contrast, **The New Seven Stars** is still very much in business and well established, a pub by the name of The Seven Stars having occupied the site since at least the 18th century. Then it was long and low, of two storeys and finished in cream wash, and its roof was of red-brown tiles. It benefited from its proximity to George Sturt's wheelwright's shop and a wayzgoose, or party, was held there every time a wagon was completed.

Owned since 1840 by the Knight family, it was offered for sale in 1888 and passed to Farnham United Breweries. Following its takeover in 1927 by Courage, it decided to rebuild the old inn and Colonel Courage offered the landlady, Doll Johnston, "the most sumptuous up to date public house in the district". She initially turned him down but the deciding factor was a pull-in for cars, the building at that time being separated from the street by a pavement-width of cobbles. Falkner and Aylwin were retained as architects and the present Tudor-style structure of 1929, set back from the road, was the result.

Farnham's first Neo-Georgian office block? St James's House dates from 1927 and was the headquarters of the Farnham Gas and Electricity Company.

The Seven Stars, pictured in 1957 when the landlord was the winner of a Courage flower competition. It dates from 1929.

But this was far from being the last pub in East Street. At 94/95 was The Royal Oak, which closed in 1914. The Green Man was at 118; this was in existence in 1823, but was shut in 1909. Probably older, The Unicorn at 120 existed in 1779 but Farnham Magistrates decreed its end in 1902.It became a bicycle shop, first run by N. Littlejohns, then William Ayling and finally, from 1942, by the Heath brothers, already at 84, who remained there until the 1960s.

On the corner of Bear Lane was what in 1857 was the East Street Brewery. From 1863 it was named The Queen Street Tavern to commemorate Queen Victoria's visit to Farnham in 1857 when an attempt was made to rename East Street in this manner. Irreverently, it was better known as Fourteen Penny House, so called because a man could drink all the beer he could consume for 14d. (about 6p), providing that he did not leave the bar to answer a call of nature! But the pub closed in 1902. In later years it became Burnett's Shoe Repair shop (125). This and number 124 were the first buildings to be demolished, on 26th August 1965, prior to the building of The Woolmead.

I cannot think of a better way to complete this chapter on East Street than to recall the words of a one-time resident, Albert Winslade, who had a tailor's shop at number 115. In his later years he set down his memories of the town in the latter half of the 19th century and they provide a nostalgic flavour of this part of East Street and of the properties located between numbers 89 to 125. This is where The Woolmead now stands.

After The Seven Stars came "Mr Johnson's house standing back with iron railings in front, Miss May's school, old cottages and kilns, the Royal Oak, Mr Poppleton's school with the school room up the passage.

"Next was Corps, the cordwainer and a rope walk in his garden, [then]...an old fashioned house where the old lady sold faggots and did mangling, then Mrs Mason's dame school, Mr Mitchell's leather shop.

"Next to my place was a private house and the first tenant I remember was Mr Baldwin, coachman to Bishop Sumner,who kept pigs in his garden...The Green Man [had] a passage through which they took the horses from market carts, which were left in the street. The passage was the only entrance to the pub which had a back way with a path through the hop ground, used a great deal by the Castle servants..."

Falkner's Fireplaces: 4

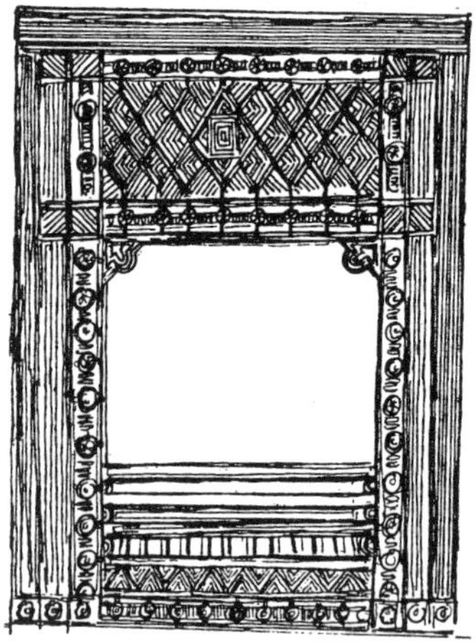

A cast-iron Victorian register grate which incorporates a damper below the front bars. This allowed the fire to be kept in overnight. There was often an additional damper that was located in the throat of the chimney.

South Street

"South Street was made by the rates, aided by donations!!!"

John Henry Knight, Reminiscences of a Country Town, *1909*

South Street, originally named New Road, was completed by 1870 at a cost of some £3000. The donations to which Knight refers amounted to £1011 while £2000-worth of loans were also required to provide Farnham with a direct route to its railway station which had opened in 1849.

From the mid-1880s until December 1965, **1** South Street was The Bush Tap and the present two-storey building was "recently erected" in 1887. It is now occupied by DNA, and prior to that by Lintern and Petters which moved from 4 Town Hall Buildings. In the 1970s it had housed Leighton's Opticians. The original Bush Tap was demolished in 1869 to make way for the new road.

Solidly built of brick with a slate roof and projecting eaves, there is generous use of stone for both the string courses and door surrounds. The latter is guarded by lions' heads incorporated in the cornice brackets. Much of what is today the street frontage of The Bush's car park was taken up by the single-storey, slate roofed outbuilding which may have survived until 1937 when the three-storey, Neo-Georgian **Bush House** was built.

This is by Guy Maxwell Aylwin, and provided staff accommodation and all-important revenue from four shops. Number 3 is now Nigel's, a men's hairdressers which took over from King and Sons who were in the same business in the 1950s. Chemist J.M. Bank was a previous occupant of 5 which is now the address of the Disking computer shop. Leighton's was once the occupant of number 7, one of its two South Street outlets. Estate agents A.W. Symonds occupied it in the 1970s and currently Castles, which is in the same business, has the premises. Oakley's newsagents

The offices of solicitors Bells Potter at 11 South Street. But were they designed (see text) by Arthur Stedman or Edward Mountford? Guy Maxwell Aylwin was responsible for Bush House on the right.

was a previous tenant of 9 Bush House, which is currently the home of Finewood Furniture.

Bells Potter, or more correctly its Potter and Crundwell predecessors, have occupied its purpose-designed offices at **11** South Street since it moved there from 47 The Borough in 1892. In the late 1920s it become Potter, Crundwell and Bridge and was renamed Potter and Kempson in 1969, following a merger with Kempson, Wright and Trimming. This in turn merged in 1987 with Bells.

Although credited to Arthur Stedman, Harold Falkner was insistent that these offices were the work of Edward Mountford, one of the most successful architects of his day and best known for the Central Criminal Court at The Old Bailey. The building accordingly won praise from Falkner, as "...a simple example of what such buildings should be in a Georgian town." Interestingly, its first two storeys are in the Classical vein while the three projecting top-floor gables are in the 16th century idiom.

The Farnham Institute completed in 1891. For many years it was occupied by the Central Club.

Falkner was less impressed by Paxton Hood Watson's Farnham Institute next door which is **13** South Street. Built by public subscription on land given by George Trimmer, the Trust deed was enlightened for the day and specified that none should be excluded "on the grounds of class, party, sex or creed". The architect submitted his plans in September 1890 and the building, begun by Patrick and completed by Crosby, was opened in October 1891. Imposing in vivid red brick with terracotta decorations, the large gables above the bay windows bear plaster relief displays. They continue under the south-facing walls as an indication that lectures and technical education was provided in the winter months. There were two full-sized billiard tables, a table tennis room and, in due course, a bar.

After the Second World War, in 1946, the Central Club was established at the Institute, and over the next 50 or so years it donated £35,000 to local charities. But a combination of dwindling membership and a rise in annual rental from £3000 to £17,500 in 1995 led to its closure at the beginning of 2001. It is to become a Macdonald Hotel's Conference Centre.

The neighbouring **15** dates from 1882 and was named Riverdale. It was the home of William Whiteley, high bailiff of the county council and clerk to the board of guardians, who moved there from 10 Downing Street. By 1901 solicitor Richard W. Mason was in residence. Mason was the son of the clerk of the Farnham UDC, also called Richard. He died in 1937 at the age of 79 but his widow continued to occupy the house well into the postwar years.

Set back a little from the road, with two storeys of yellow brick, double fronted and with a southerly bay, it was the work of Thomas Wonnacott. Today it has a colour-washed frontage and is occupied by Palladian Publications.

Mason's father had acted for the Farnham Congregational Church; his fee was £48 when it built its new place of worship in South Street. **The United Reformed Church**, as the Congregationalists have been known since 1972, had in 1793 opened their chapel in East Street, which subsequently became the Surrey Knitting Factory. With their numbers swelled by many of the town's tradespeople, it was proposed at a meeting held on 20th April 1871 that the committee should "look into the desirability for a new place of worship".

The total cost of the land was £600 and architect Thomas Wonnacott, for a fee of £204, was responsible for the design. The cost of the building, completed in 1873 and

The plaster relief details on the gables of the one-time Central Club were picked out and painted as recently as the mid-1980s when the roof was retiled.

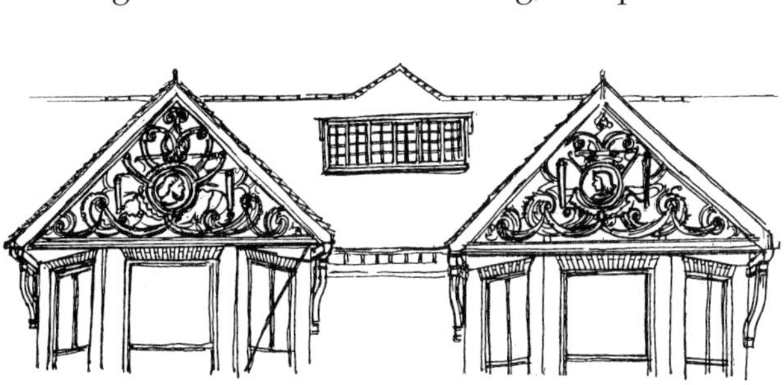

the work of Goddards, was £3698 although the eventual total of £4836 exceeded the original estimate by no less than £1138!

The church is faced in local Bargate stone, which cost an extra £86, in the predominantly Early English and also Decorated Gothic styles. The tower, also Early English, with spire, was completed for £519.

Further development took place at the church in 1893 when a large hall and vestry were added to commemorate the centenary of the establishment of the East Street Chapel. Then, in 1929, the vestry was replaced by the present ancillary rooms. In 1981 the new Victoria Road entrance was established while the Spire Coffee Bar dates from January 1993.

When the church was built, the adjoining Victoria Road did not exist: it was not adopted by Farnham UDC until 1910. The first building to occupy its south side, behind a vacant plot in South Street, was a studio for Farnham's fledgling art school which at this time was meeting in the Town Hall. The School's minutes record that on 29th October 1879 the decision was made to "accept the offer of purchase of the land…the site of the studio for £155, and a tender by Mr Goddard was accepted." It was occupied by February 1880, and was a modest affair, brick with a slate roof and four large north-lit windows. The latter have been removed in recent years and the building is currently

Farnham United Reformed Church dates from 1873 and is the work of Thomas Wonnacott. Costing £4836, the debt was not finally paid off until 1908 when an Old English Fayre in the Town Hall raised a respectable £405.

occupied by solicitors Kidd Rapinet whose offices also include **17** South Street directly in front of it.

This was originally the School of Art's extension, opened on June 1915, with two storeys and Neo-Georgian in design, later to be known as Victoria House. Brick, parapeted, with an abundance of sash windows on both floors, its entrance is in Victoria Road. Although credited to Harold Falkner, he was unusually coy in claiming responsibility, but see caption below. "Whether it was designed by the County Architect or me" he recalled, "it owes more to Lutyens' influence than either of us." This is a reference to the latter's Liberal Club almost opposite.

The art school was destined to remain at this location until 1939 when it moved to 25 West Street, into premises recently vacated by Farnham Girls' Grammar School. For its part, Victoria House was then taken over by Farnham UDC's housing and treasurer departments.

Numbers **19** and **21** South Street, at present the respective homes of Ellegance and Alhambra, comprise a two-storey brick town house, notably lacking in decoration for the 1880s, occupied by solicitor James Stevens, who moved there from 5 Castle Street. Towering above it to the south are the three storeys of **23** to **27** South Street which, on its ground floor, consists of three shops, Mr See's Oriental Fastfood (23), The Darjeeling Restaurant (25) with Trident Blinds (27) on the corner.

Comparable in scale and richness of detail to Ransom's tea rooms at The Borough end of South Street, the building was built in 1885 for R. and E. Beale of Frensham Mill as a corn store. There was originally a turret on the corner. Builder's merchants the Surrey Iron Company occupied the premises from the interwar years until the early 1960s.

Victoria Road: the building on the right was The Studio, the home of the Farnham School of Art from 1880 until 1939. The drawing shows the original windows, and while these have been reconstructed, the distinctive triangular ventilators remain. The extension on the left dates from 1915 and is the work of the then County Architect to Harold Falkner's design.

In the 1950s part of it was also briefly the home of Vernon Griffiths' "Complete House Furnishers", and more recently of the Farnham Antiques Centre. The building was refurbished in 1989.

On the other corner of Union Road stands the expanse of the Neo-Georgian **Wey Court** office block, the construction of which in 1988 required the demolition of 29 to 37 South Street. The site was previously occupied by an attractive colour-washed, three-storey, brick building, more 18th century in spirit than Victorian, which followed the curvature of the corner and thus required a neatly segmented slate roof.

At the turn of the 19th century this was occupied by photographer F. Elderfield, and accountant A. Cooper. Then it was home to Bartram's Manure Company. Quite what architect Arthur Stedman, who arrived in 1896, felt about being adjacent to the latter business is not recorded. But in 1905 he moved across South Street to his own purpose-designed offices at number 36.

Next door was coachbuilder George Heath, who had moved his business from 38 East Street to South Street in 1896. In July of that year his architect neighbour, Arthur Stedman, applied to Farnham UDC for permission to erect brick "carriage showrooms" with a tiled roof which was duly built. In 1905 Heath joined with William Charles Wiltshire to establish Heath and Wiltshire. His career had also begun in East Street and he had expanded his bicycle business to a shop at the north-eastern end of South Street. The merger of interests resulted in one of Farnham's first garages which was destined to survive until 1960.

Bridge House, a modern building in scale with its surroundings. Designed by A.G. Anderson and Partners of Bournemouth for Simo Properties, it was occupied from January 1969.

The Free Church of England's Emmanuel Church. In 1900 it replaced a corrugated iron building, situated where the bypass now runs. It had been established by the Episcopal Church, whose presence in the town dated from 1889.

Next door were the offices of another architect, Alfred Guyer, who was well-placed when the Council moved opposite. But in 1925 he sold his premises to solicitors Kempson and Wright which moved there from 121 West Street.

Then came the three-storey **Bridge House**, brick with stone dressing. By 1899 builder and stonemason Crosby and Co had moved in, although it retained its premises at 110 East Street for a time. Andrew Crosby had established his business there in 1877. It was destined to remain in South Street until May 1939 when it moved to the former Farnham United Breweries site in West Street.

Harold Falkner was responsible for the House's two shopfronts. He also essayed "the piers and railings of the bridge [now replaced] itself designed for the Local Board, of which I am especially proud." The creeper-covered Bridge House was demolished in 1968 and replaced by an office block of the same name which was opened in January 1969.

Gostrey Meadow contributes a welcome green break and a view of trees, while the presence beyond of the simple but attractive single-storey brick **Emmanuel Church**, which dates from 1900, provides yet a further religious element to South Street.

The South Street/Station Hill junction with the bypass is named Hickley's Corner because builder's merchants Hickley and Co were responsible for the construction of the three-storey, red-brick building with stone dressing which occupied the site for over 70 years. Completed in 1901 it survived until 1975, when the omnipresent through-

Before South Street
East Street tailor Albert Winslade (1864–1940) remembered, as a small boy, the gates at the junction of The Borough with East Street which led "into the meadow which is now South Street. These were closed at sunset. Inside...were the Bush Tap and stables and a path ran through the meadow to about the position of Beale's Corn Store [on the corner of what is now Union Road] while a farm yard was where the Council Offices...now is, the path turning round here, crossing by a stile the Gostrey Ditch. This ran to Downing Street, opposite the Police Station."

The first shop, on the eastern side of the street, "was a wooden one... and was kept by Doughen Williams and was called the Noah's Ark. Then followed a row of wooden shops..."

Behind the Congregational Church was "the Bush Meadow, where the boys of the Farnham Grammar School, then in West Street, used to play cricket. We often knew what a foul ditch the Gostrey was when our cricket balls had to be fished out. Our *bête noire* was old Mr Fountain, who seemed always to be on the look out for a ball knocked on to the slates of the Congregational Church – and then we knew it!"

road was widened. Architect Michael Blower incorporated some of the building's terracotta decoration in his Cobbetts Mews development in The Hart.

Hickley's had moved from premises at 68 Castle Street and the original building, somewhat severe in execution like many industrial premises with a strongly practical theme, was designed by John Kingham. It certainly did not impress George Sturt, who, fearful of change, confided to his *Journal* in December 1901: "The pile is hideous to the eyes; and spells ruin."

Hickley's occupied what was named the Burlington Buildings for over 40 years although by 1946 Dolton, Bournes & Dolton – "everything for the building trade and home repairs" – had taken over the premises and the adjoining yard. Gabriel Wade, the final occupant, was in a similar business. For **Hickley's Court** offices of 1988, architects Broadway and Malyan replaced the single corner-building with a group of three. Built in brick and tile, they clearly echo Farnham's hop-growing heritage.

This is a demonstrable end to the western side of South Street and the starting point of the Street's north-eastern prospect is the Royal Deer (see page 135) which was rebuilt in about 1929. Leonard Stedman was responsible for the Neo-Georgian, two-storey Royal Deer Buildings, which contain 2 to 8 South Street and are contemporary with the pub. (However Bill Ewbank-Smith, in *Farnham In War and Peace,* maintains that the UDC did not give Courage permission to build the shops until 1935...)

What is today Farnham Cobblers, number **2,** was in the 1950s Miss N.P. Rickard's children's outfitters which by 1971 also occupied number **6.** This is now the home of Kitchen Kapers. Men's hairdressers Les Whiting, number **4**, took over from J. Goolding, who was in the same business, while Hibberd Photographic's shop, established at **8** in 1981 and closed in 2003 is now also Kitchen Kapers.

The space which is now occupied by the entrance to **Sainsbury's** Service Area, **Les Smith's** parts shop and the supermarket itself, which opened in 1982, was previously the sites of 10 to 44 South Street. This medley of Victorian red-brick, tile-hung gables and terracotta decoration was demolished in two stages: numbers 10 to 28A came down in 1971 with 30 to 44 following ten years later.

The Royal Deer Buildings had replaced the Assembly Room with a stucco facade that chimed with the adjoining numbers 10 and 12. These were two-storey shops, both with parapets and single upper windows facing the street. Number 10 was at one time the address of the Farnham Club and in the 1960s it was best known as the home of Oxfam, the town's first charity shop. The neighbouring 12 enjoyed a far greater continuity of ownership, having been occupied by J.H. Wilcox since the firm's creation in 1883. In due course he extended his business to incorporate numbers 14 and 16.

The Chocolate Box was at 18 in the 1950s, but back in 1891 it was the original home of the *Farnham Herald*. When in 1952, the newspaper celebrated its 60th anniversary, its founder, Ernest Langham, recalled how it had all begun (see pages 160-161). But he soon outgrew 18 South Street and moved a few doors down to the larger and newly-built 24.

Numbers 20 and 22 were respectively occupied in the 1960s by the antiques business of G.E. Day and Miss Irene Tigwell's toy shop, the latter business having moved from 2 The Borough in 1929. She used to sell such items as wooden jointed Dutch dolls which cost one old penny apiece and lead soldiers for the same price. A representative of a toy firm called her business "a Dickens shop". Both of these single-storey premises contained some spiritual echoes of wooden sheds which had sprung up in South Street in the 1870s before more permanent buildings arrived.

The adjoining 24 was not only where Langham offered his services as a printer and stationer but it was also the *Herald's* offices. In 1905 he moved to 114 West Street.

The East Street Regeneration scheme of 2002 envisages returning South Street to its pre-1981 look, as below, although the sequence of apparently separate buildings on the left beyond Royal Deer Buildings accommodates a single hotel.

The eastern side of South Street pictured in 1958 in the days of two-way traffic. All the shops beyond The Royal Deer Buildings had been demolished by 1981 to make way for the Sainsbury's development.

The Birth of the *Farnham Herald*

After attending school in London's South Norwood, Ernest Langham spent three years as a printer. But, as he recalled in 1952, at the age of 21 "a friend offered to lend me money so that I could start in business on my own account… Two advertisements in *The Printers' Register* appealed to me – one of a small business at Bournemouth, the other of one at Farnham."

He decided to visit both, by bicycle. But the seaside company did not attract him, so on the way back, and in pouring rain, he cycled to Farnham. The next day he went to see the owner of the Farnham Printing Works, Frampton Ames, whose father was Crondall's school- and postmaster.

"It was in South Street in the small shop now the Chocolate Box [18], and the actual printing was done in old cottages at the back in Cambridge Place" which was entered from East Street.

"I came, I saw, and I *was* conquered" although the work at that time was mostly confined to Crookham Parish Magazine and some local timetables.

"I was troubled, and looked round for something to do. Then it occurred to me that I might do what Mr Coventry, my old master, had done…that is, bring out a weekly advertising sheet with a few items of ☛

His place was taken by F. Lawson, "Surgical Bootmaker, Repairer and Leather Merchant", who continued trading there until well after the Second World War. Next door at 26 was corn, seed and hop dealer S.A. Chalcroft. In later years these premises became another branch of G.E. Day's antiques business.

Number 28 was similar in design to its neighbour but it contained one shop rather than two. Butcher T. Stratford, who subsequently opened another branch at 2 West Street in 1904, was there in the 1890s. This business was destined to be another long-time denizen of South Street.

By 1946 grocer W.H. Cullen was installed at number 30. However, the premises, with its distinctive central tall chimney, were rather overshadowed by the adjoining 32. This three-storey, five-star, Victorian brick pile had been completed, as the terracotta plaque let into the balustrade indicated, in 1897, which was Queen Victoria's Diamond Jubilee year. Should there be any doubt of the building's function, the plaque also proclaimed *Farnham Auction Mart*. These were the offices of auctioneers Nash and Son, run by Alfred John Nash. Farnham's cattle market was now held behind his South Street offices with a gap in the fence at the back for one of his staff to squeeze through. Soon afterwards market day was switched from Thursdays to Mondays to coincide with the butchers' early closing day.

Founded in 1853, and having moved from 39 The Borough, Nash and Son continued to run the market until 1923 when it was taken over by auctioneers Hewett and Lee of Guildford. Unlike many markets which were owned by the local authority, the freehold was passed on to the Lee family. In the 1960s David Lee auctioned cattle, H.A. Lee the sheep, with P. Foggo responsible for pigs. But closure came in December 1967. The following year the site was acquired by Farnham UDC for £22,000 and was converted into a car park.

Nash's offices bore a superficial resemblance to those of its long-time neighbours, Taylor & Anderson, "the Oldest Established Coal Business in the Town", at 34 South Street. The firm also specialized in "removals, storage, packing and shipping" and had a depository at 17 Beavers Road.

After the exuberance of 32 and 34, it came as some relief to encounter the Neo-Georgian refinement of 36 with a frontage reminiscent of a late 17th-century London town house. Designed in 1905 by architect Arthur Stedman as his office, what latterly became Stedman and Blower remained at South Street until 1980, not long before the bulldozers moved in.

The block of four shops with flats above, numbers 38 to 44, represented that endangered species in Farnham, a building that was a product of the Modern Movement of the interwar years. Dating from about 1938, with steel-framed horizontal windows on the first floor, it was brick built and harmonized well with its neighbours. Happily, there was no flat roof, instead the ridge line of 36 was perpetuated in Roman tiles which were punctuated by gabled dormer windows. The chimneys were playfully banded with contrasting white bricks.

So much for the past. Today **The Liberal Club** stands well forward of the building line. Its great claim to fame is that it was designed by the eminent architect Edwin Lutyens. Although this was a popularly held local tradition, factual proof was not confirmed until 1961 when Nigel Temple sought information from the Council's Bill Ewbank-Smith. This prompted the discovery of the original plans which bore the legend *Edwin L. Lutyens, Archt., 6, Grays Inn Square, W.C. Sept 1894.*

It was 25 year old Lutyens' first essay in town architecture, probably a response to Farnham's strong Classical heritage. With a frontage of small red bricks and a central pedimented stone door, the first-floor decoration is in the form of tentative angular and curved brick pediments above the five windows. And while these are late 17th-century lead-glazed style casements, the traditional eaves-cornice usually associated with the Queen Anne style is absent. Instead the cornice doubles as a parapet. Originally topped with Roman tiles, these were found to be unduly heavy and were subsequently replaced with slate.

At the time of the Club's construction in 1895, Brightwell Road, which now runs alongside it, did not exist. It dates from 1897 and led to Farnham Swimming Pool, which was constructed to mark Queen Victoria's Diamond Jubilee.

The commemorative entrance arch, very much in the Lutyens idiom, happily survives as a fine testament to Harold Falkner's precocious architectural and practical abilities. He carved the inscription on the external beam located above the easterly window himself; perversely, he referred to the Queen as *Victoria I*!

news and a railway timetable in it – not to sell, but to give away.

"Well, we did start it, and a thousand copies of the first number of the *Weekly Herald*, four pages, 15 inches by 10 inches, were given away on July 2nd 1892. And thus began the present *Farnham Herald*.

"The type for the paper was set by hand, and it was printed on a crown Wharfedale machine. As we had no power, this machine was turned by hand. Two pages at a time were printed, and this meant 2000 runs – very good exercise for the four of us. It was something for nothing, and Farnham took kindly to the little advertising sheet. I was editor, reporter, advertisement manager and clerk of the paper and had to work hard.

"As the weeks went on we added more and more news or reading matter, and then we ceased to give it away, but made a charge of one half penny...but [I was] finding a lack of capital a brake on progress.

"At this point [solicitor] the late Mr Ernest Crundwell and others joined with me to form a small company... From this step forward we never looked back though at times, of course, there were difficulties to overcome. Health, Garden and other columns and a serial story also helped... We were certainly out of the wood."

In 1918 the Council took it over. A new pool adjoining the original, which continued in use for children, was built in 1931 and this remained open until 1983. By this time the Sports Centre at Dogflud Way was in use, and this rendered these outdoor facilities redundant.

Falkner Court, by Arthur Gomez, was built on the site of the 1931 pool but the original became derelict and overgrown with weeds. For some years Farnham Swimming Baths Trust, chaired by Michael Blower, agonized over a use for the site. Happily, a visit to Petersfield revealed the attraction of a small town-centre garden and the result is **The Victoria Garden**, opened on 30th May 1997, 100 years to the day since the pool's inauguration. The entrance arch, once sadly neglected, has been restored and a replica of the original wooden cornice faithfully recreated.

Back in South Street, the **Methodist Church**, also the work of Thomas Wonnacott, a Methodist lay preacher, dates from 1875. Like his Congregationalist Church opposite, Bargate stone is used, although only for the frontage, while the style is Early English. It was extended to the rear in 1878.

Montrose House next door, which retains its fine barge-boards and original wooden porch, is similarly faced with Bargate stone although the remaining walls are of brick. It has the appearance of a town house built for a prosperous late Victorian and that is precisely what it is, having been built by Arthur Rose, owner of Rose's Corn Store in East Street. The choice of Montrose, the original rendering, now becomes apparent.

Harold Falkner's entrance arch to the town's swimming pool dates from 1897 and was restored when the Victoria Garden beyond was opened in 1997.

It was taken over by the Council in 1926 which immediately housed its new rating and valuation department there. Accommodation had been an ongoing problem ever since its adjoining offices, today Waverley Borough Council's Farnham **Locality Office**, had been opened there in 1902. Previously Farnham UDC had met in the boardroom of the Corn Exchange in The Borough. But there was an uneasy association between the Council and Town Hall Company and matters came to a head in 1898 when the latter raised the boardroom rental to £15 per annum. A perhaps more contentious flashpoint came when councillors were also prevented from using the lavatories on the premises…

Initially the Council toyed with the idea of acquiring the Corn Exchange but an asking price of £7000 was deemed excessive. In fact the new offices eventually cost some £8000; the original estimate was £5940! After contemplating a number of possible sites, the local authority paid George Trimmer £1500 for a former skin yard in South Street on which there stood a down-at-heel cottage and some ramshackle weather-boarded buildings.

Four architects submitted designs and the Council specified that the building's cost should not exceed £2500. The entrants were Alfred Guyer and Arthur Stedman, both of whom had offices opposite the site, while West Street was represented by Harold Falkner and Paxton Hood Watson. Falkner has left us with a characteristically robust account of how the winning design came to be chosen. He does not mention Stedman's entry but recalled that "the plans had to be accompanied by the architect's

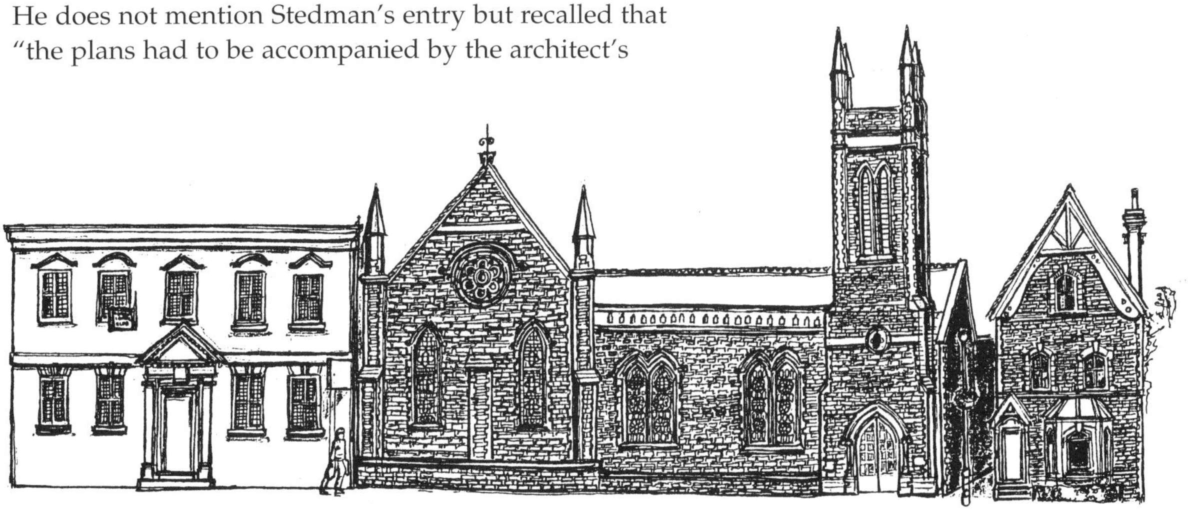

The Liberal Club *Methodist Church* *Montrose House*

The entrance arches for fire engines being enlarged in 1956 at the then Farnham Urban District Council offices. Prior to its construction in 1902, the UDC kept its fire engine in a rented shed at the rear of 12 East Street.

estimates of cost and mine was immediately disqualified on these grounds. Guyer's were impossible, so only PHW's were left."'Pack' was well on the up-and-up...he employed as a 'ghost' Arthur Cox, a very able architect...The consequence was that when the architect appeared before the Council to explain the plans, he did not know anything about them... This little contretemps was nothing to 'Pack', he could bounce his way through anything."

Whatever its parentage, the finished product, built by Tompsett, is a fine building in the Queen Anne style, perhaps inspired by Lutyens's effort a few doors down the street. With its northern gabled end and external decorative plasterwork, it not only provided a council chamber and offices but also served as a fire station. The council met there for the first time on 2nd December 1902 and the building was officially inaugurated on 13th February 1903 by the Archbishop of Canterbury.

Outwardly the building has changed little over the years although the fire station arches were enlarged in 1956. Later, in 1967, the station moved to a new building in Guildford Road. The aperture was bricked up and the windows that replaced it were a good match. However, the present cupola is made of glass fibre for in 1971 it replaced the more elaborate wooden original which had become unsafe and was removed in 1969. Today the offices of Farnham Town Council, further sympathetic additions at the rear of the building, designed by the Haworth King Partnership, were completed in 1999. These included the provision of a lift.

The one time Farnham Urban District Council offices by Paxton Hood Watson date from 1902.

Union Road

"The arrival of the resplendent Church House in 1909, followed by the elegant landscaping of the untidy Gostrey Meadow, did much to enhance the street."

Bill Ewbank-Smith, Edwardian Farnham, *1979*

Union Road, which joined the newly completed South Street with Longbridge, was to have been named Bridge Street. This was changed to Union Street and, finally, to the present name.

It is, however, of a wholly different character to its neighbour, most of its north side being residential and it has survived mostly unchanged since 1909. This contrasts with the south side of the road which adjoins Gostrey Meadow that has been the subject of development, particularly in recent years.

By 1901 H.C. Patrick, monumental masons, had a yard there and in 1906 Heath and Wiltshire, with premises in South Street, opened a "Motor Shed" with a brick frontage crowned by a high glass roof. Adjoining it, on the western side of what was named the Gostrey Works, was a separate building which housed the business's accessories department that survived until 1973.

In 1960 Heath and Wiltshire was acquired by Southern Counties Car Auctions, which pulled down the old garage and built a new one, briefly run by Swain & Jones, together with Expedier House, a five-storey office block. Opened in 1962 and built of concrete with blue Vynide-covered walls, it made no concessions to its location. Few tears were shed when what became the headquarters of British Car Auctions was demolished in June 1987.

All the other buildings in Union Road to east also went, as did those on the corner of South Street. In their place came the Neo-Georgian **Wey Court**. Its western elevation overlooks **Gostrey Meadow** with its now non-functioning drinking fountain by Harold Falkner which cost £21. The Meadow has been a popular facility since 14th September

Gostrey Meadow has been a major asset to the town since its opening in 1910. The flood plain flanking the River Wey was created in the late 1960s to prevent the regular flooding of Downing and Abbey Streets.

1910 when much of the town turned out to celebrate its acquisition by the Council. This two acres (0.8ha) of land flanking the River Wey was acquired from the Reverend M.O. Stevens, and a further acre on the east side of South Street, which had previously been a repository of rubbish, was purchased at the same time.

The Meadow is readily accessible for those residents of numbers **4** to **10**, originally Belle Vue, on the north side of the road. This is unmistakably late Victorian in character, brick, two storey with bay windows, slate and hip-roofed dormers. The neighbouring two-storey block of **12** to **18A**, once Blount Terrace, are more 18th century in inspiration.

The Old Court House

The neighbouring **Church House** makes a striking visual contribution to Union Road, and is the only example of Arts and Crafts architecture in the town centre. The work of R.B. Preston, its prominent gables and colour-washed facade provide an important focal point. It was the inspiration of the town's new rector, the Reverend Ernest Lovett, who arrived in 1908. He convinced his churchwarden, G.F. Roumieu, to donate the land which was valued at £400. By 1912 Lovett was gone. But his building, erected by Mardon & Mills at a cost of £2850, was opened in 1909 by the Duchess of Albany, who was a daughter in law of Queen Victoria.

Today it looks much as it did when built, although dormer windows in the frontage were not replaced and a simpler turret was introduced following a fire in 1943. Inside a false ceiling was introduced to cover the charred beams, this wartime renovation having been overseen by Arthur Stedman.

Sadly by 2000 the building had become a financial liability to St Andrew's Church, which found that the income it generated did not cover maintenance costs. In February it was put on the market and it might have been targeted for demolition. Fortunately in June news broke that it had been acquired for £500,000 by Sir Ray Tindle, proprietor of the *Farnham Herald*, who had been working with community leaders to ensure its preservation.

Church House

"We all believe that Church House has a positive future to play in the life of the town" he told his newspaper. A Grade II listing followed in September 2000.

Two months earlier, Sir Ray had purchased what today is named **The Old Court House**, the former police station next door, although this does not look in the least like such an establishment, being of comfortable brick, multi-gabled and tile-hung. The cells, complete with barred windows, were to be found behind. It replaced a cramped building in Bear Lane and dates from 1888. It was subsequently extended into Victoria Road to incorporate the magistrates' court.

In 1911 The Farnham Co-op at 11/12 Castle Street was also looking to expand. In May 1912 the Council agreed that the Society might erect temporary premises in Union Road on the condition that permanent buildings would be completed within a year. Work was underway by the winter of 1914 and the store subsequently appeared with a gabled frontage, Tudor-style beams and leaded casement windows. To the west it was to absorb the Primitive Methodist Chapel, opened in the mid-1870s.

But despite adopting self-service in its grocery department in the 1960s, the Co-op could not match Sainsbury's in nearby South Street, and the building was demolished in September 1989. In its place came **Gostrey House** of 1991, designed by Arthur Gomez of the Modern Design Group. Set at right angles to the road, it is replete with Art Deco themes, has a lively slate-clad roofscape and is an agreeable variation on Farnham's usual Neo-Georgian offices.

Gostrey House

West Street

"The plain, low-roofed houses, with their flat facades and crumpled, lichened tiles, succeed one another down...West Street with a delightful monotony."

Eric Parker, Highways and Byways in Surrey, *1908*

The corner of Downing Street and West Street is an important site in the town and the building which is there – now occupied by the Bradford & Bingley and Gascoigne-Pees estate agents - dates from 1929. The work of Harold Falkner and Guy Maxwell Aylwin, it carries the name of **Alliance House** because it was designed as The Alliance public house although it does not much look like one.

It replaced an establishment of the same name which in 1859 was acquired by George Trimmer. Later it came within the orbit of Farnham United Breweries. Apart from being a pub, wholesale wines and spirits were sold there. Probably dating from the early 19th century, this was a three-storey building with a slate roof. The frontage was, perhaps in the late Victorian era, clad with imitation "Tudor" beams of a similar type to those applied to the exterior of 10 The Borough.

The Farnham brewery business was sold to Courage in 1927 which commissioned the new building with a diagonal corner to improve the sight lines for motorists turning from Downing Street into West Street. Of colour-washed rendering, replete with ground-floor pilasters and a doorway flanked by Ionic columns, the first-floor windows with arched recesses above chime with those of 4 West Street two doors away. Classical detailing beneath the eaves, Roman tiles and dormer windows complete what is one of Farnham's best town-centre buildings.

Actress Jessie Matthews, who was the wife of the landlord, was The Alliance's most famous barmaid; she was there in the early 1950s. But the pub closed in 1965 and in November 1966 it was acquired by Gascoigne-Pees.

Alliance House by Falkner and Aylwin dates from 1929 and from then until 1965 was The Alliance public house. It was so designed to improve the sight line for traffic turning from Downing Street into West Street.

Numbers 5/5A West Street was timber-framed with a brick frontage and this photograph, dating fromNovember 1956, was taken after its demolition.

Millets next door occupies numbers **2** and **3**. This has three colour-washed storeys, is slate-roofed and of two bays. The third-floor windows are four-pane sashes although there are two-pane examples on the first, and all are enhanced with moulded architraves on this mid-Victorian frontage.

With its wrought-iron work and exposed canopy, it comes as no surprise to find that for many years number 2 was a butcher's shop. When in 1904 its owner, Charles Monk, retired due to ill health, the premises passed to T. Stratford, another butcher who also had premises at 11 South Street. Latterly trading as Stratford and Sons, the business was destined to remain there until the early 1960s when it was taken over by Mac Fisheries which was already at number 3. This revived a tradition as Reading and Co, which were also fishmongers, had occupied the latter premises in 1901.

MacFisheries was at 3 by 1937 and this and the neighbouring number **4**, Phase Eight fashion, have a Regency flavour, being stuccoed and three-storeyed with a parapet. In the early 1900s this was Hughes' Men's Wear shop. In the late 1930s W.R. Fletcher was there, while Dewhurst butchers were in residence until the 1970s.

Part of Holland & Barrett's health food shop at **5A** overlaps into 4, and vice versa, although this two-storey brick building with its tiled roof is Neo-Georgian and dates from 1957. It replaced 5 and 5A, respectively occupied by A. Martin and Son and the Cigar Box. The frontage was just one brick deep and this concealed a timber frame,

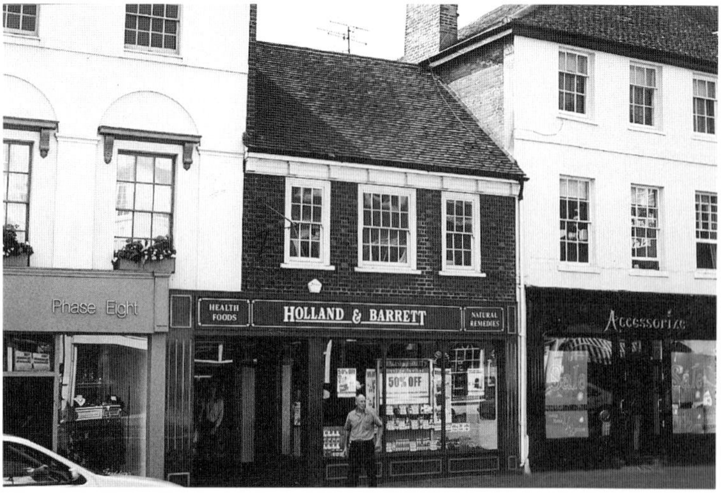

Over 45 years later its Neo-Georgian replacement appears to be completely at one with its surroundings, although Farnham lost a medieval building in the process.

to which a third floor had been added. Back in the 1890s this was Miss H. Savage's toy and china shop.

Her neighbour then at number **6** was the Home and Colonial Tea Company which was there by 1901 and was destined to occupy the premises until the 1960s when Granada TV Rentals took over. A sign of the times! It has recently been replaced by Accessorize Fashion. Between 1876 and 1884 it had been Farnham's Post Office, run by Robert Nichols.

Only the Georgian frontage is rendered, the bricks are visible on the east wall, while the roof ridge line continues to number **7** next door. From about the 1840s, this two-storey, brick-parapeted shop was occupied by Anthony Williams, who owned ten oasts and a hop-bagging room. He was also a wine merchant with a business founded in 1780. In about 1872 he moved across the road to 122 West Street.

J. Alfred Eggar, founder of estate agents Eggar and Company, was also an architect and he designed 7 West Street. It was built in 1902 as Darracott & Dunston's restaurant although the latter name was soon dropped.

By the 1890s his old shop was the butcher's premises of F.J. Gray, who was also a "wholesale and retail sausage maker" with branches at Bagshot, Crondall and Godalming. However, the business ended in bankruptcy and in 1902 the shop was acquired by T. Darracott, "baker, cook and confectioner", who was to open a restaurant there. His other outlets were at Aldershot, Farnborough, Camberley and Fleet.

He commissioned J. Alfred Eggar, who was based nearby at 10/11 West Street, to design more suitable premises and the plans of the resulting brick, two-bay building, with its arched access to Weavers Yard, were submitted to Farnham UDC in August 1902. In the best "Victorian" traditions (the Queen had died only in the previous year), it combines a *pot-pourri* of styles. In part gabled, Eggar introduced a miniature Venetian window on the third floor which echoed the genuine one at nearby 13.

Darracott's, George Sturt used to dine there, survived until the mid-1950s when it was replaced by The Queen of Hearts Restaurant which offered "Swiss Confectionery Made on the Premises." This lasted until 1968 when the current occupant, Farnham Saddlers, took over, having moved from 14/15. Tindle Newspapers occupies the first floor from where Sir Ray Tindle controls his country-wide empire of over 125 provincial papers and clutch of radio stations.

Its neighbour to the west, **8**, Halifax bank and Rosebys, is late Georgian, brick-built, with three-pane sashes, a slate roof, open eaves and exposed brackets. For many years it was a butcher's shop. James Betts lived there in 1841 and the Betts were succeeded by Ebenezer Aylwin, who kept his sheep in the churchyard behind. Next came his son, John Maxwell Aylwin, who no doubt aroused local approval when he was the recipient, on the evening of 31st May 1902, of news of the ending of the Boer War. He received these tidings over the telephone from the Officers' Mess of the 7th Hussars in Aldershot, whereupon Farnham's residents took to the streets in joyful celebration.

In due course, Aylwin's gave way to a very different establishment, Madam Emily Chilcott's gown shop, which moved in 1936 from 112. A new front, complete with non-reflective glass was, by all accounts, the talk of the town. This had evolved by 1954 into Franklin & Chilcott: "they cater for those who must be well dressed on a slender budget." By 1971 number 8 was occupied by Dugeys, which sold furniture. Subsequently the single shop was divided into the two units that exist today.

Next door number **9** is a single-bay, three-storey building with identical sash windows and margin panes on both floors. In the late 19th century it was occupied by the Misses L. and M. Legg, milliners. Their successors, Miss I. Walton (1901) and Madame E. Pashler, were also milliners and in about 1909 she advertised "High Class Millinery, Blouses and Skirts". Later, by 1949, optician Hedley Bartlett had moved from 8, where it had been by the mid-1930s. By 1957 the practice had evolved into Bartlett and Austin, which is still in occupation.

Ten West Street is the first of four shops that constitute Elphicks department store. The ground floor is mostly occupied by a brick arch, completed in 1992. This is the site, as the plaque unveiled in 1952 to the right of the most westerly first floor window indicates, of the birth on 4th November 1740 of Augustus Montague Toplady, who wrote the hymn "Rock of Ages" that was published in 1775. His parents, Major Richard Toplady and his wife, did not hail from Farnham but were passing through the town en route to the south coast where the Major was to join his ship. By all accounts the coach journey induced his wife's labour and, unable to find overnight accommodation, they found rooms at 10 West Street. This was then a humble two-storey dwelling.

Subsequently, as J. Alfred Eggar recalled, number 10 "was occupied by a tailor named Fewtrell. Mr John Knight of Bentley bought the house, pulled it down [in 1875], and

Alfred Eggar was also responsible for the design of 10 West Street, left, which was built in the 1870s to harmonize with 11 and 12, its genuine Georgian neighbours.

For over 50 years between 1904 and the 1960s, 2 West Street was occupied by Stratford and Sons butchers which offered "Best Quality English Mutton and Lamb, Prime English and Scotch Beef."

built new premises." These were designed by no less a person than architect-cum-estate agent Eggar himself, who worked and lived at 10/11. His business of Eggar and Company was established in 1870.

The house is of Georgian inspiration, built on three storeys with three bays and three-pane sashes, and no doubt it was intended to match the genuine article at 11 next door. Eggar was also responsible for the tile-hung fourth floor extension perched on the roof. When he moved in 1906 to 74 Castle Street, number 10 and the neighbouring 11 were converted into shops.

Ten became the Farnham branch of outfitters Nelson and Goodrick, who had premises at Fleet, Farnborough and Aldershot. Its neighbours at **11**, E. Canute and Co, were in a similar line. By 1937, they had been taken over by Nelson and Goodrick which survived until 1960.

Number 11 dates from the mid-18th century and it was occupied then by Robert Page, who was a member of a local family with many property interests. Later, in the 1830s, it was owned by John, William and Mary Knight. Subsequently, on 15th August 1860, it became the Farnham branch of the London and Counties Bank. This followed an approach, in March of that year, from brewer George Trimmer; the board decided that "no time be lost in opening a Branch Bank in the town."

The first manager, J.T. Edwards, came to Farnham from the company's Stratford office, although in 1862 he moved to the Bank's newly opened Guildford outlet. He was replaced by Henry Goujon, who remained as manager until his retirement in 1898. By this time the business had outstripped the confines of 11 West Street. After just five years, in 1865, it moved to purpose-built premises at 37 The Borough.

Following the departure of Nelson and Goodrick in 1960, the shops were taken over by Elphicks and reconstructed. John Maxwell Aylwin was the architect, a new shopfront was fitted and, in September, 10 and 11 became the store's Junior Shop.

Elphicks had occupied number **12**, with its easterly archway, since it acquired the property in 1969. It has a three-storey, parapeted, brick frontage, and the initials RS and a date of 1767 are visible on the rainwater head. Although this has been transferred from number 13, the date is approximately correct. This building replaced an earlier structure which was the home of another of

Farnham's lost pubs which was recorded in 1720 as The White Horse. But by the mid-18th century it had been renamed The White Lion.

The 1890s saw it occupied by Messrs Johnson & Son, who were drapers. Their shop was, remembered Alfred Eggar, "the meeting place for certain Farnham celebrities, Messrs Johnson Senior and Howard Johnson, George Trimmer, James Knight, Henry Goujon, and an occasional interloper", who we must surmise was the estate agent himself.

In 1908 the premises were taken over by Robins Brothers' Farnham Dairy Company, "all our utensils cleaned by steam apparatus", late of 16 East Street. This was a business that in 1956 advertised its cafeteria at number 12 and its dairy at Weydon Lane, opened in 1952.

Then in 1969 came the news that Elphicks had acquired the buildings and its adjoining yard, following the sale in 1968 of Robins' erstwhile business to Chichester Dairies. This gave the store a continuous frontage from 10 to 13 West Street.

Elphicks, "Not to be beaten for price, style, or quality" as the company claimed in 1906, has been an integral part of the Farnham commercial scene since 1881. It was in September of that year that George and Mary Elphick and their five children left their small London drapery business at 13 Prince's Terrace, Waltham Green, for the town. The Elphicks had acquired, for £4000, **13** West Street and the stock of the bankrupted Chilton and Scammell, which had run a drapery business there since 1869. The premises took the form of a house with a fine pedimented doorway that was located directly below the Venetian window that can still be seen on the first floor of the property. These features marked the western end of the house, part of which may be of medieval origin. It was built on the site of The Antelope back in 1604 that was to become one of Farnham's principal coaching inns in the 18th century.

In 1764 the property was acquired by Richard Sumner, a doctor, and his rebuilding dates from 1767. (Remember the rainwater head on number 12?) Subsequently, in the early 19th century, it was occupied by Richard Drinkwater, who was also a doctor, and it was acquired by Richard Chilton in 1869.

As far as the brick frontage to the west is concerned, that was occupied by a shopfront and conceals a fairly large timber-framed building which could date from the

15th century. One such aspect was revealed during work undertaken on the building in the early 1960s. But the house was gradually absorbed into the business, although the Georgian doorway, which had almost disappeared under the welter of wares, survived into the post-First World War years.

When Elphicks celebrated its centenary in 1981, Maurice Elphick, George's grandson, was chairman. Two years later work began on a major reconstruction which was completed in March 1984, and marked the arrival of Farnham's first escalator. Further changes followed in 1992. Today Maurice's son Allan is guiding this thriving family business into the 21st century.

The neighbouring Sharps Bedrooms occupies **14**, its doors being flanked by a pair of cast-iron Ionic columns. The premises had been so united by the 1890s. This is a three-storey, late Georgian frontage finished in stucco with four bays and with three-pane sashes on the third. By 1890 number 15 was the office of architect Paxton Hood Watson (see page 25). In 1901 numbers 14/15 were occupied by C.W. Jackman, a tailor and habit maker, "late Ellis from Regent Street" who was also a hatter, "all goods made on the premises". By 1906 he also had a Haselmere branch. By the 1950s it was occupied by greengrocer R. Hewitt, who survived into the 1970s.

The adjoining Church Passage runs to St Andrew's and the Church of England School, the latter dating from 1860. It is the work John Colston of Winchester, who had been diocesan architect since 1855. Executed in the familiar Victorian scholastic gothic, thankfully it is not built of brick but stone and the clunch walls harmonize with those of the nearby church.

On the other side of the Passage and now The Carphone Warehouse, number **16/17** is solid piece of Victoriana with its two-storey brick frontage, open eaves with paired bracketing and four first-floor sashes with moulded architraves. This was built in 1867 by William Kingham, who was Farnham's grandest grocer. The shop's original decorated projecting capitals can still be seen either side of the present shopfront.

Its development should be viewed in conjunction with number **18** next door, now A-Plan Insurance. Of three floors, with an early 19th-century frontage, an easterly arch once gave access to Kingham's yard at the rear. From the

A long time denizen of West Street, William Kingham was responsible for building 16/17 in 1867 and the business was to remain there until 1959. This photograph was taken in February of that year, just prior to Kingham's departure.

1820s it was occupied by Henry Gosden Gray, a grocer and cheesemonger, who on 1st May 1852 sold his business to 28-year-old William Kingham, who had "been accustomed to the London Markets". Just a week before, he had married Anne Box and they were to have 12 children, of whom three died in infancy. Four were to be directly involved in the grocery business. However, Henry Gray continued to occupy part of the premises although Kingham and his friends had "the right and use of walking in the garden". Later, ironmongery, glass and china were sold here.

To the east, 16 was a long, narrow building that ran alongside Church Passage and this and the neighbouring 17 were demolished to make way for the present shop. This development coincided with William's father-in-law acquiring number 18 and in 1876 he sold it to his son-in-law.

With quality and service as Kingham's watchwords, in 1880 his eldest son Robert became a partner, followed in 1884 by Robert's brother Howard. At this point the business became William Kingham and Sons. The two younger brothers, Herbert and Alfred, followed in 1891 and William retired four years later. Robert stepped down in 1926 and control passed to Alfred. Outside his office, remembered a former employee, "was a landing where, like a captain on the bridge, he peered down into the shop, watching for any sign that those customers were not being accorded the civility to which they were entitled."

Kingham's, renowned for its window displays, rapidly expanded. In 1910 the Lion and Lamb Hotel opposite was acquired (see page 214), a wholesale business was established in 1920 and in 1927 a functional Georgian-style brick warehouse was built at the rear of 17/18. Further afield, a Reading branch had opened in 1886, while a corporate outpost at Chippenham, Wiltshire dated from 1942.

The company celebrated its centenary in 1952 when chairman Geoffrey Kingham, who was Howard's son, declared: "We are still a family business." This status only lasted for a further 12 years for in 1964 Kingham's was acquired for some £983,000 by the Liverpool-based Morris and David Jones group.

But the days of their West Street shops were, in any event, numbered. The Southern Electricity Board was occupying 18 by 1954, while builder's merchants G.A. Day took over 16/17 in 1959. However, Kingham's continued to operate its wholesale business and in 1964 a new warehouse was built on the Farnham Trading Estate. There it ran its "cash and carry" Catering Services division with Booker Belmont continuing to operate for a time.

What since 1997 has been **Ye Olde Flyer** next door at 19 was previously, from about the middle of the 18th century, known as The Wheatsheaf. Prior to that it was named The Spreadeagle. The present two-storey brick frontage with its mansard roof dates from the 20th century. From the 1770s The Wheatsheaf was owned by the Knight family and it accordingly passed to Reid's. The presence of the nearby art school between 1939 and 1977 meant that it was a favoured

Quality was Kingham's watchword and this is no more apparent than in this robust Neo-Georgian warehouse which dates from 1927 and adjoins St Andrew's churchyard.

venue for members of its staff and students alike. But by the 1980s, the atmosphere was quiet, almost select.

Between The Wheatsheaf and 20A is what was Penfold's Yard. It was so named in the 1840s because this prosperous Farnham family, of Guildford House, Castle Street, had a cottage and kiln there. Later passing to Harold Falkner, it is at the rear of his house at 24 West Street. In 2001 it was acquired by developers, Country and Metropolitan. They sold the site to Fairclough Homes and in 2002 a small housing development, Kingham Place, was built there overlooking the church.

To the west of the entrance is what was 20 but in the 1980s that number was allocated to owner Darrell Romer's first-floor orthodontist practice and the shop became **20A**. This and the neighbouring 21 are respectively occupied by Toto Classics and Toto Tots. It is a brick, three-storey, three-bay building with a frontage which dates from the late 18th century. It conceals an earlier building of mid-16th century ancestry and 20A contains an original inglenook fireplace. At the turn of the 19th century, it was occupied by a Miss Whiten and by 1936 wool specialist Laurette was in residence. Since the 1970s it has variously played host to Whispers, Help the Aged and The Helping Hand, prior to the arrival of the current occupants in 1993.

But 20A also contains one of Farnham's hidden architectural treasures. You only need to cast your eyes upwards to view a remarkable 17th-century plaster ceiling. It came to light as recently as 1926 and was found concealed behind a Victorian ceiling when Harold Falkner was installing a new shopfront.

Following an accident when a pipe burst in the shop over the Christmas of 1986, the ceiling was restored by local builder Barry Eade. The original is reputed to be the work of John Jones, an apprentice of the architect Inigo Jones. Measuring some 10 feet x 20 feet (3 x 6m) and weighing about two tons, it is thought to be a miniature version of a ceiling commissioned by the Earl of Shaftsbury for his "small" 20 feet by 40 feet (6 x 12m) drawing room of St Giles House at Wimborne St Giles, Dorset.

The owner of 20 at the time is not known, but prior to 1716 it was London haberdasher John Watts. Later, in 1836, a one-third share in the The New Inn was owned by brewer Abraham Crowley of Alton and it may have occupied the site.

The magnificent plaster ceiling of what today is Toto ladies wear shop at 20A West Street, dates from the 17th century. Its presence was not discovered until 1926.

Next door number **21** was at the turn of the 19th century run by T. Lunn, who was a grocer, and later by a baker – the ovens survive in the cellar. From the 1930s it was occupied by A.C. Freeman's West End Radio, a business that was subsequently taken over by Mr and Mrs Edward Clayton, who permitted prospective purchasers to watch television in Lloyd Loom chairs they had thoughtfully provided. Their business closed in July 1983.

Watch repairer R.H. Marshall has occupied **22** West Street since 1968, having taken it over from Georgian Cottage Antiques. A single-bay, three-storey, pebble-dashed house, with an appropriately 18th-century frontage, a three-by-three-pane sash window on the first floor complements a three-by-two window above. Originally the doorhead was canopied. The building was a private dwelling, only being converted into a shop in about 1950 when the present bow window was installed.

Next door is the gloriously Georgian **23** and **24**, which may have been the work of Daniel Batchelour, a local builder and speculator. Dated 1790 on their rainwater heads, these were removed in recent years and, thankfully, they are now on display at the Museum of Farnham. By the

1830s both properties were jointly owned by the Knight family, namely John, William and Mary, and they remained so allied for many years. Number 23 is of three bays, on two storeys with parapet and frieze below with a pedimented doorway in the third bay. By about 1872 architect Sidney Stapley (see page 22) was in practice there.

It was also his family home and his daughter Jessie married local builder John Goddard, whose grandfather had founded the East Street business. She remained at number 23 until she died in the 1970s at the age of 96. The house subsequently became student accommodation, along with the neighbouring 24.

This is similar, although of five bays with a central doorway. As a plaque on the wall indicates, this was the home of Harold Falkner, who lived there from 1897 until his death in 1963. His mother, Mary Falkner, moved there following the demise of her husband in 1875. When Harold qualified in 1897, his niece, Miss Beryl Falkner, recalled that the first thing he built "was a bathroom for his mother on the back of 24 West Street with which she was very pleased as very few houses in Farnham – if any – had a bathroom in the early 1890s."

In later years part of the house was let for offices; The Motor Union Insurance Company had occupancy in 1952. But on Falkner's death in 1963 he left the property to the Farnham Society for use as a museum for Georgian artefacts. Unfortunately, it was unable to accept the bequest because it did not possess the funds for the necessary refurbishment. In November 1965 the property was therefore auctioned and was acquired for £9000 by Surrey County Council as student accommodation for the adjoining art school. The exception was a ground-floor room which was leased by Peter Gosling until 1971 to accommodate an antiques shop.

Sadly by the 1990s this historic house was showing the effects of neglect and vandalism, its windows were broken and its street frontage unkempt. But what had become the Surrey Institute of Art and Design expanded in The Hart in 2001 and the West Street properties were sold to developers Country Metropolitan. Number 24 was acquired by WhiteOaks Public Relations which had outgrown its premises at 26 Downing Street. It moved in June 2001 and the house has been refurbished by Arcadia Ventures.

The next door property, number **25**, since January 1978

Falkner's Fireplaces: 5

A late 19th-century register grate in which the cream and green tiles have been used to decorative and practical ends. They occupy what is called the slip, which is the space between the fireplace surround and grate. A hood, that was sometimes adjustable, is featured here.

the **Adult Learning Centre**, occupies a site that from 1758 has played host to four scholastic establishments. The present building was developed in two stages with a 19-year interval between them. Rebuilt in Victorian "modified Gothic", much favoured for schools and colleges, it replaced two houses with "Georgian" facades. Neighbour Harold Falkner regarded this construction as indicative of a lack of appreciation for 18th-century building in Farnham at this time.

With a frontage of yellow-grey bricks, the easterly section was built in 1875. It is gabled with mullioned ground floor windows, and a quartet of slim lancets above. The remainder, carefully essayed by Paxton Hood Watson, with a complementary wing, bears the date of 1894 above the front door.

Farnham Grammar School dates from 1578, when it was installed in St Andrew's Lady Chapel although this was demolished in 1758 and the school transferred to 25 West Street. At this time the western part of the timber-framed premises were jettied. Later, in the 19th century, workmen from Leadbeater's hop-bagging works in Factory Yard opposite were wont to shelter under the overhanging storey. However, headmaster Dr Samuel Locke believed that their language was particularly unedifying for his pupils so he had a false front installed which removed the protective alcove. When this house was demolished in 1894, two carved pillars were discovered.

In 1906 the School moved to its purpose-designed building in Morley Road, now Farnham Sixth Form College. In September of that year its place was taken by the Girls' Grammar School which arrived via 74 Castle Street and East Street. The cost of converting the building was £1200, of which the Farnham UDC contributed £500.

24 25

The Girls were destined to remain at 25 West Street until 1939 when, bursting at the seams, the school moved to new premises in Menin Way, now South Farnham School.

The vacuum was rapidly filled by the Farnham School of Art which had also outgrown the confines of its building in South Street. The Principal, Otway McCannell, appointed in 1928, remained there for the duration of the war. He left in 1945 and was replaced by artist and engraver James Hockey, who arrived at West Street after having taught at Kingston and Wimbledon art schools. He was destined to fill the post until his retirement in 1971. The art school evolved in 1969 into the West Surrey College of Art and Design and it remained at West Street until 1977, although the foundation course continued there into the 1990s when it too was transferred to Falkner Road.

There was a time, at around the turn of the 19th century, when the ground room of number **26** next door was used by the Grammar School boys. Dating from the middle of that century, the house, with its distinctive cement-rendered frontage, was probably the creation of professor of music Edwin Merriott. It was built on the site of a property that, in 1811, had been sold for £1050 by Richard Turner to the Marquis of Lothian. He was then living at Vernon House, a few doors further down West Street.

It was subsequently acquired in 1919 by solicitor John Robert Nash, senior partner of Hollest, Mason and Nash, who were across the road at 94. On his death in 1937 it became the home and office of Farnham architect Guy Maxwell Aylwin, who extended it to the south. The practice was continued by his son, John, until the 1980s. Since 2000 it has been occupied by his daughter, solicitor Joanne Aylwin.

Number 26, for a time acted as an overflow to the school for the clergy at 27 next door, which is now **The Bishop's Table Hotel**. Similarly cement-rendered with an 18th-century frontage, it was acquired in 1808 by the fifth Marquis of Lothian. This meant that the family owned a large block of West Street, from number 25 to Willmer House. There were other acquisitions on the north side.

The fifth Marquis died in 1815 and 27 was acquired by John Newman, a local doctor, whose family provided medical practitioners in Farnham and its immediate vicinity. It subsequently passed to S.G. Sloman, who was listed in 1891 as a surgeon. By 1901 it was a training school for the clergy with Reverend T.G. Gardiner in occupation.

Ceasing to be the Bishop's Hostel in 1919, it was acquired in that year by Charles Borelli and in the 1930s it became Mrs Summers Cox's Newnham House guest house. This closed in 1961 and it passed to Oliver Moxon who re-named it The Bishop's Table. The present owners, Kass and Mariam Verjee, arrived in 1986.

Vernon House, now occupied by **Farnham Library**, is a many-faceted house although the once creeper-clad West Street frontage is perhaps the least prepossessing aspect. Both wings were cut back in 1721, hence the blank end walls; the date appears on both rainwater heads. Another date, 1881, can be seen above them which may indicate when the frontage was rendered in cement. At the rear is a late Victorian south-western extension which dates from the Knight family's occupancy of the house. Built of yellow-grey bricks with a full-length bay window at its western end, it replaced a lower two-storey, Georgian-style frontage with a parapet and dormer windows

This is 28 West Street and it is named Vernon House because Sir Thomas White left the property to Henry and Joan Vernon in 1635. At that time it was named Culver Hall, a name that persisted for some 150 years. It may have indicated the presence of a dovecot, culver being an old name for a dove or wood pigeon. It remained in the Vernon family until 1804, when Anne Vernon died. In 1764 she had married Dr John Butler of Winchester, who became Bishop of Hereford.

26 **_The Bishop's Table_**

Anne was the last of the line and what was now named Vernon House was acquired in 1806 by the Marquis of Lothian. His son William, the sixth Marquis, sold it in 1844 to local banker and brewer James Knight. He may have been responsible for rendering the West Street frontage. In 1891 his son John, a solicitor, was living there.

It was subsequently acquired by Duncan Norfolk Bethune, a relative of the Knights. However, between the wars it became run down and neglected. In 1928 Alfred Eggar proposed that it should house the town's library, then squeezed into Brightwell House off East Street, and a museum. By 1936 the building was empty and Charles Borelli headed a committee to pursue Eggar's idea. But in the meantime, Bethune was negotiating with builder Arthur Mardon to convert Vernon House into a garage (!) and he submitted plans to Farnham UDC to that effect. Thankfully, in April 1937, these were rejected.

Mardon then hinted that if the Council would pay him and his wife a £200 annuity for the remainder of their lives, the property would pass to them. Instead a price was fixed, later reduced to £1500, and in 1939 the councillors agreed, but in the face of protests from the Ratepayers' Association.

Surrey County Council's Farnham Library was transferred from Brightwell House in 1949, although a much needed single-storey extension was not completed until 1990. Taking a Victorian garden room as his inspiration, County Architect Chris Jolley created a building wholly in sympathy with Vernon House and its grounds.

Farnham Library

Farnham's Royal Roof

Westminster Hall's magnificent roof, credited with being the finest hammer-beam structure in the world and the largest in northern Europe, was constructed in Farnham in the late 14th century.

We have the Bishop of Winchester, William Wykeham, to thank for the fact that it was constructed here because he had already commissioned Hugh Herland, who was King Richard II's chief carpenter, to design the roof for his college chapel at Winchester. Herland would have also been able to examine the fine 13th-century scissor roof of the Bishop's Camera at Farnham Castle.

Also executed by royal command, work began in 1394 No less than 660 tons (670 tonnes) of oak were used. This came mainly from Alice Holt Forest but also from as far afield as Hertfordshire and Sussex. Erected at "the Frame by Farnham", it was then dismantled and in mid-1395 transported by wagons to a wharf at Hamme, near Chertsey, from where it was taken down the Thames by barge to Westminster. It was completed by 1400.

But where was "the Frame"? It is thought to have been located at what today is Arundell Place, off West Street which was previously known as Timberclose. And the carpenters may have resided nearby at ☛

To the immediate west are numbers **29**, **30** and **31**. They are deceptive because, outwardly, they appear to be colour-washed brick-faced cottages. In fact they were once one building, a three-bay medieval house with an easterly gabled end, jettied on the first floor which housed the solar, an adjoining open hall with smoke bay and a service area at its western extremity. In 1806 it was described as "formerly called Timber Hall" and in the 14th century may have housed the carpenters who were constructing the great hammer-beam roof that was destined for Westminster Hall (see accompanying notes).

A timber-framed building is also concealed by the mid-19th-century frontage of **32/32B** and **32C**. For much of the 19th century 32 was a baker's shop, first occupied by William Pullinger and later (prior to 1850) by Stephen Smither. By 1901 it was the home of another bakery and grocer's shop; West Street Stores, as it was named, survived into the 1970s, latterly under P.A.G. Elsmore's ownership. It occupies two separate timber-framed buildings, one positioned behind the other. The rear structure is almost complete. The roof frame is said to date from the early 16th century.

Three storeys, four-pane sash windows and pedimented doorways might suggest a late Georgian house but **33** and **33A** conceal a timber-framed structure of much greater age. Like 29/31 to the east, it was also known as Timber Hall. This was the home of Stephen Elmer who is listed as having lived there in 1769. Unusually, he succeeded in combining the trade of maltster with being an Associate of the Royal Academy. The son of an artist, Elmer's speciality was paintings of fish and game, whether dead or alive. He was also responsible for *The Last Supper,* once an altarpiece in St Andrew's Church, which today can be seen on the staircase wall at the Museum of Farnham.

The refronting, which was cement-rendered from the outset, had been completed by 1822 when John Hassell made a painting of the property. This shows 33 with a shopfront and, if you stand on the opposite side of West Street, its outline is still discernible. In 1867 it was occupied by Thomas Turner, who made boots and shoes, "orders by post promptly attended to", and who also sold furniture. His business expanded into a double-fronted shop but the property was sold in 1931, following Turner's death, and it subsequently reverted to private occupancy.

Numbers **34** to **37** date from 1834 and were built, speculatively, by James Garfath, whose yard was at 85 opposite. The frontages of 34, **35** and **36** survive today much as they were built. Of three storeys with two bays apiece, Garfath may have been concerned about the window tax because there are no sashes above the pedimented front doors.

Number 37 has been twice altered. In 1872 it was listed as a public house called The Holly Bush. William Orford was named as the landlord in 1901. Fake beams were applied to the exterior to "Tudorize" it in the way that the Alliance on the corner of Downing Street had been decorated. Two years later it was acquired by Farnham United Breweries. It consequently passed to Courage in 1927 and survived for a further ten years.

In the 1950s it was converted into a shop, horizontal windows replaced the original sashes and the frontage was rendered. In the 1970s it was Bits and Pieces junk shop, and until recently it was a Tindle Enterprise Centre. It is currently the home of Back to Front Exterior Design.

Flanking the adjacent Bishop's Mead is **Willmer House**, home of the Museum of Farnham. Unlike many of the properties in West Street, this is not a re-faced older structure but was built new in 1718. However, a Tudor brick cellar just behind the property on a north-south axis survives at the western end of the site which suggests the presence of an earlier building.

This is one of the town's two Grade I listed houses, the other being The Grange in Castle Hill. Unfortunately the name of its perhaps London-domiciled architect is not known. Of robust Baroque design, there are three storeys and five bays, the frontage being built of small, soft bricks with a high sand content that could be easily rubbed or sawn into shape. These are used to produce what Ian Nairn has described as "one of the finest cut brick facades in the country". This particularly relates to the architraves of the first-floor windows which, along with the slightly projecting central bay, help to prevent the frontage from being repetitious. The sash windows appear to be of the same dimensions throughout; in fact those on the second floor are slightly shorter than the rest.

Each floor is marked by a string course and there are rusticated pilasters at the extremities of the frontage. Behind the panelled parapet are five small pitched

Timberhall, what is now 29-31 West Street. An alternative theory places the Frame at Farnham Castle. Whatever its exact location, this majestic roof, which covers a huge span of 69 feet (21m) without supporting pillars remains a tribute to Herland's formidible skill and to the carpenters who were each paid 6d. (2.5p) a day.

The greatest threat that the roof encountered, apart from the ravages of death-watch beetle, which in 1914 necessitated the introduction of unobtrusive steel beams, was during the Second World War.

In an air raid on the night of 10/11th May 1941, the Hall, along with the House of Commons chamber, was hit by German incendiary bombs. There were not sufficient pumps or water to save both buildings, to the concern of Conservative MP, Colonel Walter Elliot, also director of public relations for the War Office, who was present.

In consultation with Chief Superintendent C.P. McDuell of the London Fire Service, they decided to concentrate the efforts of the fire fighters on saving the medieval building. In this they were successful and Westminster Hall and its magnificent 14th century roof survived, at the expense of the Commons, which was destroyed in the conflagration. Although a magnificent Victorian Gothic building, it only dated from 1852.

roofs that run diagonally across the property.

While "rubbers" are used for the frontage, they contrast with those of the remainder of the walls which are of a conventional size and quality. The door surround is of wood and flanked by stone Tuscan pilasters. Interestingly, the architrave bears what Nairn describes as "the favourite London mason's motif of a central upward cusp" which might suggest the influence of the capital city.

Inside, the panelling is mostly of pine, although oak is used in the eastern back room and for the mantelpiece which incorporates a broken pediment, another Baroque feature. The staircase is also of oak and has turned banisters and ogee mouldings beneath the steps. It is thought that it might have been intended for another house because, on the landing, the accompanying panelling awkwardly projects above a window sill. Alternatively the staircase might have been moved during an internal reworking of the house in the 19th century.

Outwardly it appears today much as it was built although the "annexe" on the western side which houses the Museum's local history collection, with offices above, dates from 1866. The site had previously been occupied by a brew house.

Willmer House was completed for John Thorne, his initials and the date of 1718 can be seen on the drainpipe heads. He was a maltster and hop merchant with hop

Willmer House, right, which today houses the Museum of Farnham, dates from 1718. Its rubbed brick frontage is of national stature, although the architect is unknown.

grounds at Runwick, Dippenhall and The Ridgeway. The affluent Thorne was also for a time owner of The George Inn at the north-eastern end of West Street. But in 1739 he filed for bankruptcy, although his home was held in trust for his wife and children. By 1747 the house had passed to his son, also called John, although by 1756 it was owned by Samuel Slater, who was a brewer. He sold off some of the house's grounds to John Manwaring, who was his hop-merchant neighbour, and he built what is now Sandford House next door. Following Slater's death in 1780, the house passed to Stephen Elmer, the artist, although not apparently a struggling one. He lived at 33 West Street, and continued to do so until his death. In 1787 this fine property was acquired by brewer Robert Trimmer, who had occupied the brew house since 1765.

The building takes its name from two sisters, Fanny and Nancy Willmer from Petersfield, who purchased it in 1808. Both were fluent in French and in 1810 they opened the Willmer House School for Young Ladies. This lasted until 1842 and the scholastic tradition was maintained by the establishment of Thomas Hunter's School for Boys which survived until about 1860.

At this point it reverted to being a private residence when it was acquired by Mrs Caroline Paine, who was step-daughter of Nancy Willmer, and also owned the adjoining Sandford House. Later it was leased to the Misses Potter and in 1876 the "very substantially built" residence was sold to James Sidney Longhurst, a dentist and erstwhile pupil of the boys' school. He lived and practised there from 1876 and it remained in his family until his son Sidney died in 1924.

It was bought at auction in 1925 by Mrs Charles Burke who on her death in 1939 left it to her sister, Mrs Holmes. She did not wish to live in it and, during the war, it housed a unit of the Canadian Army. When the owner died in 1943, Willmer House was acquired by Canon Campbell Crum, rector of Farnham in the years between 1912 and 1928, when he departed for the canonry of Canterbury. He lived in Willmer House until his death in 1958. To his family's eternal credit, they felt that it should be made available to the local authority with the result that the property passed to Surrey County Council in 1960. It opened as the town's museum in the following year. Charles Borelli would certainly have approved.

Sandford House dates from 1757, and like the neighbouring but earlier Willmer House, was built by a member of the town's affluent hop-growing community. The extension on the right is Victorian.

The neighbouring **Sandford House** was completed some 40 years later than Willmer House in 1757, and built, as already noted, for John Manwaring, a member of a local family which progressed from tanning leather to the more lucrative trade in hops. Of five bays and three storeys, like its neighbour it possesses full-length sashes throughout. The centre projecting bay is surmounted by a stone pediment and coping which is repeated in brick above the third-floor window and on the door surround. This is another Baroque frontage.

Apart from the west wing, which is a 19th-century extension, the front of the house appears much as it did when it was built. But alterations were made in the Victorian period to the rear when a veranda with metal supports and canopy was built across the full width of the building. This involved bringing the ground-floor windows of the westerly back room forward to align with the front of the veranda which projects some six feet (1.8m).

Inside the entrance hall is wood-panelled, as is the north-west room on the first floor. Like its neighbour, it has a fine oak staircase with turned and fluted banisters.

The name of Sandford House is relatively recent. When in 1936 the Reverend and Mrs G.S. Bird acquired the property it was plain 39 West Street, although local tradition named it The College because the forerunner of the Royal Military Academy, Sandhurst once stood opposite. The new owners thought that a name was more appropriate and Mrs Bird chose Sandford House after her previous home, Sandford House, at Kirkstall near Leeds. It had been named after Sir Sandford Graham, who acquired it from Lord Cardigan, of Crimean War fame, in settlement of a gambling debt.

The Birds left in 1946 and by 1952 Major G.V.H. Gough was in residence. In 1957 Mrs Douglas Gordon, granddaughter of Richard Combe of Pierrepont, Frensham, purchased the house and lived there for some 12 years. In October 1969 Captain J.A. Venables successfully applied to have the ground floor changed from a residential designation so that it might be used as an antiques shop. In 1986 it was on the market for £300,000 and during that year it became the Surrey Language Centre which occupies the property today.

Sandford House's westerly neighbour, **Wickham House**, is not quite what it appears to be. Of three storeys and three bays with a parapet, featuring sashes with exposed surrounds and a canopied door-case, its frontage might be thought to date from the early 18th century. In fact it was completed in 1931 to the design of Harold Falkner. It does, however, complement the rest of the house which dates from this time.

At one time it belonged to the Manwaring family next door, but by 1872 it was occupied by brewer Sampson Sampson, previously of 18 Bridge Square. A Captain Garnier was the occupant in 1891 and solicitor Edgar Kempson was there in 1901. From the late 1940s until the 1960s it was the home of Sir Alwyne Ogden, who from 1912 until 1948 was in the consular service in China.

The Manwaring family also for a time owned what is now numbers **41** and **42** which was named Elmer House. This property was built in two phases. The eastern portion of five bays dates from about 1780 to 1785 with blind arcading on the ground floor, also seen in 61 Castle Street. The second section, which was attractively built at an angle to the original to follow the line of West Street, was completed in the 1850s in the same style. This is probably when the original multi-pane sashes were replaced by the two-pane windows that both properties still retain.

Sold by the Manwarings in 1834, it passed, via William and George Knight, to Richard Mason in 1869. A solicitor, clerk to the Local Board since its formation in 1866, he continued in that position with Farnham UDC until his death in 1910. Mason named the property Elmer House after artist Stephen Elmer of 33 West Street, and his collection of that artist's paintings was displayed there.

Wickham House with its frontage by Harold Falkner, who is reputed to have also carved the decorated brackets supporting the door canopy.

Wright's Lion Brewery Stores, an off-licence that dates back to 1893 when Farnham United Breweries occupied this part of West Street. The Brewery's erstwhile entrance is in the left foreground.

In 1936 number 41 became the First Church of Christ, Scientist, which occupied the building until 1956 when it moved to East Street and later, in 1965, to a purpose-designed church in Bear Lane. From 1952 the West Street premises housed St Christopher's preparatory school which closed in 1992. In 1993 the building, now named St Christophers House, was divided into luxury apartments. During the conversion, original Adam-style fireplaces were discovered behind panelling. A former coach house and the one-time school gymnasium at the rear of the property were similarly enhanced.

Numbers **43** and **45**, two storey with a mansard roof, also date from the 19th century. In 1891 R. Wicks, butcher, baker and grocer, was listed at 43 and 44. This business was taken over by Frost and Co., who then occupied 44 to 46. By 1901 it was Bond & Jerome, grocer's and butcher's shop. In the 1950s and 1960s The Empire Stores was located at 43.

Next door, **46,** is an 18th-century cottage-style property although the abruptly curtailed easterly wall suggests that it was once a larger building. It is thought that The Black Horse alehouse was here and in the mid-18th century and it was the home of Thomas Westbrook, who also owned The Spreadeagle further down West Street. It still existed in 1785 but does not appear in an 1839 Farnham directory. From the interwar years until the 1950s it was Davis's confectioners.

The creeper-clad, brick, two-storey shop now occupied by Venus Video, number **46A**, dates from the 1950s and replaced modest premises with a distinctive Dutch-style gable. Between the wars this was G. Hopper's Carmen's Café which was still there in 1954.

The Farnham Tandoori Restaurant, **47**, which opened in 1983, occupies a mid-19th-century, two-storey building on the western side of Mead Lane which once housed The Rose and Thistle pub. By 1872 it was owned by George Trimmer, then it became a Farnham United Breweries property and it survived as a Courage house until 1934. At the time of its closure it was reputed to be smallest licensed premises in the country! It evolved into the Farnham Fish Bar which lasted until the early 1980s.

The adjoining building, Meads Guest House and L. and G. Stylists hairdressers, which are both numbered 48, date from the mid-1950s. At the turn of the 19th century,

A.W. Davis, a boot- and shoemaker was at **48**, as was James Burchett, who had taken over the business of Thomas Trusler, a nurseryman, florist and seedsman. Burchett's house and shop, which he purchased in 1916, were set back from the road. There was a long greenhouse in front of them which flanked the pavement and ran parallel with West Street. His business closed in 1953 and the present property, which was brought forward to align with 47, was built in its place probably by F.E.G. Brockway and Sons which was then based at 48. Its works were in Mead Lane behind its offices. The adjoining **Vernon Court** flats, also by Brockway, date from 1956 and were built on the site of Burchett's nursery garden.

What is now **Old Town Mews** was built in 1997 where a shop and beer house called The White Hart, owned after 1809 by John and James Knight, once stood. The Farnham Brewery offered it for sale in 1891. In 1901 J.Spencer was named as licensee and not long afterwards the building was destroyed in a fire. It was then acquired by George Elliott, an "engineer and millwright, van, wagon and cart builder", owner of the nearby Reliance Works, who lived at 44 Downing Street.

Elliott died in December 1912 at the age of 83 and in the following year Heath and Wiltshire purchased 49 West Street and converted it into a garage. This company occupied the premises until 1960 when the business was taken over by British Car Auctions. But it was empty in June 1994 when an application was made to demolish it.

George Elliott's name (although it could refer to his father) also appears on the gable of **50** West Street, a no-nonsense industrial building of brick with stone dressing and at one time double doors opening on to West Street. A plaque, unveiled in 1985, indicates that it was there in 1895 that George Parfitt built John Henry Knight's car that was one of Britain's first petrol-powered automobiles.

Following Elliott's death, the property was sold in 1913 but it is best remembered, from 1946, as the St John Ambulance Station which, in July 1963, was transferred to The Hart. In 1985 the Middlesex-based Griffon Land Estate

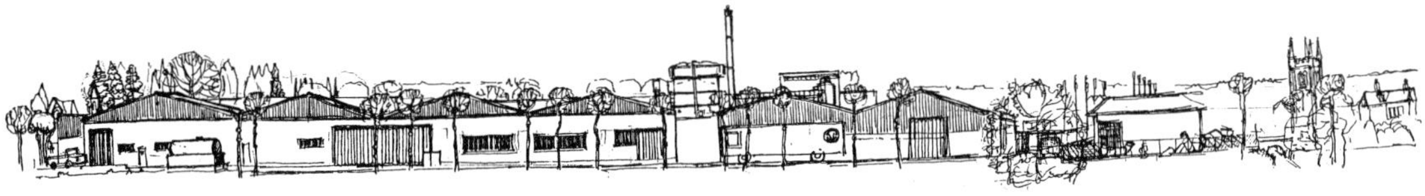

Crosby occupied its West Street location from 1939 until its closure in 1991. Now only the name of Crosby Way, which has been built on part of the factory site, is a reminder of its one-time presence.

applied to redevelop the site into offices, having retained Farnham architects, the Haworth King Partnership. Waverley Borough Council agreed, although it specified that changes to the exterior of Elliott's former premises should be kept to a minimum. Since 1992, number 50 has been occupied by accountants, Wise and Company.

Moving on, past the site of The Fox and Hounds pub, which was 57 West Street from the 1850s until it closed in August 1967, we arrive at Crosby Way. It is named after the last occupant of the Lion Brewery site. This was established in 1857 by George Trimmer, principally to serve the newly established army camp at Aldershot; it was destined to be the hub of his Farnham United Breweries empire. It would eventually encompass 161 tied houses. But what had become the town's largest employer was, in April 1927, acquired by Courage and the brewing ceased there on 30th June 1928. This was thereafter concentrated at Alton, Courage having acquired Hall's brewery there in 1903. However, the new owners continued to use some of the Farnham buildings as a local depot.

Then, in May 1939, Crosby moved from South Street to the former brewery site. After the war it concentrated on the manufacturer "of panel and flush doors for the building industry" at the Lion Works and consequently much altered the premises. The old brewery buildings flanking West Street were demolished in 1969 but Crosby's brutally angular, dark-bricked replacement, built in 1970, was much disliked.

There was great surprise when in October 1990 Crosby announced the closure of its factory after 114 years in the town and with a loss of 214 jobs. This was completed in April 1991. In 1994 the Council approved the construction of 89 new homes on the eastern part of the site.

The Millennium Centre, by Haworth King, occupied some of the westerly section. Completed in June 1999, it consists of four two- and three-storey, brick, slate-roofed

The Millennium Centre

office buildings built around a central courtyard. It was the work of John Monk, who sadly died just prior to its opening. Although traces of Crosby's presence have all but disappeared, a fragment of George Trimmer's enterprise does survive. Alongside the old Brewery entrance is the **Lion Brewery Stores** (see page 191), opened as an off-licence in 1893, which has been run ever since by four generations of the Wright family.

Historically you are never far away from beer in Farnham and a block of three almshouses on the north-west side of West Street all owe their endowments to a trio of local brewers. **Sampson's Almshouses** date from 1933-34 and were built by Mills & Sons to the designs of Harold Falkner. These replaced similar houses in Mead Lane which had become obsolete. They were demolished after the Second World War, having been fortified during hostilities. After The Chantrys housing estate, built on former hop grounds in 1969, comes **McDonald's Almshouses** erected in 1906 at the behest of hop merchant George McDonald. They were built by Mardon & Mills and designed by Arthur Stedman. **Trimmer's** Tudor-style almshouses were built in 1893 although they are bisected by Mount Pleasant which dates from the mid-1890s.

Further to the east and set back from West Street are a complex of hop kilns which are survivors of the scores that were once scattered throughout the town. These are named **Newnhams**, after the hop-growing family which built them. They consist of an original square kiln joined in the mid-19th century by two of the latest circular type. A second and larger pair were added in about 1890. By this time owned by George Trimmer, in 1920 Newnhams passed to building contractor W.J. Wilkinson, which used them until this business closed 1972. They passed to Crosby and were converted into its head office by John Chandler of Orman and Scott of Guildford and opened in October 1977. Newnhams is currently undergoing refurbishment as office accommodation.

Number **60** West Street, on the opposite side of Crondall Lane, is interesting because, although "Georgian" in appearance, it actually dates from about 1850. Built by Henry Harding, the bay window is a later addition. In 1901 the house was occupied by auctioneer J.W. Burningham, who was also parish clerk. Along with **61** next door, it was the home of Nigel Temple, author of *Farnham Buildings and People*.

The Jolly Sailor, cement-rendered and colour-washed, is numbers 62 and 63. It was created from a stone terrace dating from the early 19th century. The bay windows on either side of the entrance are of a later date. There was a beer house on the site by 1839 and although it was not known as The Jolly Sailor at that time, it certainly was called that by 1848 when it was owned by Barrett and then Farnham United Breweries. Number **65** next door is brick-faced although stone is apparent on the end wall.

The neighbouring **65A** is what by 1936 was named The New Bungalow. You might expect it to be domestic accommodation, which it is. However, closer inspection reveals it also to be a public convenience!

The adjoining numbers **66** and **67** with their cement-rendered frontages appear to date from the 1860s but are in fact older. In the late 1830s the latter was occupied by Charles Vince, a grocer, who had a shop at 66. By the turn of the 19th century it was the home of J.H. Nash, who was a builder, undertaker and monumental mason.

Sixty-eight was restored in the mid-1930s by architect Guy Maxwell Aylwin, when the present front windows were introduced. In 1981 its owners traced its documented history back to 1763. Then it was sold by Stephen Baker, a shepherd of Moor Park, to William Dowden, a grocer, who acquired it for £44. However, the Surrey Domestic Buildings Research Group found traces of jettying behind the brick facing, along with evidence of an open hall, and dated it to the late 15th century.

More recently, in 1864, it was acquired by George Trimmer for £250 and remained in his family's hands until 1920, at which time it commanded a rental of 8s. (40p) per week. Trimmer did not, of course, live there but he was the occupant of **69** West Street next door, now the home of the Farnham Orthodontic Practice. Of three storeys and five bays, it was conveniently located for Trimmer's Lion Brewery almost opposite. This is a stuccoed 19th-century reworking of an earlier property which in 1832 served as a boys' school. Trimmer died on 15th November 1892 leaving a fortune of £380,385. The house became the Farnham High School for Girls, although by 1910 it was the Cambridge House Private School for Girls.

The cottages, numbers **70** to **73**, colour-washed with tile roofs, have 18th-century brick frontages. In 1959 numbers 70 and 71 were sold for £500 and the neighbouring 72 and 73 attracted a price of £350.

The Plough is 74 West Street although the present building dates from 1933-34. Like The Marlborough Head in East Street, this was owned by Crowley and Company of Alton and is a variation on architect John Howard's half-timbered Tudoresque style. The pub is in truth considerably older, a fact which is apparent from the rear of the premises. In 1839 Mary Cole was listed as the landlady and a succession of breweries owned it prior to Crowleys acquiring the property in 1908. Although still named The Plough, in 1994 the complementary pub sign was replaced by a representation of Edvard Munch's famous picture "The Scream".

Next door, number **75** is outwardly of 19th-century origins, rendered, with moulded architraves to the windows and a fine tiled roof and tile hanging. In the 1890s, as indicated by the still existing shopfront, it housed Miss E.P. Cole's dairy.

It's back to brick for numbers **76**, **77** and **78**. These have two storeys, with dormer windows but no parapet: they date from 1799. Miss E. Trusler was the occupant of 76 in 1901. She was a stay and corset maker. Later, it was the home of artist Rowland Hilder. Next door 77, now Captain Yorke's tobacconists and newsagents, was The Rainbow, which in 1872 was a public house owned by Thomas Mathews and later Farnham United Breweries. It survived as such until 1911.

Potters Gate *76* *77* *78* *Beaver House*

Its later Victorian neighbour, **79**, dates from about 1870 and was built for Charles Attfield, who was a maltster and corn dealer. Named Beaver House, it overlooked Beavers Yard, which was named after a family of important hop planters in 18th-century Farnham. Brick built with stone dressing and a stuccoed ground floor, its open eaves with paired brackets echo those of the neighbouring block, although they are less obtrusive. The house passed to George Trimmer and his family continued to own it until 1905.

By 1887 the Misses Stroud were running their "boarding school for young ladies and preparatory school for boys" there. This subsequently moved to 1 Station Hill. Sidney German established an estate agency at Beavers House in 1903 although in 1923 he moved to Kenmure House, Abbey Street.

What was once Beavers Yard is now **College Gardens**, so named because the precursor to the Royal Military Academy at Sandhurst was, for seven years, located there. This came about because by late 1812 work on building the Academy had not progressed at the expected rate. While the Junior Department had made a move from its High Wycombe premises, its Senior counterpart could not be so accommodated. So a house in Farnham was purchased for £1355. It does not appear to have been a good buy because repairs absorbed a further £2500, the work being completed by the end of 1813. The building in question was a long, single-storey structure of ten bays with a frontage that faced West Street.

A mere 30 officers were accommodated there between

College Gardens *80* *82*

1814 and 1821. But the site was still cash-hungry and a further £80 was spent on the garden. When the Department moved to Sandhurst, the Treasury sold the Farnham premises which only realized £347, a loss to the exchequer of a substantial £3588. The "College" was then demolished and in 1835 the site was sold to William Pink Paine for £300. In 1837 it was named College Yard. It soon passed to Charles Attfield, who later built Beaver House there. What are now gardens was once occupied by cottages which may have been used for housing the officers.

In 1957 the site was acquired by Farnham UDC under the terms of a £30,000 bequest from Joseph Ewart, for many years a member, for the erection of old people's dwellings. This quiet backwater also provides a welcome element of greenery to this part of West Street.

Although the brick frontages of numbers **80**, which now incorporates 81, respectively suggest late 18th-century and early 19th-century styles, they do in fact conceal earlier timber-framed buildings. It is occupied by Guitar Village and in 1991 its owner, Derek Eyre-Walker, restored the property and uncovered the smoke-blackened beams of a type of house rarely seen in Farnham. It is a so-called "half Wealden" with a service area and cross passage running through beneath the solar. An early 17th-century wall painting was discovered and is visible on the first floor. The property was previously known as Abbotts Cottages.

Number **82** next door, which shares the same roof, has a frontage of a similar date although possessing a 19th-century shopfront. All three properties were owned in 1839

Fox Yard *83* *84* *85*

Mixed grilles, above, below and opposite: *The iron grating framed within a miniature Classical arch in the wall of 1 Potters Gate, off West Street, a house, as the plaque on its south wall indicates, that was built in 1909. The road is said to have been so named because potters used it to reach the clay pit in the Old Park.*

Variation on a theme: this time the grille is square with a border of Gothic quatrefoils.

by Thomas Hunter and Ann Savage, the former having run a boys' school there before moving to Willmer House opposite. George Elliott, more usually associated with the Reliance Works further down West Street, in 1882 advertised himself as an agricultural implement maker at 82. In the 1890s the shop was occupied by baker and grocer W. Stewart. In the 1950s it was a business named The Mecca. By 1971 it was D. and E. Freeman Antiques and, more recently, Bits and Pieces Antiques, removed from 37 opposite, which stayed until 2002. It is now the premises of Moyst eastern antiques.

Fox Yard takes its name from the nearby Fox pub, although it was previously known as Hunter's Yard after a previous occupant of 82. Almost out of sight is Bars, Wells and Fox Yard Cottages, which all date from the late 18th century and reputedly were used as accommodation for the nearby military college.

For much of the 19th century The Fox occupied the two-storey, colour-washed **83**, now Kall-Kwik, which, like its westerly neighbours, is a refronted timber-framed building. Early in the 19th century it was owned by the Patrick family, who were then builders, and in 1839 it was a Knight pub. John Henry Knight offered it for sale, along with the adjoining 84, in 1888. It was acquired by Barrett and thus in due course by Farnham United Breweries. It was described as a lodging house in 1851 but this was closed down in 1902. By 1937 this was The Cosy Café which lasted into the 1950s. It was later Pearson's estate agents and, in the 1970s, Farnham Heating.

Although number **84** is closely allied with its neighbour and similarly timber-framed, its frontage is of exposed brick rather than colour wash. In the 19th century it was variously occupied by Charles Waterman, a tailor, and Alfred White who in 1891 was listed as a "cooper and dealer in baskets". It was in the ownership of Farnham United Breweries until the property, by then occupied by the British Legion, was sold in 1928. Soon restored, the present bay windows date from about this time. Inside a Tudor fireplace "in excellent condition" was discovered. Subsequently occupied by The Old Mitre tea rooms and then The Old Mitre Restaurant, in later years it was Krug's Austrian Restaurant. The present Italian Caffé Piccolo dates from 1995.

Dwarfing its two-storey neighbours, the early Georgian

three-storey number **85**, Lane Fox estate agents, was in 1901 occupied by the Benefit Building Society. Outwardly the building has changed little over the years although before the Second World War the first-floor windows were unusual six-pane sashes. These were subsequently replaced by the more conventional three-pane type. The shopfront and door were also in place in the 1930s when it was occupied by Willcox and Sons. Between 1949 and 1962 it was the home of H.G. Mutch's Health Food Shop, then Farnham Carpet's showroom and, later, Village Pine.

Adjoining 85 is **Fenn's Yard** which takes its name from aerated water manufacturer Messrs Fenn and Company, established in 1860, that produced soda, seltzer, lemonade and ginger beer "in patent or cork stoppered bottles". Prior to that it was occupied by builder James Garth, who built 34 to 37 opposite. Fenn occupied the weather-boarded building until the early 1930s with the premises subsequently passing to building contractors Sherfield Brothers. This firm later moved to Park Row. In 1951 what is 85A was taken over by the Farnham Carpet Company which is still there.

The style of numbers **86**, **86A** and **87** – two storey with a tiled roof, good unadorned brick and three-pane sashes – suggests mid 18th century. By 1818 they were owned by solicitor James Shotter, who lived at 88. These were properties once favoured by maiden ladies. In 1878, they were respectively occupied by Miss Randall and Miss Hooper; by 1909 it was Miss Lewis and Miss Merriott.

Creative Solutions is the current occupant of **88A** which probably dates from the early 19th century and was a later addition to 88. But in 1950 it was separated from it by the Misses Pennington who acquired 88 following the death of its owner, Lt-Colonel Henry Vallentin. It contained only one ground-floor window but in that year the present pedimented doorway was fitted by Mills & Sons. Previously it had graced an 18th-century London house that was bombed during the war and came from Crowther's yard at Isleworth (see page 208). Its arrival was witnessed by Nigel Temple and this change to the house's appearance was one of the reasons why he began to chronicle the histories of Farnham's buildings.

Number 88, better known as **Bethune House**, is one of the buildings that endows West Street with its dignity. Dating from the 1780s, it is of five bays and three storeys

The shape is circular and the grille's tracery has ecclesiastical undertones. Here, as with many Farnham walls, ironstone is successfully juxtaposed with brick.

Originally what is now 88A was part of the neighbouring 88 and it possessed just one ground-floor window, a sash with margin panes. Look carefully at the brickwork and you can see where it was. It was removed in 1950 when the present window was fitted to make room for the door which was added to make the building a self-contained unit.

with sashes of the same height throughout and a centrally positioned pedimented doorway. There is no decoration, save for a cornice below the parapet. This contrasts with the rear of the property which presents a combination of differing roofs and extensions. A rainwater head there is dated 1807. The oldest part is the north-eastern corner where there is evidence of timber framing.

In the 1830s James Shotter, a solicitor, lived at 88 and he was probably there when he died in 1852. Lt-Colonel John Luard, who founded Farnham School of Art, resided there for a time. A Mrs Oakes is listed as the occupier in 1891 but the *Farnham Directory* gives a street number, rather than the name Bethune House which presumably came later. Paradoxically, at this time Mr and Mrs Duncan Bethune, a relative of the Knights, lived in Vernon House opposite!

Soon afterwards 88 was the home of Lady Mary Arkwright and her husband Richard, sometime MP for Leominster, Herefordshire. By 1909 G.F. Roumieu J.P. was there. Between the wars, and after, it was Lt-Colonel Vallentin, who was a member of Farnham UDC in 1923-26. Following the occupancy of the Misses Pennington, Bethune House later became the offices of chartered accountants R.H. Hackett and Milne, Eldridge, the latter being still in occupancy. Fortunately the frontage has remained essentially unchanged over the years, although in the 1950s the present three-pane ground-floor sashes were fitted in place of two-pane ones.

The neighbouring number **89** is of similar character, perhaps a little later in date, but is built of yellow-grey bricks in a street mostly of reds. With its doorway on the eastern side, this could easily be a London town house. Like its neighbour, it has three floors but three bays with

Fenn's Yard ***86-87*** ***88A*** ***88*** ***89***

tall first-floor windows. The sashes on the third floor are smaller than the others and, arguably, the building looks the better for them. At the rear there are no less than two Venetian windows, one above the other. Yet another also features above the garage but this and the room it serves are relatively recent and is now annexed to number 90.

By 1796 this was the home of Mrs Harrison, a widow, but George Bury owned it in 1840, it being occupied then by William Alexander, a hop planter. For the latter half of the 19th century it housed a school, "*an educational home* [author's italics] for daughters of gentlemen" run by the Alexander family. Harold Falkner and his sister were pupils. The school later moved to 96 West Street. In the 1950s it was the occupied by Captain A.M.H. Fergus and Dr Margaret Falconar.

Next door, number **90** has what Nigel Temple describes as "among the very best local small Georgian facades". Dating from 1784, it is of five bays and two storeys with a central pedimented doorway and decorated cornice below the parapet. An element of individuality is provided by a central round-headed window (with Adamesque tracery), a feature that is shared with 61 Castle Street which, it is suspected, is by the same hand. It was built on the site of two houses, later made into one, and held in trust by John Hearn, a grocer, in 1721. In 1781 this property was sold to Daniel Bristow the elder, a mercer (a silk merchant), and he initiated the construction of the present building.

In 1810 the house was purchased for £687 by the Marquis of Lothian, who owned Vernon House. It passed to his second son Lord Charles Beauchamp Kerr, and then to Mark, his brother. He soon sold it to John Townsend and it remained in his family by the time William Hollest,

90 91 92 93 94

The door-case of 90 West Street with its prominent volutes indicates the Ionic architectural order. The scalloped Adamesque tracery in the fanlight is echoed in the window directly above the door.

solicitor, was listed as the occupant in 1839. Harriet Andrews, widow of wealthy hop grower Samuel, died there in 1859. She had shared the house with her son Charles, owner of The Grange, following the death of his young wife in 1845.

Later, in the 1950s, it was Mrs C. Leveson Lane's home and she initiated repairs to the door-case on which the original Ionic capitals, by then badly rotted, were replaced with copies carved by a local craftsman. The steps were rebuilt and railings added. Subsequently occupied by P. and B. Jordan's antique shop, it is currently the home of Sir Ray Tindle, chairman of Tindle Newspapers and proprietor of the *Farnham Herald*, and his wife.

Its easterly neighbours, numbers **91** and **92**, were originally one house, but it was divided into two prior to 1818. The appearance – three storeys and four bays with four-pane sashes and a tiled roof – suggests late 18th century. Both were owned in the 1830s by William West. Later, in 1891, number 91 was the home of Mrs James Nash. Ernest Heath, a corn merchant, was living there in 1915. If you look carefully, you can see a change of brick which indicates the presence at one time of a shopfront. In 1952 it was the home of a Miss Bradford and it is currently occupied by The Vanilla Room.

John Nichols, a printer and bookbinder with a shop at 41/42 The Borough, lived at 92 in the late 19th century. In 1911 it was sold for £450 to builder Arthur Mardon, late of 68 Castle Street. It was the home of Mrs Coomber in the 1950s and by 1971 was T. & H. Venables' antiques shop.

Number **93** was the offices of solicitors Hollest, Cotterell, previously Hollest, Mason and, later, Nash, from about 1876 until 1996. It is now Old Chambers offices. The firm's origins reached back to 1794 when Captain Jacob Hollest set up in partnership with his brother. They were joined by Richard Mason, who was Farnham UDC's first clerk. He had in 1847 been articled to John Hollest, then of 107 West Street. John Nash arrived in 1881.

Of two storeys and five bays with a central pedimented door, 93 was probably built by Thomas Buddle in about 1781 on the site of an existing house and kilns. William West was living there in 1818 and, as well as being the aforementioned solicitor's premises, in 1891 it was also the county court office.

This was soon transferred to **94**, which dates from 1895,

and is the work of Paxton Hood Watson, who had recently completed the Grammar School extension at 25 West Street. It replaced a small house occupied by the Misses Fewtrell, who were dressmakers. Instead of perpetuating the Georgian theme of the neighbouring properties, Watson opted for a semi-circular gable, with a 17th century-style eaves-cornice, that echoed the contours of the Venetian window featured on the first floor.

Today 94 successfully marks a demonstrable end to this part of West Street. This was also the case when it was built, because in 1895 the stuccoed, two-storeyed 95 was demolished. Its absence permitted the building of The Hart, opened in 1904, which gave access to the hopfields beyond.

Next is **Sequel House**, that was named Craven House on its completion. The northerly section is **Maritime House**. It dates from 1967 and was the first of Farnham's postwar Neo-Georgian office blocks and the last building to be designed by Guy Maxwell Aylwin, whose practice at 26 was directly opposite. Its construction required the demolition of 96 and 97, the latter having retained its Georgian frontage. In 1891 number 96 was occupied by Richard King, while the neighbouring shop played host to James Smith, a corn dealer in occupancy since 1850.

However, on Christmas Day 1892, number 96 was devastated by a severe fire and it was rebuilt as a lofty, three-storey, brick property with a prominent gable facing West Street. Initially used by Miss Alexander's school, recently removed from 89, it was subsequently converted into a shop. Butcher B.W. Toop, "purveyor of high class meat", occupied it for many years before he ceased trading in the early 1960s.

Yet the shop at 97 survived as a reminder of what 96 had once looked like. Disney, a jeweller, was there at the turn of the 19th century and after the Second World War Gladys Hardingham sold books from this address. Later came Dennis Collett's Old House Bookshop, who subsequently moved to 87 East Street. The days of both buildings were numbered. In January 1967 they were demolished.

The Neo-Tudor **99**, Association House, formerly Corner Piece, stands on the site of The Prince of Wales pub, which was 98. The entrance of this is now around the corner in Timber Close. Opened by George Trimmer in 1860, it survived until 1893 and the premises were subsequently occupied in 1901 by Mrs J.Cumber, bootmaker.

Her neighbour, next door at 99 in the same property, was Mr Mansfield's greengrocery and sweetshop, although in the 1930s wine merchants Aylward and Sons were there.

The present building, completed for them in 1937, was the work of Leonard Stedman and he reverted to the premises' pre-Georgian appearance, it having originally been a two-storied, timber-framed structure. A third floor was subsequently added and the original frontage concealed behind a brick facade. These later additions were removed and Stedman incorporated many of the original beams in his reconstruction. After the war Aylward's business was acquired by Tyler and Co which was there until the 1970s.

Numbers **100** and **101** and **102** and **103** should be seen in the same context. They all date from 1812 and were built as a speculative venture by Daniel Batchelour. With stuccoed frontages, three storeys, sash windows and slate-roofed, their side walls are built of local ironstone. The development also included Factory Yard, of which more anon.

At the turn of the 1890s, number 100 was still a private house being occupied by a Mrs Gates, who was a grocer with a shop at 36 East Street. By the 1950s it was The Mandarin and then A.G. J. Smith, who was a confectioner. The present occupant is Serena ladies' wear.

Timber Close ***99***

The neighbouring 101, now 101 Collectors Records, was in 1901 occupied by Mrs W. Lindsay's registry of servants. In 1952 it was the home of The Galleon and between 1981 and 1990 of The Vienna Restaurant.

Next is **Arundell Place**. Also developed in 1811/12 by Batchelour, there were in total 12 buildings, which included eight cottages that were so named. But Batchelour was soon bankrupted. In late 1831 John Leadbitter of 5 Castle Street acquired the premises at the rear of the site and from there he wove hop bags, sailcloth, wagon and rick cloths. He accorded it the Dickensian name of Factory Yard. His business was discontinued well before the end of the 19th century although it may have been acquired by George McDonald, around the corner at 104 West Street, who in 1901 was listed as a rick-cloth manufacturer.

By the 1950s Factory Yard was occupied by builders F.W. German and Son and, later, East Hants Builders, a company that was established in Crondall in 1947 but which ceased trading in the late 1960s. The site and the moribund business was acquired by property developers Ellis Campbell of nearby Craven House. In January 1975 it submitted its plans to redevelop the site. These required the demolition of most of the buildings, including cottages which at their backs were identified as 5 to 10 Factory Yard, although the fronts were named Timber Close!

In 1977 Ellis Campbell's Michael Campbell and developer Andrew Sturt acquired East Hants Builders and renamed it Arundell House Securities. They retained architect John Maxwell Aylwin and he was responsible for their headquarters, Arundell House, completed in 1977. Today renamed Craven House and a prestigious office development of good brick in the Classical spirit, it imaginatively incorporates ironstone in its westerly wing. The vestibule contains a stone tablet which bears the legend of *Arundell Place 1812*. Factory Yard accordingly reverted to its original name. The company remained there until 1986 when it moved into offices in its Lion and Lamb development.

Numbers 102 and **103** are the remaining part of Batchelour's 1812 speculation. By 1878 Miss Caroline Biddick was running her Ladies School at 102 but shops did not arrive until later. Ernest Ranger's pawnbrokers business occupied 102 and his drapery store was later extended to include 103 which remained there until the 1970s. That shop had been occupied by hairdresser Lionel

The fanlight of 104 West Street, another example of the fascinating variety of designs found throughout Farnham. Such tracery was often crafted by chair makers who were familiar with the discipline of bending wood into intricate shapes.

The Crowther Connection

The 18th-century shopfront, replete with Adam details and a Gothick cornice, that so enhances the frontage of 104A West Street was brought to Farnham by Harold Falkner. It came from Crowther's Architectural Antiques of Syon Lodge, London Road, Isleworth, Middlesex and, when discovered, was forming part of proprietor Bert Crowther's office! The firm was established in the 1930s and survived at that location until as recently as 2002. There was another branch in Fulham, and it continues in business from a Pimlico address. Crowther's also supplied the door-case of 88A West Street and there are no doubt other Georgian architectural artefacts in Farnham that came to the town via its Isleworth premises.

As stated in the text, there is a similar Birch shopfront dating from about 1770 in the Museum of London. But there can be little doubt that they are both genuine. Despite Ian Nairn in "Pevsner" dismissing the Farnham shopfront as a "19th century copy", Nigel Temple recalls seeing the name *Birch, Birch and Co*, after the top layer of paint had been removed, prior to it being installed. It is inconceivable that this lettering was not original. However, the westerly door of 104A is a replica and dates from when the shopfront was fitted.

H. Smith, also a "perfumer and wig maker", who in 1920 moved down the road to 1 The Borough. Today 102 is Greenwood's estate agents while the Curtain Agency is at 103. The green glazed tiles at the base of the latter shopfront probably came from the Wrecclesham Pottery.

Although number **104A**, Asset Recruitment, is about the same height as its neighbour, it is much narrower, and the brick frontage of what has been dubbed "the giraffe house" is dominated by two high arches. It dates from the mid-19th century, was built as a malt house by Charles Attfield and subsequently became a warehouse where hops were bagged. However, from 1875 George McDonald was running his related rick-cloth manufacturing business at what was then 104.

The arches were later bricked in and shortly after the Second World War the property, and neighbouring 104, were occupied by senior staff at the Farnham School of Art which was located almost opposite. At this time Robin Ball and his wife occupied the top flat of what is now 104A, together with their son Gareth, whose illustrations so enhance this work.

In 1951 Charles Borelli and Harold Falkner decided that the property was ready for "the treatment" which involved knocking out the brick infilling and then introducing a shopfront into the resulting ground-floor recess. Falkner's original idea was to remove *all* the bricks from the arches until the Ball family tactfully pointed out that they would take with them their sitting room floor! So a short section of the arches remain. In 1952 what was now 104A became the offices of the *Surrey & Hants News*. In 1978 the paper was purchased by Tindle Newspapers, it remained there until 1992 and subsequently moved to new premises in Lion and Lamb Yard.

104A ***104*** ***Malthouse Yard***

Falkner had acquired a London shopfront from an Isleworth dealer which Wilkinson installed at 104A. But when the paint was removed the name of *Birch* was revealed. Just to confuse matters, there is a similar well-documented 'front in the Museum of London. In the 18th century this proclaimed the presence of Samuel Birch's pastry shop at 15 Cornhill that was demolished in 1926. This suggests that he occupied a site with two entrances and therefore required two "fronts".

Next door at **104** is a town house of five bays and two storeys with a parapet which contains five blind recesses. It dates from the early 18th century. Pioneer Farnham hop grower Robert Bicknell was 104's first known owner in 1719. W.S. Hart was there by 1936 and solicitors W.H. Hadfield and Son, today Hadfields, Butt and Bowyer, arrived in the 1960s.

The adjoining stone-flagged Malthouse Yard at the rear is another delightful Farnham backwater which contains the octagonal brick office from where the talleyman is believed to have paid the hop pickers. Nearby is Malthouse Yard Cottage which was sensitively restored in the 1980s.

Numbers **105** and **106**, with three storeys and three bays apiece, date from the 1830s and both properties have blind windows in their middle bays. Number 105 was for many years a private residence. It was named Lombard House between the wars.

By 1891 Henry Loveless was the occupant of 106, where he had a furniture warehouse, and he had evidently been there for many years by then. He was also a "pawnbroker, silversmith and general salesman" and was succeeded in 1894 by Ernest Ranger and Son, who were in much the same line of business. They survive today as Ranger's Furnishing Stores. Its shopfront, by Alfred Guyer, dates from 1906 when he made further alterations to the property.

The Post Office next door, number 107, was officially opened in January 1973, the supervising architect having been D.C. Wye of the Ministry of Works' Southern Region headquarters. It was an attempt to create a building in sympathy with the West Street's architecture yet still incorporate contemporary features. In this it has been reasonably successful.

The brick and tile elements of the frontage and scale of the structure chime with its immediate neighbours and the three shallow oriel windows do not offend. However,

The 18th-century shopfront being installed at 104A West Street by W.J. Wilkinson and Sons, a builder with a good reputation in the town.

Leigh House, demolished in 1969, that became Farnham's Post Office in 1904, provides the backdrop for a mayoral review of the town's Civil Defence Parade held in May 1953.

a discordant note is struck by the concrete lintels beneath them which, with the passing of time, have become discoloured. A noteworthy feature is an abstract mural executed by West Surrey College of Art and Design lecturer Michael Fairclough, which was intended to reflect the town's geographical location. It covered a blank wall, behind which was the strong-room. There was also an enlarged sorting office and telephone exchange at the rear.

Farnham's Post Office had been temporarily moved to Bear Lane for four years, the staff having vacated the premises in January 1969. But work on the construction of the new building did not begin until November 1970. It replaced Leigh House, a two-storey, three-bay, cement-rendered property dating from the early 19th century. In 1841 John and Mary Hollest lived at 107. He was a solicitor and she the daughter of Thomas Leigh of 9 Castle Street, hence the name. For a time it became the home of Major-General Herbert Plumer, late of the Sudan expedition and Matabele campaigns and a Boer War hero. He later moved on to the grander environment of Firgrove House.

In 1884 Robert Nichols, who ran the town's Post Office, had taken a 21-year lease on 114 West Street which was due to expire in 1905. Already outgrowing those premises, it was decided to move the Post Office to Leigh House and in May 1904 the Council approved plans for the new facility. Paxton Hood Watson, in one of his last commissions in the area, was responsible for the conversion and the work was undertaken by Tompsett.

Completed by the end of 1904, the public now had access to what had once been the General's dining room and hall. The staircase was removed but preserved and it later graced 40 The Borough. Behind was a new sorting office which was three times the size of that at 114. Lit by gas, 350 bags were ready for the expected Christmas rush.

The shop at number **108**, now occupied by Cancer Research UK, was once part of the neighbouring 109 and 110 and its cement rendering belies the fact that behind it is a medieval building which was once The Swan Inn. This was a hostelry of great antiquity; in 1604 it was mentioned having paid dues "beyond the memory of any man that now liveth". But by 1652 the land at the rear had been given over to hops and by 1687 the property had been divided into three.

Over 200 years later, in 1897, it was the home of

Thomas Andrews and Co's "pianoforte and music warehouse" which had originated in Guildford in 1857. Andrews had died in 1895 but two years later his successors, the Donn family, opened their Farnham branch and this continued to trade for nearly 65 years. It was replaced in the 1960s by The Furniture Mart and later became Foster Brothers Clothing menswear shop.

Pullingers at **109**, of colour-washed brick with its distinctive tile-hung gable, is the town's oldest business still occupying its original premises. In 1979 it was acquired by Langham's and thus came within the orbit of the *Farnham Herald*. In 1795 William Keet was a hairdresser there, as was his son, also called William. In the 1820s he introduced stationery as a secondary line, and when he died in 1841 his wife Ellen continued the business. Their daughter, Emily, married George Pullinger, a grocer, and she subsequently inherited the property.

Later toys were added, a line that continued through to the years after the Second World War. Still trading in 1886 as W. Keet at 109 and 110 West Street, by 1901 the business had become Geo Pullinger (Keets Bazaar) but by 1906 the suffix had been dropped. There was by then a "fancy needlework department" across the road at 12 West Street. The presence of an art college in the town has meant that artists' materials have long been a popular line.

Don't be deceived by the rather anonymous colour-washed brick parapeted frontage of number **110** which is Help The Aged's shop. This is the eastern segment of the

108 *109* *110*

Most busy shoppers have probably never noticed it. But the date of 1537 in bricks, sheltered from the elements on the east wall of the archway entrance to Lion and Lamb Yard, may refer to the foundation of an inn on the site which became the Lion and Lamb Hotel.

timber-framed Swan Inn and its jettying can be seen encased in the western wall of the adjoining archway. This was the rented offices in the late 1930s of estate agents German, Addy, who advertised themselves "for all Houses (large or small)". An uncle and nephew partnership forged in 1939, it had moved from Kenmure House, Abbey Street, a property that was demolished in anticipation of the expected bypass. Sidney German had acquired the neighbouring 111 and 112, and he moved next door to 111 while The Farnham Dairy took over 110. It later, by 1956, introduced a "cafeteria and self-service" grocery, which may have been a first for Farnham.

However, in 1969 the Dairy withdrew from the retail business (see 12 West Street), and the shop closed on 1st March of that year. Acquired by Cavendish Offices & Houses Investment Company, it was let to Hugh Stockman of Alton, who opened his House of Hugh menswear shop there.

The adjoining three-storey property, number **111**, was built new in about 1803 by Richard Attfield, although the top floor appears to be a late 19th-century addition. It is of particular interest because from 1828 the shop was occupied by Clemente Borelli, who practised as a silversmith there. In 1853 he acquired the property from James Longhurst, a cheesemonger. But by the 1860s the Borelli business had moved to 11 East Street.

For many years the West Street shop was occupied by jewellers and watchsellers Harrington's who arrived in 1885, but by the 1890s it was Miss Crow's "baby linen and ladies underclothing" outlet. Subsequently James Dann, another jeweller, took over and occupied it for many years.

German, Addy was there by 1946 but German died in 1954 and Addy remained until 1965 when the business was taken over by Pearson's, which moved into 112. By the 1970s number 111 was occupied by optician P.E. Leapman. C.E. Hall, who has been there since 1978, is in the same profession.

Some five years earlier than its neighbour, **112** was built by Richard Attfield at some time between March and August 1799. A saddler and harness maker, he lived in the house, which has two floors, three bays, with mansard roof and flat-topped dormer windows, until about 1820. It was bought in 1826 by John Wells, a cornwainer, and his family was destined to remain there for 99 years.

In 1925 the house ceased to be a family home and

became a shop at which point a plate-glass front was introduced to accommodate Emily Chilcott's millinery business. This remained there until 1936 when she moved across the road to 8 West Street. However, in 1950 the 25-year-old shopfront was replaced for German, Addy by a more appropriate triple bow window. It was the work of Guy Maxwell Aylwin and was inspired by his family butcher's shop, previously at 8 West Street.

This alteration was to accommodate Biggs of Farnham, already occupying Lion and Lamb House a few doors down, but here with a "Leather Shop for Revelation and Antler Luggage". As already noted, Pearson's arrived in 1965, but it was taken over by the Prudential in the 1980s and 112 stood empty for a year. In 1989 came The Granary and Brasserie which was succeeded in 1990 by The Vienna Restaurant, the present occupant, that moved there from 101.

Its sign, suspended by a fine wrought-iron bracket, was designed by Harold Falkner and incorporates the date of 1903. This harks back to the time when Sidney German opened his first estate agency, and it followed him through no less than four moves in the town.

Next comes **Lion and Lamb House** which takes its name from the inn that bore this name from at least the early 18th century. A deed of 1761 relating to the adjoining 114/115 West Street, refers it being on "the east side of…an Inn, formerly The Hart [an abbreviation of White Hart] but now called or known by the name of The Lyon and Lamb."

On the eastern side of the archway to Lion and Lamb Yard is the date, recorded in brick, of 1537. Although unverifiable, it could record the foundation of the earlier building. This was a coach stop from the 18th century, but by the 1900s the Lion and Lamb Commercial Hotel, with accommodation for 20 and stabling for 15 horses, was

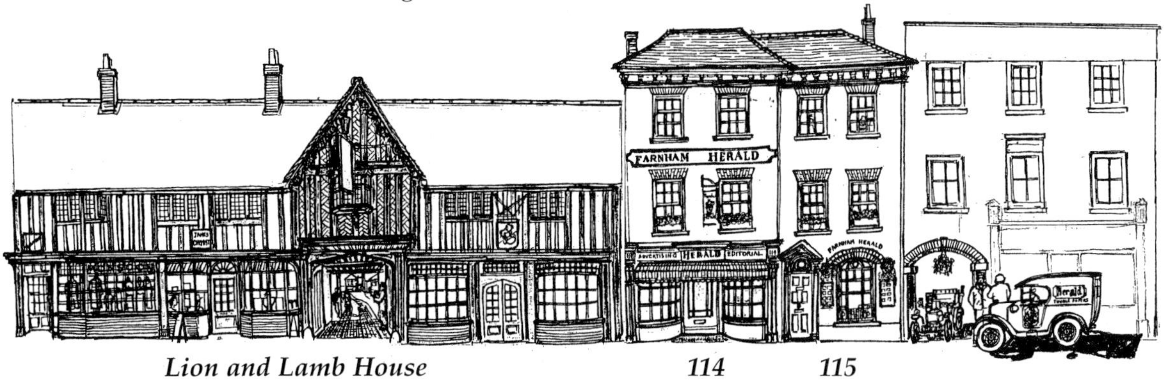

Lion and Lamb House *114* *115*

A world away from the Lion and Lamb Yard we know today, framed by the archway of the then Lion and Lamb Hotel, Mathews' brewery – the building was said to date from about 1810 – survived various financial reconstructions. In 1886 it was bankrupted with substantial debts of £36,170. It closed in 1910 when the hotel and its yard were sold to William Kingham and Sons.

shabby and run-down. It had a stuccoed, two-storey, Regency frontage, with sashes and a Venetian window above the entrance arch which led to the yard beyond. There was a commercial room at its west end and a coffee room on the opposite side.

In 1838 its landlord was Thomas Mathews, a man who went on to establish, in 1845, the West Street Brewery in the yard. Against a background of financial problems, by 1877 it was renamed the Lion and Lamb Brewery, although by 1882 it had reverted to its original name. There he produced ale, stout, porter and pale ale. It finally became Thomas Mathews and Son but it closed in 1910.

The Lion and Lamb had been offered for let by estate agents Kingham and Kingham of Aldershot, a practice in which architect John Kingham, one of grocer William's sons, was a partner. It was sold in 1910, in-house as it were, to William Kingham and Sons opposite. The purchase included the yard beyond and a garage was built there to accommodate Kingham's growing fleet of vans.

John Kingham, with input from Charles Borelli, was responsible for the design of the Neo-Tudor Lion and Lamb House dates from 1921 but retains some original timbers. Mardon, Ball undertook the work. Kingham kept the property until 1936 when it sold the premises to the Farnham Market and Town Hall Company. But it retained the yard, having in 1925 built a warehouse there. A second one was constructed at the end of the property, in The Hart. It was completed in 1955 and extended in 1957.

The "new" building fronting West Street contained

Lion and Lamb Yard ***Monsoon*** ***Cromwell Chocolatiers***

three shops. Number **113** was to be occupied from the 1930s by Martin and Sturt, latterly of 41/42 The Borough, from which sprang The Farnham Printing Company for "printing, die stamping, commercial and letterpress bookbinder". It remained there until 1986 when it moved to the Farnham Business Centre. The shop is currently occupied by Monsoon ladies' wear.

At **113A** next door was Trimming and Company, and today is Vaughan James Chemists, but on the eastern side of the arch of Lion and Lamb House is the double-fronted shop which from 1937 was the home of E.T. Biggs and Son Jewellers, "Silver…watches of quality…Glass and Leather". The Misses Mary and Margaret Biggs retired as co-directors in 1975 when it was acquired by a Wolverhampton -based company. In 1982 it was sold to Goldsmiths and the Farnham business has been called this since 1998.

When Kingham rebuilt the property, it perpetuated the Neo-Tudor theme with a range of timber-framed buildings at the south-eastern end of Lion and Lamb Yard. This consisted of five further shops, one of the most enduring being the Lion and Lamb Café in premises which currently houses the Lion and Lamb Bistro. Another business that predates the development of the Yard is Karel Weijand's Persian Carpets shop on its westerly side. He established it there in 1975.

The archway provides access to Lion and Lamb Yard shopping centre, begun in 1984 and officially opened in November 1986. Architect Max Lyons imaginatively

e Lighting Agency and Trading Co *Persian Carpets* *CCA Galleries* *Laura Ashley*

Natural variety: the new shops in the foreground easily co-exist alongside the older ones in Lion and Lamb Yard. The former locally established Hammicks, now Ottakar's Bookstore, is one of the original occupants, having arrived in August 1987.

complemented the ten existing brick, clunch and weather-boarded buildings with 15 new shops and offices of the same materials, so it is difficult, some years on, to see where the old finishes and the new begins. All are further bonded by a pathway of ironstone and granite setts.

There were parallels with the Town Hall Buildings in The Borough in 1931 when, on 3rd March 1986, a representation of the recently preserved Tudor warship *Mary Rose*, made of copper covered with £500 of gold leaf and the work of Dippenhall-based David Gillespie, was mounted on the cupola of the tallest building in the complex.

Kingham's former warehouse in The Hart was demolished and a car park for approximately 250 cars created for the new supermarket. Initially this was operated by Presto, which opened in March 1986, but from 1987 it became a Safeway store.

Back in West Street, since 1905 number **114** has been the home of the *Farnham Herald*, Ernest Langham having moved his business there from South Street. This and the neighbouring **115** were originally two houses which had been in single ownership since at least 1744. One hundred and forty years later, in 1884, it was leased for 21 years by Robert Nichols, who moved the Post Office from number 6 opposite and it remained there until 1904. At this time 114 was owned by George Ransom, who had tea rooms at 22 The Borough. In July 1905 he submitted plans for its conversion to a shop with a printing facility at the rear. Crosby did the work, the *Herald* moved in September and Ernest Langham's stationery business occupied the shop later. In 1912 he would advertise "I have one of the most complete Printing Plants in this part of Surrey" adding, almost as an afterthought, "printer and publisher of the *Farnham Herald,* Splendid paper for 6d [2.5p]."

Expansion followed at the rear in 1924 and in 1949 the business grew into number 115 next door which, during its neighbour's Post Office years, had been occupied by the postmaster. While its frontage has remained essentially unchanged, in about 1952 the plate-glass window of 114 was removed and replaced by the present double-bow front which was the work of Harold Falkner. At the same time the Victorian two-pane sashes were removed and replaced by original three-pane examples.

One of the joys of West Street are the alleyways and yards that can be found on both sides of the road. Harts Yard runs to The Hart via Long Garden Walk and is located between 115 and 116 West Street.

In 1969 Ray Tindle, as he was then, organized the purchase of the *Farnham Herald* through the *Surrey Advertiser* of which he was a shareholder. Then, in 1974, he bought the balance outright.

Next door number **116** dates from the early 19th century. By the 1890s it was occupied by Thomas Mathews, of the nearby West Street Brewery. In 1900 the International Tea Company arrived here from 39 The Borough and it remained at 116 until 1927 when it moved down the road to number 121. By the 1950s dry cleaners Flinn and Sons were established there, and now it is occupied by Johnsons, also a dry-cleaning business.

Ernest Jones jewellers, number **117**, occupies a shop that by 1891 was Frederick Hart's ironmongers, who was also a cutler and oil and colour merchant. It was briefly a branch of Tily & Brown's ironmongers of 6/7 Castle Street. In 1933 Lipton, the grocer, moved there and occupied it well into the postwar years. But by the 1970s it was S. Hiltons and Sons' shoe shop.

It is rather dwarfed by **118**, its three-storeyed, cement-rendered neighbour with dominating first-floor pedimented sashes, which dates from the 1850s. Harold Falkner believed that it was the work of Farnham builder Harding. In the 1890s this was Mrs Cummings's "fancy and stationery repository" while Miss R. Cummings' wool and haberdashery shop was still there in the 1950s. In 1960 the ground floor was extensively altered. The Victorian double shopfront, complete with six large panes, was removed and Currys bicycle shop moved in from next door at 119. It still occupies the premises although electrical appliances are now sold rather than two-wheelers.

Brick with three flush-fitting sashes on its first floor and an eaves-cornice might suggest "Queen Anne." In fact the frontage of **119** was reconstructed in the manner of the original in the early post 1945 years. In 1891 it was Hammond's Refreshment Rooms. He also ran the Royal Deer, although by 1901 both had passed to W. Clarke. In 1946 it was Currys, then The Wallpaper Centre, and by 1971 was a Freeman, Hardy and Willis shoe shop. It is now Specsavers opticians.

In 1891 number **120**, rendered and of similar appearance but with two sashes, was A.G. Dawson's fishmonger and poulterer, but by 1901 it was the Central Meat Company's butcher's shop. This evolved into the

Classical survivor: the mid-Victorian 118 West Street photographed in 1954. Then it was occupied by Cummins' wool shop. Currys, next door at 119 did not move in until 1960 and it still occupies the premises.

The date of 1924 above the door of the building in the left foreground refers to when Ernest Langham's Farnham Herald *expanded in Harts Yard. Today it is Tindle House and is the office of the chief executive of Tindle Newspapers. Beyond, the single storey building with the saw-tooth roof used to house the presses that printed the* Herald *although this activity ceased in 1992 with a move to a Press Centre at Monkton Lane. Since 1999 printing has been undertaken at the Surrey Press Centre, Blacknest.*

London Central Meat Company which remained there until the late 1950s. By 1963 it was occupied by Baxter's the butcher and is now the Sanity record shop

Although it is not apparent today, number **121**, now occupied by Argos, and The Edinburgh Woollen Mill at **122** was once one building. The former has two storeys and six bays, five sashes, plus a blind window, a cornice, a parapet with six recesses and a slate roof. This was The George, an old established coaching inn which in the 17th century clearly took the comfort of its customers seriously. In 1664 William Clifton, the owner, had to pay tax on no less than 11 hearths. His inn must have been one of the warmest buildings in Farnham! There was a yard at the rear, with access via an archway at its westerly end. Its width is marked by two of the four Ionic pilasters of more recent date which today grace the frontage. Both the archway and yard survived into the 1960s.

The George had closed by the end of the 18th century, the building having become in 1788 the home of Andrew Collyer, who owned Collyers Coaches. His family occupied the property well into the 19th century. Alfred Tennyson met his future wife, Emily Sellwood, there in the 1850s. She lived with her family at Hale Place, and they married in 1868 after a 17-year engagement.

In 1865 numbers 121 and 122 were divided and the former was occupied by solicitors Knight, Saunders and Kempson. They remained there, latterly as Kempson and Wright, until September 1925 when they moved to South Street. The frontage remained intact with the first-floor sashes to the east of the arch repeated at street level.

Sold by the executors of one William Wells to Herbert Bide, it was then converted into a shop for International Stores, which moved in 1927 from 116. It was destined to remain at this address until January 1984. Shamefully, in 1964 it applied to demolish the building, an event which did not happen. But as a consequence the floor space was increased by annexing the old carriageway. A new shopfront replaced the original and outbuildings at the rear were demolished. While the property was being converted in 1984 for Argos's occupancy, a fine plaster ceiling, which may have dated from The George's great coaching days, was uncovered.

When the building was divided in 1865, the neighbouring 122 was refronted and first-floor bay windows and a third storey added. The ground floor had already been converted into a shop. In about 1872 it was acquired by Anthony Williams of 6 West Street, who was a wine merchant and this business remained there until 1962. Later, in a similar line of trade, came Fairdeal Vintners, while the present occupant has been there since 1995, having followed on from Hammick's children's bookshop.

The frontage of the one-time George Inn, today Argos, as it appeared from the 18th century until 1927 when it was converted into a shop for International Stores. The archway on the left provided access to the yard, both features surviving into the 1960s.

Author's Note

The dating of historic buildings is not, alas, an exact science as there are exceptions to practically every architectural rule. Farnham, where the Georgian style has lingered for so long, makes this a particularly challenging exercise and I would ask for the forbearance of readers for the instances where I cannot be as precise in a dating attribution as I would wish. *J.W.*

Glossary

Architecture has its own language, and whilst I have endeavoured to keep its use to a minimum, there are instances when only the right word will do!

architrave A plain or decorated moulding which frames either a window or door.

balustrade A series of short posts or pillars which support a rail or coping of a roof, terrace, balcony or staircase.

barge-board Inclined, sometimes decorated boards, which conceal the ends of the roof timbers, that are secured against a gable beneath the tile or slate line.

Baroque An exuberant European flowering of Italian Renaissance architecture, as practised in Britain during the late 17th and early 18th centuries.

bay External divisions of a building usually marked by windows.

bracket A wooden, usually ornamented, supporting member projecting from a wall in timber-framed buildings.

coping A capping, usually of stone, that protects the top of a parapet or wall from rainwater.

Corinthian One of the eight Classical Orders, originally Greek, adopted by the Romans, which features a column with acanthus leaves on its capital.

cornice A projecting ornamental moulding that runs along the top of a wall, or above a window, on a Classical building.

eaves-cornice A cornice which incorporates the eaves in Queen Anne architecture.

Gothic The architecture of the pointed arch, a style that evolved throughout the Middle Ages, from Early English (late 12th century to c1300), Decorated (c1301-c1350), the latter overlapping with Perpendicular (c1350-c1500).

Gothick A whimsical interpretation of Gothic, as revived in the second half of the 18th century.

Ionic A Greek Order, also adopted by the Romans, with a column which features volutes on its capital.

jettying A projecting upper storey found in timber-framed buildings.

lancet A slim, sharply pointed window, a feature of Early English Gothic.

lintel A horizontal wooden, or stone, beam bridging an opening.

mansard roof A type of pitched roof with each aspect executed in two planes, the lower being steeper than the upper. This allows more room space, together with an attendant dormer window, than could be accommodated in a conventional roof.

margin panes Flanking narrow windows positioned around the edges of sashes in the late 18th and early 19th centuries, sometimes enhanced by coloured glass.

motte and bailey Norman castles usually consisted of a mound (motte) surmounted by a wooden tower set within an enclosure protected by a palisade (bailey).

mullion An upright post which divides a window into two or more segments.

ogee arch A double or S-shaped curved moulding used in pairs to form a pointed arch.

oriel window A type of bay window on an upper floor which is supported by brackets, or a pier, to the wall below.

parapet A shallow projection in Classical buildings at the base of a roof, an extension of the wall below.

pediment A triangular low-pitched gable in Classical architecture usually supported by a row of columns. A variation is a segmental pediment with a curved upper section and both versions often appear in miniature forms above windows and doors. On a broken pediment the apex of the triangle is absent.

pilaster A shallow rectangular column attached to a wall which conforms to one of the Classical Orders.

quoin Dressed stones at the corner of Classical buildings that are usually laid with alternate long and short faces.

rendering A finish, usually of plaster, stucco, or pebble-dash, applied externally to a surface that was not intended for exposure.

rubbed brick A soft brick which contains a high sand content that could be rubbed or sawn into shape. The fine joints are filled with lime putty rather than the usual mortar.

strapwork Decoration that featured in the late Elizabethan and Jacobean periods with narrow, flat straps or bands designed to resemble leather.

string course A continuous horizontal moulding, or narrow band of slight projection, on the face of a building.

stucco An external finish used instead of stone. Of two types, one is made from lime and the other plaster.

Tuscan A Roman, as opposed to a Greek, Order, with a column crowned by a simple undecorated capital.

Venetian window A window, introduced in the 18th century, topped by a semicircular arch and flanked either side by a narrow flat-topped window.

volute The spiral scroll on the capital of an Ionic column although it also appears in reduced forms on the Corinthian and Composite Orders.

Bibliography

FARNHAM AND SURREY

Budgen, Christopher, *West Surrey Architecture*, Heritage of Waverley, 2002

Eggar, J. Alfred, *Remembrances of Life and Customs in Gilbert White's, Cobbett's and Charles Kingsley's Country*, Simpkin, Marshall, Hamilton, Kent and F. Sturt (no date)

Ewbank-Smith, B. (editor), *Bumbledon*, 1960-1963

Ewbank-Smith, B., *Edwardian Farnham*, Charles Hammick, 1979

Ewbank-Smith, W., *Farnham In War and Peace*, Phillimore, 1983

Ewbank-Smith, B., *Victorian Farnham*, Phillimore, 1971

Farnham Chamber of Commerce, *The Book of Farnham*

Farnham and District Museum Society *Newsletter*

The Herald Press, *Farnham and District Directory*, 1937 to 1963/4

The Herald Images of Farnham, Breedon Books, 1997

Home, Gordon, *Farnham and its Surroundings*, Frank Sturt, 1900

Kelly's *Directory of Farnham*, 1970, 1971

Knight, John Henry, *Reminiscences of a Country Town*, Martin and Sturt, 1909

Manning, Elfrida, *Saxon Farnham*, Phillimore, 1970

Nairn, Ian and Nikolaus Pevsner, *The Buildings of England, Surrey*, Penguin Books, 1962, 1995

Nichols, John, *The Farnham Almanack and Directory*, 1872–1909

O'Rourke, Valerie D., *Hop Growing and its Decline in the Parish of Farnham (Surrey)* 1873-1973, Thesis for Teachers' Certificate, 1976, Farnham and District Museum Society, 1986

Parker, Eric, *Highways and Byways in Surrey*, Macmillan, 1908

Parratt, Jean, *Around Farnham in Old Photographs*, Alan Sutton, 1990

Parratt, Jean, *Bygone Farnham*, Phillimore, 1985

Parratt, Jean, *Farnham A Photographic History of Your Town*, W.H. Smith, 2001

Parratt, Jean, *Farnham by the Wey*, Chalford, 1995

Parratt, Jean, *Farnham Past*, Phillimore, 1999

Parratt, Jean, *Licensed Farnham*, Pollyphonics, 1999

Parratt, Jean, *Yesterday Today – More of Around Farnham in Old Photographs*, Alan Sutton, 1992

Pigot and Co's ...*Directory...of Surrey 1839*, Local History Reprints, 1996

Radley, Robin, *A Sketch History of Art in Farnham*, Farnham Art Society

Robo, Etienne, *Medieval Farnham*, E.W. Langham, 1935

Smith, Caroline I., *Harold Falkner*, B.A. Arch (Hons) Dissertation, 1983

Sturt, George, *A Small Boy in the Sixties*, Cambridge University Press, 1927

Sturt, George, *The Wheelwright's Shop*, Cambridge University Press, 1923

Temple, Nigel, *Farnham Buildings and People*, E.W. Langham, 1963 and Phillimore, 1973

Temple, Nigel, *Farnham Inheritance*, E.W. Langham, 1956

Verney, Sir John Bt., *John Verney's Farnham*, The New Ashgate Gallery Trust, 1982

GENERAL

Brodie, Antonia et al, *Directory of British Architects 1834-1914*, Continuum, 2001

Clark, Kenneth, *The Gothic Revival*, John Murray, 1962

Curl, James Stevens, *Oxford Dictionary of Architecture*, Oxford University Press, 1999

Dixon, Roger and Stefan Muthesius, *Victorian Architecture*, Thames and Hudson, 2001

Filmer, Richard, *Hops and Hop Picking*, Shire Publications, 1998

Hammond, Martin, *Bricks and Brickmaking*, Shire Publications, 2001

Harris, Richard, *Discovering Timber-Framed Buildings*, Shire Publications, 2001

Summerson, John, *Georgian London*, Barrie and Jenkins, 1988

Who's Who of British Architects, Architectural Press, 1926

NEWSPAPERS AND MAGAZINES

The Architectural Review

The Builder

Country Life

The Farnham Herald

Surrey County Magazine

Surrey & Hants News

Index

The figures in *italic* type indicate an illustration